UNDER THE INFLUENCE

Under the Influence

Putting Peer Pressure to Work

Robert H. Frank

PRINCETON UNIVERSITY PRESS

PRINCETON AND OXFORD

Requests for permission to reproduce material from this work
should be sent to permissions@press.princeton.edu

Published by Princeton University Press
41 William Street, Princeton, New Jersey 08540
6 Oxford Street, Woodstock, Oxfordshire OX20 1TR

press.princeton.edu

ISBN 9780691193083
ISBN (e-book) 9780691198828

British Library Cataloging-in-Publication Data is available

Editorial: Joe Jackson and Jacqueline Delaney
Production Editorial: Lauren Lepow
Jacket Design: Matt Avery (Monograph LLC)
Production: Erin Suydam
Publicity: James Schneider and Caroline Priday

Jacket art: iStock

This book has been composed in Adobe Text and Gotham

Printed on acid-free paper. ∞

Printed in the United States of America

10 9 8 7 6 5 4 3 2 1

Example, whether it be good or bad, has a powerful influence.

—GEORGE WASHINGTON, MARCH 5, 1780

CONTENTS

PART I

Introduction

Prologue

That we are more closely connected to one another than most of us realize is an old idea. An important variation dates from 1929, when the Hungarian writer Frigyes Karinthy published a short story titled *Láncszemek* ("Chains"). Two of the story's main characters speculate that any two living people can be connected by a chain involving no more than five acquaintances. That *some* such chains exist is hardly surprising, since most of us can think of people in distant locations to whom we are connected through a small number of intermediaries. The man-bites-dog aspect of Karinthy's conjecture is that almost *any* two people A and E could be linked by a chain like A knows B, who knows C, who knows D, who knows E.

One of the first systematic attempts to test this claim came in the 1960s with a series of experiments by the psychologist Stanley Milgram. In one, he sent packages containing a small booklet to ninety-six people chosen at random from the Omaha, Nebraska, telephone directory. His cover letter asked them to try to forward the booklet to a specific resident of Boston, Massachusetts, through a chain of personal acquaintances. He told them the name and address of the Boston resident, that he worked as a stockbroker, and that the first person in their chain should be someone they knew on a first-name basis. Milgram also advised them to choose someone they believed (presumably based on the target's location and occupation) could be socially closer to the target than they themselves were. Subsequent recipients in the chain were asked to forward the same instructions.

Many of the Omaha recipients undoubtedly tossed Milgram's booklet in the trash, so it is remarkable that the Boston target received eighteen of the ninety-six packages. The average number of links in the eighteen chains was 5.9. But the now-familiar expression *six degrees of separation* would not gain broad currency until many years later, when John Guare's play by that name premiered on Broadway in 1990.

The concept became a meme in full when four Albright College students introduced "Six Degrees of Kevin Bacon" in 1994, a game designed to measure the professional proximity of an actor, living or dead, to the American film star Kevin Bacon. An actor has a Bacon number of 1, for example, if she or he appeared in the same film with Bacon. Someone who appeared in a film with another actor who appeared in a film with Bacon has a Bacon number of 2, and so on. The average Bacon number is 2.955 among actors who have one. In that group, even the actor most distant from Bacon, William Rufus Shafter, has a Bacon number of only 7. Shafter, a Union Army officer during the Civil War, appeared in two films in 1898.

For academics who study social connectedness, the six-degrees concept gained little traction until 1998. That's when the sociologist Duncan Watts and the mathematician Steven Strogatz published their landmark paper, "Collective Dynamics of Small-World Networks," in *Nature*. In the years since then, this paper has provided the mathematical foundation for the analytical tools that social scientists have been using with such remarkable success to study how ideas and behaviors spread through populations like infectious diseases. It has already been cited by other scholars more than thirty-eight thousand times and is one of the few papers ever published to be among the most widely cited works in multiple disciplines.

In his 1976 book, *The Selfish Gene*, the evolutionary biologist Richard Dawkins coined the term *meme*, which Webster now defines as "an idea, behavior, style, or usage that spreads from person to person within a culture." The meme is to cultural transmission, Dawkins argued, as the gene is to biological transmission.

One of Charles Darwin's central insights was that natural selection favors genetic variations that enhance the individual organism's ability to survive and reproduce. Much of the time, the same variations also benefit larger groups. But often not. For example, an inclination to cheat when no one is looking might benefit individuals, but widespread cheating almost always makes matters worse for groups. It is the same with memes. The memes that propagate most successfully are often ones that benefit both individuals and groups. But here, too, not always. As the legal scholar Jeffrey Stake has argued, "Ideas should not be treated as inert products but as living things that sometimes exert some influence over their environment. Some of the ideas are more adept at surviving than others, and the ones that survive will not necessarily be good for humans."[1]

It is often hard to evaluate whether a specific behavior even qualifies as a meme, and if so whether its consequences, on balance, are positive or negative. Yet sometimes the evidence is clear.

We know, for example, that the strongest predictor of whether people will take up smoking is the proportion of their close friends who smoke. Smoking is thus clearly a meme. The negative health consequences of smoking are also conclusively documented, and most smokers themselves express regret about having started. By definition, then, smoking unambiguously qualifies as a socially destructive meme.

On the other side of the ledger, we have compelling evidence that the adoption of photovoltaic solar panels is both socially contagious and almost uniformly positive in terms of environmental consequences. Accordingly, few would object to calling the practice a socially beneficial meme.

Adam Smith, widely considered the father of economics, is often cited in defense of the claim that competitive markets produce the greatest good for the greatest number. But that was never Smith's position. His signature insight was that the pursuit of narrow self-interest often leads to socially beneficial outcomes, but not always.

The same holds for competition among ideas. Good ideas often triumph, but there is no presumption that the marketplace of ideas reliably promotes the common good, especially in the short run. My central claim in *Under the Influence* is that we therefore have a powerful and legitimate public policy interest in encouraging socially beneficial memes and discouraging socially harmful ones.

Many insist it is solely the individual's responsibility to choose which ideas to embrace, which behaviors to mimic. Some who hold that view are likely to oppose my claim. I am sympathetic to the sentiments that underlie their position. No one wants to live in an Orwellian nanny state. But my aim will be to explain not only why it is compellingly in our interest to exert at least some collective control over the social forces that shape our choices, but also why failure to do so may threaten our very survival.

The existential threat we face is the climate crisis. In October of 2018, the United Nations' Intergovernmental Panel on Climate Change reported that in the absence of decisive measures to curtail greenhouse gas emissions, we are now on track to catastrophic increases in average global temperatures by 2040. The forecasts of climate models are notoriously imprecise. Temperatures might well rise by less than predicted, but they might also rise by considerably more. And even the current temperature rise of only 1°C (1.8°F) has already produced floods, droughts, and fires on a scale unseen in human history. As David Wallace-Wells put it in the first sentence of *The Uninhabitable Earth*, "It's worse, much worse, than you think."[2] If temperature increases come anything close to the IPCC's projections, many hundreds of millions of people will die, and much of the earth's wealth will be destroyed.

Reactions to this threat vary greatly from country to country. In the United States, supporters of the Green New Deal have proposed an expansive legislative agenda that attacks climate change and economic inequality simultaneously. Critics, including many from the left, have objected that tackling both problems at once will simply make failure in both domains more likely. Green New Deal proponents counter that unless we include policies to mitigate rising inequality's impact, it will be impossible to assemble a sufficiently broad political coalition to overcome our current gridlock.

A deeper understanding of the power of behavioral contagion, which psychologists define as a tendency to mimic others' behavior, suggests that the Green New Deal is less impractical than many critics think. One of the most costly ways we influence one another is by reinforcing individual spending decisions that are highly wasteful. A simple example: we buy heavier cars because driving a relatively light car is more dangerous, yet when all buy heavier cars, everyone's risk of injury and death goes up, not down. Understanding how contagion amplifies such spending patterns, we will see, helps identify simple policies that would redirect trillions of dollars annually in support of carbon-free energy sources, all without demanding painful sacrifices from anyone. Those same policies would reduce economic inequality and stimulate the creation of good jobs. Or so I will argue.

But before launching that attempt, I digress briefly about my choices of what to include in the pages ahead. Most books on writing celebrate brevity. Rule 17 in the renowned *Elements of Style*, for example, exhorts writers to "Omit Needless Words." For the most part, I try to follow this rule, both sentence by sentence and in my choice of topics to omit. But for reasons I will explain shortly, I have also included material whose omission would have made the book significantly shorter.

The original edition of *The Elements of Style* was written by Professor William Strunk in 1918. In 1959, thirteen years after Strunk's death, it was revised and expanded considerably by his former student and *New Yorker* magazine stalwart, E. B. White. In the revised edition, popularly known as *Strunk & White*, White's preface contains this remarkable passage describing Strunk's presentation of Rule 17 to his students: "When he delivered his oration on brevity to the class, he leaned forward over his desk, grasped his coat lapels in his hands, and, in a husky, conspiratorial voice, said, 'Rule Seventeen. Omit needless words! Omit needless words! Omit needless words!' "[3]

If it's good to omit needless words, why did Strunk speak the phrase three times? White suggests it was because his professor was so ruthlessly effective at omitting needless words: "In the days when I was sitting in his class, he omitted so many needless words, and omitted them so forcibly and with such eagerness and obvious relish, that he often seemed in the position of having shortchanged himself—a man left with nothing more to say yet with time to fill, a radio prophet who had out-distanced the clock."[4]

My own experience in the classroom suggests an alternative interpretation. In chapter 13, I will mention studies showing that introductory courses in economics, my own discipline, appear to leave no lasting imprint on the millions of students who take them each year. The principal reason for this dismal performance by dismal scientists, I believe, is that we almost always try to teach our students far too much. Many instructors ask, "How much can I show them today?" and feel pleased with themselves when they manage to zip through more than a hundred PowerPoint slides in an hour. But in their effort to cover every idea that economists have written about during the past two centuries, all goes by in a blur for most students.

Learning theorists counsel against this approach. Because we are bombarded by terabytes of information each day, our brains are equipped with a subconscious filter that directs our conscious attention only to information that reaches our senses repeatedly. Only then do our brains conclude that something may be important enough to merit the construction of new neural pathways.

In short, my conjecture is that Professor Strunk stated Rule 17 three times because he understood intuitively that repetition fosters learning. In the case of economics, at least, that's a liberating insight, because only a handful of basic principles do most of the heavy lifting. My experience has been that students who see and use these principles repeatedly in a variety of familiar contexts are able to master them at a high level in just a single semester.

I cite that experience to explain why I have invoked the meme of smoking not only in these introductory pages, but also in more than half the chapters that follow. It embodies perhaps the simplest and least controversial illustration of my case for public policies that influence the social contexts that shape our lives. Some of the other examples I will discuss are more likely to provoke disagreement. But as I will try to explain, each is analogous in every relevant detail to the smoking example.

Another phrase I'll repeat more than once in the pages ahead is *the mother of all cognitive illusions.* I use this phrase to describe the belief, held by many wealthy voters, that higher top tax rates will require painful sacrifices of them. That belief is demonstrably false. As the wealthy themselves would be quick to concede, they already have far more than anyone might reasonably be said to need. But what many don't understand is that higher taxes would also not compromise their ability to buy the special extras they want. Because those extras are invariably in short supply, getting them requires bidding against others who also want them. What the rich have utterly failed to recognize is that their ability to bid successfully depends only on their relative disposable income, which is completely unaffected by higher taxes.

The rich think higher taxes would hurt them because they know higher taxes would reduce their disposable incomes in absolute terms. But almost every income decline they have actually experienced was one in which their own income fell while the incomes of peers remained unchanged—as happens, for example, when someone experiences a business reverse, home fire, health crisis, or divorce. In the wake of such events, it really is harder to bid successfully for what you want. But things are totally different when the rich all pay higher taxes. The same full-floor apartments with commanding 360-degree views end up in the same hands as before.

I'll mention two other elements of repetition that appear in the book for a different reason. Much of my research over the decades has focused on two questions: How does context shape spending patterns? And how could genuine honesty be sustainable in even the most bitterly competitive environments? Because my answers to both questions rely heavily on social forces, writing a book on behavioral contagion that made no reference to these issues seemed out of the question. Chapter 6 briefly summarizes my work on the emergence of trust, with application to the increasingly worrisome issue of tax evasion. Chapter 8 recaps my work on how social context shapes spending patterns and describes how we might alter those patterns to our advantage.

Only a minuscule proportion of the world's population has read my work on these issues. Members of this group might reasonably decide to skip those two chapters.

1

The Argument in Brief

I have four adult sons, none of them a smoker. I once told a friend that if they'd grown up when I did, at least two of them would have taken up the habit.

My son Chris, who was present during this conversation, immediately asked, "Which two?" "David (my oldest), almost certainly," I said, "and probably also Hayden (my youngest)." I added that Jason would have been unlikely to smoke no matter when he'd been born.

Chris feigned offense. He'd been a musician in New York City for almost a decade, where, in his circle, smoking was almost as fashionable as when I was young. He thought that he, too, might have become a smoker if he'd grown up when I did.

When I started smoking at age fourteen in 1959, many of my friends had already been smoking for several years. My parents didn't want me to smoke, but as they were smokers themselves, their objections rang hollow. In those days, more than 60 percent of American men were smokers, and almost as many women. Smoking was just something that most people did.

Yet even then, most people who smoked didn't seem happy about it. Today, roughly 90 percent of smokers say they regret having started, and about 80 percent express a desire to quit.[1] Almost half of all smokers try to quit each year, but fewer than 5 percent succeed.[2] Several of my own attempts to quit failed. So I count myself fortunate to have abandoned the habit before leaving for college.

The reason I succeeded in raising nonsmoking children and my parents did not is that today's environment is different from the earlier one. By far the strongest predictor of whether someone will smoke is the percentage of her closest friends who smoke. If that number rises from twenty to thirty, for example, the probability that she will smoke rises by about 25 percent.[3] Whereas most of my teenage friends were smokers, relatively few of my sons' friends were. In 2017, only 18.6 percent of American men were smokers, only 14.3 percent of women.[4]

Today's environment is different mostly because of the taxes, prohibitions, and other regulatory measures we have taken to discourage smoking. In the 1950s, a pack of Camels could be had for as little as twenty-five cents in some parts of the country (about $2.15 in today's dollars). But in many areas today, taxes have pushed that price north of $10, and in New York City a pack of cigarettes cannot be sold legally for less than $13. In the intervening years, we have also banned smoking in restaurants, bars, and public buildings. Some jurisdictions have prohibited smoking even in outdoor public spaces. We have spent billions of dollars on media campaigns to discourage smoking.

Given the long-standing American hostility to social engineering, each of these steps faced heavy pushback. When called on to justify them, regulators offered their time-honored response: restricting individual freedom is often the only way to prevent undue harm to innocent bystanders.

By a wide margin, the example of harm to others most often cited by regulators has been that secondhand smoke causes injuries that bystanders cannot easily avoid. This explanation resembles the rationale for requiring catalytic converters on cars: we need them to prevent pollution that would otherwise cause undue harm to others.

Even strict libertarians concede the legitimacy of this rationale in principle. As John Stuart Mill, perhaps the Western world's most

THE ARGUMENT IN BRIEF 13

eloquent champion of individual freedom, memorably wrote in *On Liberty*, "the only purpose for which power can be rightfully exercised over any member of a civilized community, against his will, is to prevent harm to others. His own good, either physical or moral, is not sufficient warrant. . . . Over himself, over his own body and mind, the individual is sovereign."[5] That a desire to parry libertarian objections influenced regulators to invoke secondhand smoke in defense of antismoking measures is also consistent with their insistence that their aim is not to protect smokers from harming themselves. And health hazards from exposure to secondhand smoke have in fact been conclusively documented.[6]

But are those hazards sufficient to justify extreme measures to discourage smoking? Unless you worked in a crowded bar with no ventilation, the damage caused by secondhand smoke was extremely small compared to that from being a smoker. For example, more than 85 percent of American deaths from lung cancer are attributable to smoking, but only a fraction of the remainder has been linked to passive smoke exposure. In terms of their actual impact, then, smoking regulations do vastly more to protect smokers from themselves than to protect innocent bystanders from secondhand smoke.

A second rationale for regulating smoking was stated in the lawsuits brought against tobacco companies by forty-six state attorneys general and others in the 1990s. Damage claims in these suits were based on the assertion that smoking imposed a burden on Medicaid, which is paid for by taxes on smokers and nonsmokers alike. These lawsuits resulted in the Master Settlement Agreement of 1998, judgments from which had the effect of raising the price of cigarettes by about twenty-five cents a pack.[7] But considerable controversy remains about whether smokers do in fact burden taxpayers. As the economist Kip Viscusi has argued, for example, smokers tend to die early, around age sixty-five on average, thereby saving both federal and state agencies a great deal of money.[8]

The narrow focus on secondhand smoke and fiscal effects greatly understates the harm that smokers impose on others. By far the greatest injury caused by someone's decision to become a smoker is the harm caused by making others more likely to smoke as well.

When someone becomes a smoker, every friend of that person will have one more smoker in his or her peer group. Every member of every one of those groups will then become more likely to smoke. Those who take up the habit will then make each member of their own peer groups more likely to smoke, and so on. And in addition to causing still others to become more likely to smoke, every one of those new smokers will inflict the real, albeit smaller, harms associated with secondhand smoke.

In short, when a regulation discourages someone from smoking, the harm to others that would have been caused by that person's secondhand smoke or by pressure on government health-care budgets is only a minuscule percentage of the total harm actually prevented.

Today's environment is different from the one I grew up in mostly because of the taxes and other regulatory measures we have adopted to discourage smoking. Yet more than 15 percent of American adults still smoke, and in some groups—low-income adults, for example—the share is considerably higher. Should regulators enact even stricter measures against smoking? On the strength of the harm caused by budgetary effects and secondhand smoke alone, that would be a hard sell. But the balance of costs and benefits looks different if we include a full accounting of the harm caused by behavioral contagion.

Many opponents of regulation are quick to argue, however, that behavioral contagion is not a proper justification for government intervention. It is one thing, they say, to protect someone whose asthma is aggravated by secondhand smoke, but quite another to penalize people merely because their behavior makes others more likely to smoke. People have agency, they insist, and it is the individual's responsibility, not the state's, to decide whether to smoke.

These observations have obvious rhetorical force. People faced with the decision of whether to smoke do indeed have greater agency than those who are damaged by secondhand smoke. And all else equal, the regulators' burden of proof clearly should be heavier in the first case than in the second.

Yet smoking that results from behavioral contagion also harms many people who have no practical means to avoid injury. Consider, for example, parents who have already taken every reasonable step to discourage their children from smoking. Given what we now know about the health consequences of smoking, could anyone second-guess their pursuit of this goal? Yet it is a statistical certainty that more of them will fail to achieve it in environments with higher proportions of smokers. These parents, like the victims of second-hand smoke, have no way to escape the anguish they suffer from failure to achieve their goal. Although that harm may be hard to quantify, it is surely considerable. And parents aren't the only ones who suffer. Every smoker who dies prematurely also injures a host of friends and other relatives.

Consider, too, that stricter measures to discourage smoking appear to make even smokers themselves happier. In a 2005 study, the economists Jonathan Gruber and Sendhil Mullainathan found that people with a higher propensity to smoke were significantly happier in places with higher cigarette taxes.[9] That finding seems less strange when we recall that most smokers wish they'd never started, and that stricter regulations make their efforts to quit more likely to succeed.

When legitimate aspirations are in conflict, people's freedom to do as they please will be limited no matter which way we turn. The claim that behavioral contagion constitutes a legitimate rationale for regulatory intervention against smoking is thus difficult to dismiss with slogans about individual rights and agency. Clearer thinking about behavioral contagion requires careful analysis of the trade-offs between competing types of freedom, which in turn requires difficult conversations about free will and other thorny philosophical issues.

Are these conversations worth having? This question becomes easier to answer once we examine the central role that behavioral contagion plays not just in the choice of whether to smoke, but also in a host of other important life decisions.

The environments we inhabit shape our behavior in powerful ways, sometimes for the better, but often for the worse. Behaviors that promote good health, which include eating prudently and getting regular exercise, are often difficult to muster. The benefits from these behaviors, after all, come not right away but only after substantial delay, and humans share with most other animals a tendency toward myopia. We place far too much emphasis on immediate rewards and penalties, far too little on those that occur with significant delay. For most people, healthful behavior is easier to achieve in communities where such behavior is widely practiced. In contrast, a recent study found that members of military families who are posted to places with high obesity rates were more likely than others to become obese themselves.[10]

———

As social psychologists like to say, "It's the situation, not the person." What they mean is that when we try to explain what others do, we often place undue emphasis on internal factors, such as traits of character or personality, and too little emphasis on external or situational factors. Psychologists call this the *fundamental attribution error*.

The error was on vivid display in experiments conducted in the 1950s by the psychologist Solomon Asch.[11] His aim was to discover the extent to which certain environmental cues might influence people to ignore the clear evidence of their own senses. In one experiment, a subject and seven of Asch's confederates were asked which of the three lines in the box on the right side of figure 1.1 is the same length as the line in the box on the left. As even a brief glance confirms, line 2 is the only possible correct answer. Yet when Asch instructed his seven confederates to say line 3 had the same length, the subject agreed with them 37 percent of the time. When others were asked the same question in the absence of the experimenter's confederates, the error rate was less than 1 percent.

Virtually all people who read about the Asch experiments feel confident that their own judgments could not have been manipulated in this way. Yet as Asch demonstrated, a substantial number of them are almost certainly wrong about that. What people say and do often depends surprisingly heavily on social circumstance.

A decade later, the psychologist Stanley Milgram conducted a series of experiments that further dramatized the power of social context.[12] The laboratory setting was one in which the experimenter

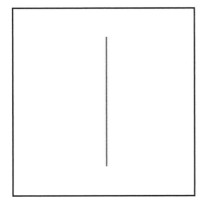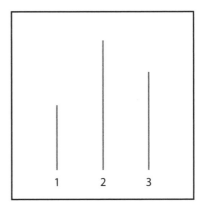

FIG. 1.1. The Asch experiment. Adapted from Solomon E. Asch, "Opinions and Social Pressure," *Scientific American* 193, no. 5 (November 1955): 31–35.

enlisted a subject to help administer a learning exercise. Three people were involved in each trial. The experimenter (Milgram himself, labeled E in figure 1.2), the "teacher" (who was in fact the subject of the experiment, labeled T in the diagram), and the "learner" (who was described as another subject but was actually Milgram's confederate, labeled L in the diagram). The experimenter posed a question to the learner, and when the learner responded correctly, the experimenter asked another question. But when the learner responded incorrectly, the experimenter instructed the teacher to press a button on a machine that would administer an electric shock to the learner. (Unbeknownst to subjects, no shocks were actually delivered.)

The teacher was told that with each additional incorrect answer given by the learner, the machine would increase the intensity of the shock delivered. And as subjects continued to administer successive shocks, learners began to cry out as if in agony. Yet 65 percent of subjects continued to administer the shocks up to the highest level, which they were told was 450 volts.

Most people who read about these experiments say confidently that they themselves would have discontinued administering the shocks much earlier than Milgram's subjects had. Yet there is no reason to believe that those subjects were any less empathic or morally responsible than others.

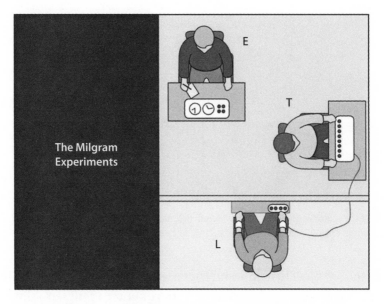

FIG. 1.2. Adapted from Stanley Milgram, "Behavioral Study of Obedience," *Journal of Abnormal and Social Psychology* 67, no. 4 (1963): 371–378.

The more likely explanation is that many who read about this experiment fall victim to the fundamental attribution error. We greatly underestimate how the details of social context—in this case, being instructed to act in a specific way by an established authority figure—would have influenced our own behavior. (Many of Milgram's subjects were in fact visibly upset by the learner's apparent suffering, and it is almost certain that this experiment would not be approved by today's human subjects committees.)

The power of context to shape behavior has long been evident to astute social observers. In an 1842 speech delivered to the Springfield Washington Temperance Society in Illinois, for example, Abraham Lincoln urged his listeners to reflect on the power of social influence. The temperance movement of that day stressed character flaws as the most important explanation for problem drinking, but in the following passage, Lincoln, then thirty-three years old, argued for a more context-oriented approach:

> But it is said by some, that . . . [social] influence is not that power-ful engine contended for. Let us examine this. Let me ask the man

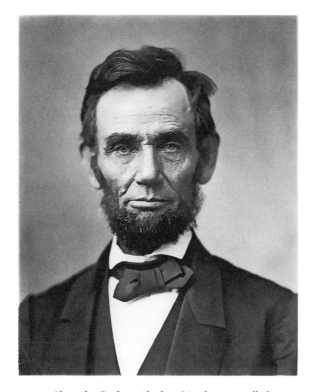

FIG 1.3. Alexander Gardner, *Abraham Lincoln*, matte collodion print, November 1863.

who could maintain this position most stiffly, what compensation he will accept to go to church some Sunday and sit during the sermon with his wife's bonnet upon his head? Not a trifle, I'll venture. And why not? There would be nothing irreligious in it: nothing immoral, nothing uncomfortable. Then why not? Is it not because there would be something egregiously unfashionable in it? Then it is the influence of fashion; and what is the influence of fashion, but the influence that other people's actions have [on our own] actions, the strong inclination each of us feels to do as we see all our neighbors do? Nor is the influence of fashion confined to any particular thing or class of things. It is just as strong on one subject as another.[13]

The results of the Asch and Milgram experiments clearly would not have surprised Mr. Lincoln.

Context matters in part because every human decision depends heavily on evaluative judgments, which in turn depend heavily on the contexts surrounding those judgments. Context shapes our judgments about mundane physical quantities, such as distance. Suppose, for instance, that you're driving with your six-year-old to visit her grandparents and she asks, "Are we almost there yet?" You'll say no if 10 miles remain on a 12-mile journey, but you'll say yes if those same 10 miles remain on a journey of 120 miles.

Context also shapes judgments about temperature. If someone asks whether it is cold out, your answer will be different if it's sixty degrees on a sunny March afternoon in Montreal from what it will be if it's a sixty-degree November evening in Miami. I grew up in Miami, and at high school football games on such evenings, we'd wear the heaviest coats we owned.

Although the link between context and evaluation is uncontroversial among behavioral scientists, its importance goes almost completely unacknowledged in many public policy discussions. In large part, that's because traditional economic models, which supply the theoretical underpinning of most policy discussions, completely ignore how context shapes human judgments.

In a move that resembles the willingness of Solomon Asch's subjects to ignore the clear evidence of their own senses, most of my fellow economists assume that people's purchases are completely independent of what others buy. Yet context clearly influences our evaluations of economic goods and services no less than it influences our evaluations of distance and temperature. Many car buyers, for example, want to purchase an automobile with spirited performance. But the same car that would have been experienced by most drivers as having brisk acceleration in 1950 would seem sluggish to drivers today. Similarly, a house of a given size is more likely to be viewed as adequate the larger it is relative to other houses in the same local environment. And an effective interview suit is simply one that compares favorably with those worn by other applicants for the same job.

Taking account of the link between context and evaluation does much to undermine Adam Smith's celebrated theory of the Invisible

FIG. 1.4. Findlay / Alamy Stock Photo.

Hand. Smith himself was actually much more circumspect about his theory than many of his most enthusiastic modern disciples, who insist that market forces can be trusted to harness narrow self-interest to create the greatest good for the greatest number.

This view of the Invisible Hand is greatly overblown. For example, consider business owners faced with the decision of what kinds of signs to erect. Is the mix they choose molded, as if by an invisible hand, to best serve the interests of the broader community? There are grounds for skepticism. Although judgments about what constitutes aesthetically pleasing urban landscapes are obviously contestable, there is broad agreement that business decisions often fail to produce them.

It would be a mistake, however, to conclude that the visual blight we see in some cities results from deficient aesthetic sensibilities, or from monopoly, or from other commonly cited market failures. In most cases, the problem is simply that a sign's ability to do its job depends on context. To be noticed, it must stand out in some way from neighboring signs. If it sticks out farther, or is taller or brighter, than others, it succeeds. Otherwise, it fails. That simple fact explains why a visual cacophony of signs is the almost inevitable result of unfettered competition among rational business owners for the attention of passing motorists.

Of course, what some see as blight, others may see as evidence of the bracing vitality of capitalism. Disagreement about the efficacy of the Invisible Hand is all the more certain when, as here, individual interests conflict with those of broader groups. Each business owner wants a more conspicuous sign, but such signs are not necessarily best for the broader community.

Here, too, as in the case of smoking, the mere fact that a regulation limits the freedom of some people is not evidence that it is ill-considered. If case law is any indication, both business owners collectively and the broader communities they serve would often prefer that commercial signs be less costly and obtrusive than the ones we see in unregulated environments. Most cities, after all, enact zoning laws that limit the size, placement, and other features of signs, often with widespread support not just from citizens, but also from the very business owners constrained by those laws.

Are some zoning laws too heavy-handed or misguided in other ways? Undoubtedly. My point is only that when individual and collective interests are in conflict, slogans about rights and freedom provide little useful guidance. In these situations, it is often impossible to avoid harming one group without causing even greater harm to others. A well-considered position on regulations of this sort requires grappling with the relevant trade-offs between competing freedoms.

To forestall possible misunderstanding, I should emphasize that I am an enthusiastic admirer of the Invisible Hand. My assertion that it falls short of others' overblown claims for it is not to deny the importance of Adam Smith's insight. Others before Smith understood that firms develop product-design improvements and cost-saving innovations not to serve humanity, but to increase their profits by capturing market share from rivals. But what Smith saw more clearly than others was that the story doesn't end there. Rivals are quick to copy new designs and improvements in production methods, and the resulting competition drives prices down to levels just sufficient to cover the new, lower costs of production. The ultimate beneficiaries of this process, Smith explained, are consumers, who enjoy a continuing stream of better and cheaper products. Smith's Invisible Hand is the most important single explanation for why incomes are so much higher today than they were throughout the bulk of human history. But that doesn't mean that market forces reliably harness self-interest to produce the greatest good for the greatest number.

―――

The argument I will defend in this book, implicit in several of the examples already discussed, is summarized in the following seven premises:

1. Context shapes our choices to a far greater extent than many people consciously realize.
2. The influence of context is sometimes positive (as when people become more likely to exercise regularly and eat sensibly if they live in communities where most of their neighbors do likewise).
3. Other times, the influence of context is negative (as when people who live amidst smokers become more likely to smoke, or when neighboring business owners erect ugly signs).
4. The contexts that shape our choices are themselves the collective result of the individual choices we make.
5. But because each individual choice has only a negligible effect on those contexts, rational, self-interested individuals typically ignore the feedback loops described in premise 4.
6. We could often achieve better outcomes by taking collective steps to encourage choices that promote beneficial contexts and discourage harmful ones.

7. To promote better environments, taxation is often more effective and less intrusive than regulation.

Among behavioral scientists, the first five of these premises are completely uncontroversial. It is only 6 and 7 that provoke disagreement.

Regarding 6, even when everyone acknowledges that behavioral contagion causes harm, as in the smoking example, it is often hard to reach consensus on collective actions that would modify the contexts that shape our actions. In part, the difficulty is that individual incentives and collective incentives often diverge so sharply. But objections to premise 6 are also rooted in the long American tradition of hostility toward regulations generally. Nor can there be any presumption that regulation always improves matters. Markets sometimes fail to deliver optimal results, but government interventions are also imperfect.

Premise 7 is controversial simply because many people dislike being taxed. Yet a moment's reflection reveals that the only interesting questions in this domain concern not whether we should tax but rather which things we should tax and at what rates. Whether you're a small-government conservative or an expansive progressive, tax revenue is necessary to pay for valued public services.

Currently, we raise much of our tax revenue by levies on activities that not only cause no harm to others but actually improve people's lives. Most of us, for example, think it a good thing when businesses hire more workers, yet we tax business payrolls heavily, which discourages hiring. A better option would be to use taxes to discourage activities that cause harm, including those that alter the contexts that shape our choices in unfavorable ways.

Context is heavily implicated, for example, in questionable decisions about safety. When my son Chris was fourteen, he had a serious bike accident. The emergency room physician who treated him showed me the helmet he had been wearing, the left front quadrant of which had been shattered. He told me that if Chris had not been wearing it, we would be discussing funeral arrangements instead of the precautions necessary to prevent further injury to his broken collarbone.

Despite considerable effort, I had never been able to get Chris's older brothers to wear bike helmets. None of the other kids wear them, they correctly insisted, and unless I was physically present, they would often ride without one. I'm therefore extremely grateful to the New York State legislators who, several years after my older sons had left home, enacted a law requiring helmets for bicyclists under the age of eighteen. Except for that law, Chris probably would not be alive today.

Even many libertarians agree that paternalistic laws of this sort may be justified for minors, who often lack the experience and knowledge to make responsible decisions about their own well-being. But wisdom and immunity to peer pressure do not magically ignite at eighteen. On what grounds might such laws be justifiably applied to mature adults?

During a sabbatical year I spent in France, I worked with a colleague who rode helmetless through heavy Paris traffic during her forty-five-minute daily bicycle commute to our office. When I once teasingly suggested that concerns about fashion prevented her from wearing a helmet, she took umbrage. And in fairness, she was in fact the least fashion-conscious of the researchers in our office.

A few weeks later, however, she knocked on my office door to tell me about having tried on some bicycle helmets at Galeries Lafayette over the weekend. She confessed sheepishly that, on seeing herself in the mirror, she realized instantly that she would be unwilling to be seen in public wearing one. As Abraham Lincoln understood clearly, fashion is a force that affects even those who believe themselves least susceptible to it.

Some rationalize helmet requirements by saying that they save society the expense of caring for those who are injured in cycling accidents. Yet many such accidents result in deaths that are both premature and quick, obviating large government outlays for Social Security and chronic illness treatment under Medicare. On balance, those who ride without helmets probably save the government money (as noted earlier, the same probably holds for people who smoke).

When I owned a motorcycle, I loved to ride with the wind in my hair and was glad that I lived in a state that didn't require helmets. Yet many of the same reasons for thinking that laissez-faire might not be our best choice with smoking seem also to apply with helmets. If my young Parisian colleague had been killed or seriously injured in a cycling accident in Paris, her friends and family members would have suffered grievous injury. And beyond having urged her to wear a helmet, they could have taken no other practical steps to avoid that injury.

Whether wearing helmets seems unfashionable depends on how many other people are wearing them. When a cyclist rides without one, she contributes—albeit imperceptibly—to the impression that wearing a helmet is unfashionable. Her choice thus entails not only potential harm to herself, but also a small increment in harm to others who are influenced by it. From the perspective of society as a whole, her own personal cost-benefit analysis makes riding without a helmet seem misleadingly attractive.

This way of framing the problem suggests that the most straightforward remedy is not to mandate helmets, but rather to make riding without one less attractive. For example, we could permit someone who wants to ride with the wind in his hair to pay a modest annual fee for a medallion that, when affixed to his cycle, would entitle him to ride legally without a helmet.

People for whom riding without a helmet is really an essential part of their cycling experience might find it worthwhile to pay this fee. But those who feel less strongly—in most cases, a substantial majority—would elect not to. And once enough people were seen with helmets, wearing one would no longer seem distressingly unfashionable. An added bonus is that each dollar collected from the fee would mean one dollar less that would need to be collected from taxes on beneficial activities. It's not a perfect solution, but it's far less intrusive and more flexible than mandating helmets for everyone.

Economists define *externality* as a cost or benefit incurred or received by third parties who have no control over its creation. Those who have taken a decent course in economics will recognize that my proposed solution to the helmet problem is exactly analogous to orthodox economic solutions for environmental externalities like air and water pollution. For those problems, the standard remedy is a tax on each unit—or, equivalently, a requirement to purchase a marketable permit for each unit—of effluent emitted. When economists first proposed this way of attacking the problem of acid rain in the 1960s, critics derided them for advocating giving rich firms a license to pollute to their hearts' content.

But that view reflects a complete misunderstanding of the economic forces that cause excessive pollution. When firms are permitted to discharge toxins into the air and water for free, they do so not because they derive pleasure from polluting, but rather because filtering out the toxins is costly. Put another way, firms in unregulated environments find polluting misleadingly attractive. Charging them for each unit they emit attacks the problem by making polluting less attractive.

Almost thirty years elapsed between economists' first calls for marketable sulfur dioxide permits and the actual implementation of their proposal under amendments to the Clean Air Act in 1990. But once the new incentives were in place, firms quickly discovered effective ways of reducing their sulfur dioxide emissions. The acid rain problem, which once dominated the news, was solved much more quickly and cheaply than it would have been under a traditional system of prescriptive regulation.

Society's interest is in achieving any given pollution-reduction target at the lowest possible cost. Pollution taxes serve that goal by concentrating abatement efforts in the hands of firms that can reduce their emissions most cheaply. That's because firms with access to the least expensive clean production processes will find it attractive to adopt them rather than to pay the higher taxes they would owe if they stuck with their current processes. Firms that have no such alternatives will continue to pollute and be taxed accordingly. In this manner, a tax on pollution achieves the target reduction levels at the lowest possible cost.

Precisely the same logic supports fees for those who cycle without helmets and taxes on those who smoke cigarettes.

———

Compelling evidence suggests that context shapes our behavior in ways more powerful than most people realize, sometimes for the better, but often for the worse. The link between context and choice is also reciprocal: context not only shapes our choices but also is the collective result of them. The effect of each individual choice, however, is too small to seem worth considering. As a result, we face a pervasive set of "context externalities," or "behavioral externalities." Behavioral externalities are analogous in every respect to traditional externalities like air and water pollution.

Many of the problems we currently attack with taxes and regulations, such as smoking, have been portrayed as traditional externalities. But as careful examination of the sources of damage from smoking makes clear, the most important harms that antismoking measures prevent are caused by a behavioral externality.

In the chapters ahead, I will describe evidence that behavioral externalities plague not just decisions about whether to smoke, to erect ugly signs, and to cycle without helmets, but also a host of other important choices. In each case, we will see, the resulting losses are large in absolute terms. But in two specific domains, they are larger than in other cases by many orders of magnitude.

The first concerns how behavioral contagion influences overall spending patterns. Although economists generally assume that people are the best judge of how to spend their incomes, it is now well understood that rational individual spending decisions are often mutually offsetting in ways analogous to military arms races. Nations build additional weapons hoping to gain an edge on rivals, but when all follow that strategy, the balance of power is unaffected. All would be better off if each spent less on weapons and more on schools and hospitals. Yet unilateral disarmament would put a nation's political sovereignty at risk.

In similar fashion, individually rational spending decisions are often counterproductive. For example, the wealthy build larger mansions in the perfectly rational expectation that they will find the additional living space sufficiently pleasurable to merit its cost. But the standards that define "spacious" are quintessentially context-dependent. When all mansions expand, the bar shifts accordingly. Beyond some point, larger properties entail greater hassle, so the additional outlays may actually leave the rich less happy than before. As we will see, the economic waste associated with mutually offsetting spending patterns of this sort likely exceeds several trillion dollars a year in the United States alone.

But we will also see that even losses on that scale pale in comparison with those we are on track to experience from climate change. According to one authoritative estimate, global per capita income projects to be almost one-quarter lower by century's end than it would have been in the absence of warming.[14] The good news is that a clearer understanding of behavioral contagion's role in both greenhouse gas emissions and wasteful spending patterns helps identify ways to avert both sources of loss.

When the problem is that a specific context encourages behavior with negative consequences, the best solution will often be to alter the individual incentives that gave rise to that context in the first place. This approach has worked spectacularly well in the domain of smoking, despite our having offered spurious reasons for the actual policies we have adopted. Our policy responses are also bound to be more effective in other areas if they rest directly on our best understanding of the actual sources of the problems we're trying to solve.

PART II

The Origins of Behavioral Contagion

2

How Context Shapes Perception

Which of the three ellipses shown in figure 2.1 is darkest? Suspecting a trick, you may say they're all the same. If so, you're right. But if you think they actually *look* the same, you should schedule an appointment with your neurologist. To the normally functioning brain, the ellipse on the left looks darkest because of the contrast between it and its surroundings.

Unless you're a psychologist, the sensory processes that led your brain to that conclusion probably occurred completely outside of conscious awareness. To survive in difficult environments, we must be able to evaluate large quantities of complex stimuli on the fly, and, just as with visual stimuli, we're hardwired in many other ways to be influenced by context in social settings. Reliance on relative comparisons plays a central role in this process.

It is a role that practitioners in my own discipline have largely overlooked. There are of course exceptions. As the economist Richard Layard memorably wrote, for example, "In a poor country, a man proves to his wife that he loves her by giving her a rose, but in a rich country he must give a dozen roses."[1] But among contemporary economists, Layard is an outlier. Unlike researchers in other behavioral sciences, most economists ignore that virtually every

FIG. 2.1

perception and evaluation is heavily influenced by frames of reference.

Much of the time, the frames that matter most are those that spring from our immediate surroundings, including the behavior of peers. But if peer behavior and other contextual cues influence our every evaluation, they must also affect every choice we make. That's why a better understanding of the link between context and perception is a key step toward understanding the power of behavioral contagion.

Although social psychologists have long focused on our general tendency to underestimate the importance of social influences, they have said less about the reasons for this tendency. The asymmetry exists in part because people are generally better able to command our attention than situational factors are.[2] People are vivid. Situational factors are boring, at least by comparison. But another reason for the difference, I believe, is that social forces and other contextual cues typically influence us only subliminally.[3]

Because of the sheer volume of decisions we confront each day, the sensory mechanisms that enable our nervous systems to interpret environmental information must respond to stimuli automatically and be extremely fast.[4] Both the anatomical complexity of the perceptual mechanisms themselves and the speed with which they must process information require that they operate almost entirely outside of conscious awareness. It is thus hardly surprising that we give social forces and other contextual cues little thought. We're largely unaware of them.

My aim in this chapter is to demonstrate how our senses render judgments about the social and physical environments that surround us. Those judgments are often only approximate, and sometimes even misleading. Yet because it would be impossible even to function without these assessments, it would be an error to conclude that our reliance on both physical and social contextual cues is harmful on balance. Despite important examples to the contrary, then, the safer presumption is that our senses draw inferences from the environment in largely adaptive ways.

———

How bright a light seems or how loud a note sounds also depends critically on the contexts in which those stimuli occur. The headlights of an oncoming car, for instance, are little noticed by passing motorists in the daytime, but are often bothersome at night, because our perception is far more sensitive to contrasts in luminance than to absolute intensity.

Our senses are likewise far more attuned to changes in the relevant contexts than to their absolute levels. That's why a man can fall asleep even with a television blaring, yet will awaken abruptly when his wife turns it off. Sensitivity to change also explains why our attention is much more strongly drawn to movements in a visual field than to static elements. Again, that these contextual forces operate almost completely outside of conscious awareness helps explain why we often underestimate their importance.

Contrast and adaptation play similar roles in perceptions of smell. When dinner guests first arrive, for example, they immediately remark on the wonderful aromas from the roast in the oven. But for

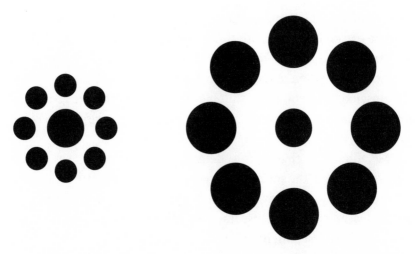

FIG. 2.2. Adapted from Andrew M. Colman, "Titchener Circles," *A Dictionary of Psychology* (New York: Oxford University Press, 2009).

the cook who has been working in the kitchen for several hours, those same aromas are scarcely noticeable.

Consider, too, our perceptions of the sizes of objects. In figure 2.2, the middle circle on the left is the same size as the middle circle on the right. Yet because the middle circle on the left is large relative to the circles surrounding it, it appears significantly larger than the middle circle on the right, which is much smaller than its surrounding circles.[5]

Artists with at least an implicit understanding of the workings of human perception are often able to create profoundly disorienting images. The brain employs systematic contextual rules for interpreting what two-dimensional images convey about the three-dimensional objects they represent. Consider the Penrose triangle, shown in figure 2.3, which was created by the Swedish artist Oscar Reutersvärd in 1934 and later popularized by the British psychiatrist Lionel Penrose and his mathematician son Roger Penrose. When the brain applies its perceptional rules of thumb to infer the nature of the three-dimensional object depicted, it hits a brick wall. The Penroses described this drawing as "impossibility in its purest form."[6]

The Penrose triangle figures prominently in perhaps the best-known of the many disturbing images created by the Dutch artist

FIG. 2.3. The Penrose triangle.

M. C. Escher: his 1961 lithograph *The Waterfall*. As shown in figure 2.4, the walls of the aqueduct clearly step downward, suggesting that it must slope downhill. But then the water exits the aqueduct at a point exactly above where it first entered. How can that be?

The website opticalillusion.net goes behind the curtain to show how the Penrose triangle underlies Escher's magic.[7] The right side of figure 2.5 depicts the essence of the aqueduct that our brains find so troubling. As in Escher's lithograph, the water appears to be flowing downhill before ending up at a point right above where it started. But as the small image in the center of the illustration makes clear, the drawing at the right is just two Penrose triangles (ABC and CDE), one stacked atop the other, with an extra vertical member (BD) connecting them.

The left panel of the diagram renders the aqueduct again, this time with the vertical pillars sawn off at mid-height. With the posts

FIG. 2.4. M. C. Escher's *Waterfall*, © 2019 The M. C. Escher Company—
The Netherlands. All rights reserved. www.mcescher.com.

thus truncated, our brains easily interpret the tops of them as lying
in roughly the same horizontal plane. And with no need to connect
them to other points in the structure, we interpret the path of the
aqueduct as receding horizontally in an unambiguous way, rather
than returning, impossibly, to a point exactly above where it started.

That artists can fool us with optical illusions does not mean we
are stupid. On the contrary, the links between context and perception that underlie such illusions serve us reasonably well most of the
time. As organisms struggling to survive in often hostile environments, we have a strong interest in perceiving the world as it actually
is. That our species has survived for so long is thus at least weak evi-

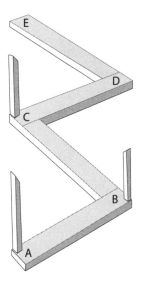
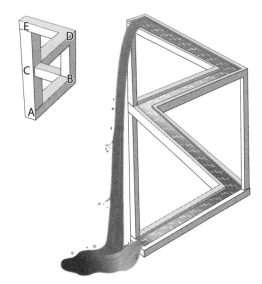

FIG. 2.5. Opticalillusion.net.

dence that the links between context and perception are best understood as evolution's attempt to make strategic use of the information available to us.

But as Charles Darwin saw clearly, natural selection is a crude instrument. The perceptual systems it molds should be understood as broadly adaptive, not as instruments that render reality with perfect accuracy in all circumstances. That we are sometimes vulnerable to optical illusions is better viewed not as a flaw in these systems but as evidence of the difficult trade-offs that arise in almost every engineering design problem.

The nature of the dilemmas often posed by these trade-offs is clearly illustrated in our assessments of faces. The two photographs in figure 2.6 are of the same person. Yet when people are asked to identify the sex of this person, most say that the image on the left is of a female, the image on the right of a male.

In this illusion, offered by the psychologist Richard Russell,[8] the female appearance of the image on the left stems from the skin tone in that image being significantly lighter than the skin tone of the image on the right. This difference creates greater contrast between the darkest parts of the face—the lips and eyes—and the lightest

FIG. 2.6. Richard Russell, "A Sex Difference in Facial Contrast and Its Exaggeration by Cosmetics," *Perception* 38, no. 8 (2009): 1215. SAGE Publications.

parts, the skin. Most of us may not be consciously aware that facial contrast is on average higher in females than in males.[9] But that does not prevent us from employing that difference to make inferences about gender identity that are correct most of the time.

In short, virtually every assessment we make rests on an explicit or implicit frame of reference. One particularly important reference point is the absolute level of whatever stimulus we are attempting to evaluate. According to a relationship known as Weber's law of psychophysics, our perception of the change in any stimulus depends on the size of the change measured as a proportion of the original stimulus.[10] Thus a change seems large only if it is large in proportional terms.

The law gives rise to the related concept of a *just noticeable difference*. Most people, for example, would not be able to identify which of two lightbulbs was brighter if one was rated at 100 watts and the other at 101 watts. But suppose that if we increase the wattage of the second bulb gradually, half of all judgments correctly identify it as brighter only when its wattage reaches 105. Weber's law would then identify 5 percent as the just noticeable difference for brightness discrimination. A bulb would thus have to be rated at 210 watts before most people would correctly perceive it as brighter than one rated at 200 watts.

Weber's law applies across multiple modes of sensory perception and works in similar ways across almost all vertebrate species. One

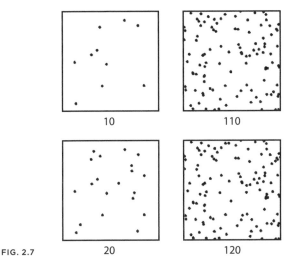

FIG. 2.7

implication of the law is that our ability to make fine distinctions between stimuli declines with intensity, irrespective of whether we are evaluating distance, temperature, loudness, pitch, weight, pain, brightness, numerosity, or a host of other signals.

The lower-left square in figure 2.7, for example, contains ten more dots than the upper-left square, and almost everyone perceives at a glance that the dots in the lower-left square are more numerous. But the lower-right square also contains ten more dots than the upper-right square, and people find it much more difficult to render a comparable judgment about the dots in those squares.

Evidence suggests that the patterns of perception implied by Weber's law are innate rather than learned. Young children will place the number 3 at about the midpoint of a scale that runs from 0 to 10, but by the time they are in the fourth grade and have been exposed to more formal instruction about numbers, most will place it closer to the 30 percent mark on that same scale. Adults in remote areas with little formal education treat the number scale much as young children do.[11]

Again, human senses are evolved structures. When biologists try to explain their properties, their point of departure is the same as for any other aspect of our structure and behavior: over the millennia, natural selection has systematically favored variants that make us more likely to function efficiently in our quest for the resources necessary for survival and reproduction. For example, this perspective sheds light on why specific design features of insects' compound eyes achieve an optimal balancing between resolution and diffraction of natural light; it also illuminates why mammals shift their gaits from walking to trotting to galloping at precisely those points that minimize the energy cost of locomotion.[12] Similar Darwinian reasoning informs biologists' understanding of human senses.

Why might an ability to make finer distinctions between small numbers have been more useful than a similar ability for much larger numbers? As the computer scientists Lav Varshney and John Sun speculate, "it could be more important to know whether it is five lions facing you or three than to know if the deer herd you are chasing contains 100 animals or just 98."[13]

A major problem confronting perceptual systems is that signals about our surroundings contain not just relevant information but also considerable noise. In another paper, Varshney and his colleagues show that perceptual systems that obey Weber's law have the desirable property of minimizing the relative noise levels in the statistical distributions of the signals we most often encounter in practice.[14] Their findings thus provide theoretical justification for the claim that our perceptual systems are broadly adaptive.

But that does not imply that seeing the world in relative terms is always advantageous. In some contexts, at least, it can lead us astray. The importance of a cost-saving action, for example, depends not on the proportion by which you reduce an expense but on the absolute dollar amount. Should you drive across town to save $10 on a $20 lamp? Confronted with this question, most people say they would, in part because saving 50 percent off the purchase price of an object seems like a significant achievement. But ask those same people whether they would drive across town to save $10 on a $4,000 TV and almost all will say no, because the savings is such a trivial percentage of the purchase price.

Although there is no uniquely correct answer to these questions, a rational person's answer to both questions should be the same. In both cases, after all, the benefit of driving across town is exactly

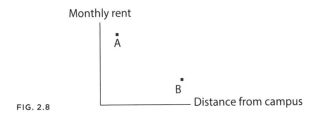

FIG. 2.8

$10—the amount that will be saved on each purchase. So if the drive counts as more than $10 worth of hassle, the answer to both questions should be no. But if the hassle of the drive is less than $10, it makes sense to drive across town in both cases.

Contextual cues can also lead us astray in other ways. In the parable of Buridan's ass, a starving donkey stands equidistant from two identical bales of hay. But because his attraction to each bale is exactly equal, he is unable to decide which bale to approach and therefore dies of starvation.[15] Although it is difficult to imagine such indecision causing a human to starve, many people experience significant anxiety when forced to decide between two options that are roughly equally attractive. If the options were in fact equally attractive, it would of course not matter which one was chosen. But the anxiety some people experience in such situations is real and can make them more vulnerable to contextual cues that provoke error.

Suppose, for example, that you were a student faced with a choice between the two apartments labeled A and B in figure 2.8. The attraction of A is that it's conveniently close to campus, but its rent is fairly high. In contrast, the attraction of B is that its rent is lower, but it is farther from campus. By suitable manipulation of the rent and distance values, we can generate hypothetical pairs of apartments like A and B between which a given individual would be essentially indifferent. The interesting thing, however, is that this doesn't mean she would find it easy to choose. On the contrary, like Buridan's ass, many people experience significant anxiety when confronted with such choices.

Now suppose we assemble a large group of people and manipulate the distance and rent values of A and B so that, when forced to

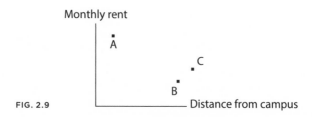

FIG. 2.9

choose, half pick A and the remaining half pick B. What do you think would have happened if we had asked that same group to choose among three apartments—the same A and B as before, plus a new option at C, as shown in figure 2.9? According to traditional rational choice theory, the apartment at C is an irrelevant option, since it is worse along both dimensions than B. And in fact when C is added to the set of options, no one chooses it.

Yet the presence of the option at C has a profound effect on the observed pattern of choices between A and B. This time, many more people choose B, and many fewer choose A.[16] The apparent explanation is that people find it easy to choose B over C, and that invests option B with a halo that leads people to favor it when confronted with the anxiety-inducing choice between A and B.

Experienced salespersons may exploit this pattern when dealing with people who have difficulty choosing among hard-to-compare alternatives. To close the deal, it may be enough to expose the client to a new option that is worse along every dimension than one of the original options.

Another contextual cue that heavily shapes our perceptions is a pronounced asymmetry with which we tend to view events with positive attributes as compared to those with negative attributes. The consistent finding is that the amount of effort people will expend to resist being stripped of something they already possess is significantly larger than the effort they will devote to acquiring something they don't already have. This asymmetry is known as *loss aversion* and is among the most deeply rooted human tendencies known to behavioral scientists.[17]

When the possession in question is an insignificant material object, such as a coffee mug, people must be offered roughly twice as much to part with it as they would have been willing to pay to acquire it initially.[18] If the possession is something more important, such as health or safety, that ratio becomes dramatically larger.

In one experiment, subjects who were asked to imagine having been exposed to a rare fatal disease—there was a 1 in 1,000 chance they had caught it—were willing to pay only $2,000 for the only available dose of the antidote.[19] The same subjects said that, under identical conditions, they would have to be paid 250 times as much to induce them to voluntarily expose themselves to the disease if there was no available antidote. This asymmetry is striking, since in both cases, people would be buying a one-in-a-thousand reduction in their likelihood of death.

Another vivid illustration of how loss aversion colors our perceptions comes from an experiment that began by telling subjects that the United States is preparing for the outbreak of an unusual disease that is expected to kill six hundred people if we take no action, and that two alternative programs to combat the disease have been proposed.

One group was told to assume that the consequences of the two programs would be exactly as follows:

If Program A is adopted, two hundred people will be saved.
If Program B is adopted, there is a one-third chance that six
    hundred people will be saved, and a two-thirds chance that
    no people will be saved.

When subjects were then asked which one they would favor, 72 percent chose A and 28 percent chose B. Subjects in this version of the experiment appeared to be risk-averse, preferring to save two hundred lives for sure rather than choosing a risky prospect with the same expected number of lives saved.

After describing the same disease to a second group of subjects, the experimenters then asked for a choice between these two options:

If Program C is adopted, four hundred people will die.
If Program D is adopted, there is a one-third chance that
    no one will die and a two-thirds chance that six hundred
    will die.

This time, 22 percent chose C and 78 percent chose D. Unlike the first group, who appeared to favor the safer choice, the second group appeared to favor the riskier one.

In general, when people are given a choice between options with the same expected value, as here, most people choose the safer option. That's of course what the first group, whose options were framed in terms of the number of lives saved, actually did. But those in the second group, whose options were framed in terms of the number of lives lost, chose the risky option. What's so interesting about this finding is that, as a moment's reflection reveals, Program A is the same as Program C, and Program B is the same as Program D. Even though the pairs of options available to the two groups were functionally identical, the second group defied convention by choosing the risky option, the one that preserved an opportunity to avoid any losses. The experimenters made no claim that the second group chose irrationally. But they saw the observed pattern of choices as clear evidence of the strength of people's aversion to losses.

No serious behavioral scientist disputes that context heavily shapes our perceptions and evaluations. Most scientists also agree that although natural selection favored perceptual systems that deliver accurate information about the environments we inhabit, those systems are far from perfect.

As we have seen, for example, certain kinds of stimuli reliably induce many of us to draw faulty inferences about reality. Scholars in the field of behavioral economics, which lies at the intersection of psychology and economics, have focused largely on mistakes of this type. As Amos Tversky, whose work strongly influenced this vibrant field, liked to say, "My colleagues, they study artificial intelligence. Me? I study natural stupidity."

My focus in the coming chapters will have little to do with natural stupidity. I offer the examples in this chapter as illustrations that the perceptual and cognitive mechanisms by which we draw inferences about our environments operate largely outside of conscious awareness. That's true not only when those mechanisms support accurate judgments, but also in the occasional instances when they do not.

The most important harms caused by behavioral contagion, I will argue, stem from the tendency of our evaluations to rest on relative magnitudes. "Hot" means hot in relative terms. "Far" means far in relative terms. And "rich" means rich in relative terms. Anyone who did not rely heavily on contextual evaluations of this sort would be at a severe competitive disadvantage.

As will become clear, however, such reliance often generates enormous losses for groups. In the chapters in part IV, I will describe simple policies whose adoption would eliminate the most serious of those losses without demanding difficult sacrifices from anyone. On its face, that might strike many as an implausible claim. If such policies exist, why haven't we already adopted them? As I will argue in chapter 12, it's because so many of us suffer from what I call the mother of all cognitive illusions.

3

The Impulse to Conform

Johann von Goethe's *The Sorrows of Young Werther* is a loosely autobiographical novel presented in the form of letters written to a friend by a sensitive young artist. The protagonist has fallen in love with a woman who is engaged to another man. The anguish provoked by unrequited love eventually becomes more than the young Werther can bear, and in the end he takes his own life.

The novel was published in 1774 to widespread critical acclaim, but in the ensuing years, a wave of suicides swept across Europe. Investigators discovered that many of the victims had been strongly influenced by Goethe's narrative. Suicide had become a meme. As the psychologist Paul Marsden described the reaction of policy makers, "In an attempt to stem what was seen as a rising tide of imitative suicides, anxious authorities banned the book in several regions in Europe."[1]

In the ensuing two centuries, scholars have been actively exploring what has been called the behavioral contagion thesis—loosely, the idea "that sociocultural phenomena can spread through, and leap between, populations more like outbreaks of measles or chicken pox than through a process of rational choice."[2]

Much of the resulting literature views imitative behavior with a critical eye. During the more than three decades I have spent thinking about this subject, I have not come across a more vivid example that seems to support this characterization than one portrayed in Alan Funt's 1970 film, *What Do You Say to a Naked Lady?* The film is a series of vignettes like those portrayed in Funt's long-running television series, *Candid Camera*. In one, Funt places an ad inviting candidates to interview for a high-paying position, then arranges appointments to meet with those who respond. As the scene unfolds, the camera focuses on a candidate who arrives for his interview and is directed to a waiting room in which several others are already seated. The man naturally assumes that the others are also there to be interviewed, but viewers know them to be confederates of Mr. Funt.

After some moments elapse without incident, the confederates rise unbidden and begin removing their clothing. The camera zooms in on Funt's subject, whose face initially conveys bemusement but gradually transforms into an expression of concern as he struggles to figure out what's going on. But after a few more moments pass, he appears to reach a tipping point. He, too, rises and begins taking off his own clothing. As the scene ends, he and the others are standing naked, waiting for some indication of what comes next.

Many people who witness this scene feel confident that they would not have behaved as Funt's subject did. And since we don't know how many times Funt ran this experiment before he got the footage he wanted, perhaps they are right.

Yet we should not be too quick to ridicule the man's behavior. He was hoping, quite reasonably, to land a job that paid significantly more than he was earning. Because others in the experiment arrived before he did, he would have assumed, plausibly, that they were better informed than he was about what came next. It would thus have been reasonable for him to have concluded that the next step in the interview process required taking off his clothes. The others had already begun doing so, and since it was reasonable for him to believe that they knew more than he did, it was also reasonable to conclude that they believed the next steps in the protocol were worth taking. His apparent options were thus either to conform or else to abandon his chance at a substantial pay raise. If he thought that conformity entailed only a risk of minor embarrassment, it might well have seemed prudent to go along.

More recent scholarly work on herd behavior has been similarly open to the possibility that it is broadly consistent with individual rationality. At any rate, few researchers would deny that it is useful for people to make periodic progress assessments. Indeed, it's difficult to see how someone who didn't ask, "How am I doing?" from time to time could have thrived in the competitive environments we inhabit. Our responses to this question depend heavily on the frames of reference we summon for thinking about it. But because important decisions must often be made without time for careful reflection, many of those frames lie almost completely out of conscious awareness.

Consider a Pleistocene hunter-gatherer busily foraging for berries when two members of his clan run by at full speed with looks of terror on their faces. What should he do? Possibly the runners are being chased by others in a dispute that doesn't concern the forager. In that case, he should simply continue with the task at hand. But it's also possible that the runners are fleeing from an angry tiger. The forager's best option would then be to experience the men's fear vicariously and immediately take flight. Since inaction would be so much more costly in the second case, running away is probably the prudent choice.

This perspective suggests why the psychological forces favoring conformity are often so powerful, even when, as in the case of Solomon Asch's subjects described in chapter 1, no obvious reasons favor conforming. But that's completely consistent with the idea that our inclination to emulate others serves us well on balance. After all, without drawing on the wisdom and experience of others, we would find it almost impossible to cope with the stream of complex decisions we confront.

A tendency to mimic others, for example, might be helpful in calling our attention to useful new opportunities. If I had never heard that LED lights save significant amounts of energy, seeing neighbors adopt them might lead me to consider them. Alternatively, seeing others engage in a practice that had previously been frowned upon might make me less apprehensive about trying it. Visiting an acupuncturist, for instance, was once regarded in the West with suspicion. Learning that friends were seeing one might liberate me from the fear that others would think ill of me for doing so.

Failure to mimic may sometimes entail social costs. If my host at dinner orders a cocktail, it may be socially awkward for me not to join him. Mimicry may also help deepen social ties, which are valuable not just intrinsically, but also in conferring material advantages. Imitative behavior may help support social identity as well. Being knowledgeable about professional basketball, for instance, could be part of a social identity that my coworkers share, which could mean that lack of interest in the sport would make me less likely to become a trusted colleague.

In sum, there are many reasons that a subconscious impulse to mimic others might have served us reasonably well, on balance.

No matter what the evolutionary origins of imitative behavior may have been, a burgeoning scientific literature suggests that in both humans and other animals it is powerfully rooted in what has been called the brain's mirror neuron system (MNS).[3] This system has been likened to a camera that records in real time the gestures, facial expressions, body language, vocal tones, and eye movements of others with whom we interact, in the process priming our own nervous systems to mimic what we've seen and heard. When we see someone smile, for example, the MNS records activation in the two major muscle groups that produce the smile, those that pull the corners of the mouth upward (zygomaticus major), and those that cause the eyes to narrow (orbicularis oculi). When we see someone lift a cup to her lips, the MNS mimics the nerve impulses that would produce the same muscle movements in us. When we see someone yawn, we too are more likely to do so.

Experiments conducted by the psychologists John Bargh and Tanya Chartrand suggest that the mirror neuron system plays a central role in human communication and bonding.[4] In one of their studies, subjects in a treatment group were assigned to perform a collaborative task with others they hadn't previously met. Unbeknownst to them, these others were confederates of Chartrand and Bargh, graduate assistants who had been trained to suppress their tendencies to mimic their task partners. In a control group, different subjects performed the same task in collaboration with graduate assistants who were instructed not to suppress their natural tendency to mimic their partners. In postexperiment debriefings, subjects who had interacted with the mimicry suppressors reported substantially less favorable feelings about their collaborators.

On reflection, this difference in evaluations may not seem surprising. Even though our tendency to mimic one another lies almost entirely outside of conscious awareness, it affects electrical activity in our brains in measurable ways. We are aware, at least subconsciously, whether a conversation partner mimics us in the conventional manner. A partner who fails to mimic may convey that she doesn't care or isn't paying attention.

Other researchers describe a related phenomenon called emotional contagion, according to which people tend to experience the emotional states of those with whom they interact closely. The psychologists Elaine Hatfield, John Cacioppo, and Richard Rapson described emotional contagion as a primitive, automatic, and unconscious process that occurs through a series of afferent feedback steps that cause conversation partners to experience similar emotional states.[5] Such reactions are adaptive insofar as they facilitate relationship formation. But they can also produce harmful effects, as when early-career psychotherapists report feelings of depression in the wake of sessions with patients they have been treating for the illness.

Not all imitative behavior involves emotional contagion. As economists have long recognized, it can also be motivated by informational factors alone, and there is now a large literature on the related topics of "information cascades"[6] and "availability cascades,"[7] whose implications have been insightfully explored in a 2019 book by the legal scholar Cass Sunstein.[8]

One of the earliest and most influential academic papers in this literature is by the economist Abhijit Banerjee,[9] who demonstrated formally that because other people often possess relevant information that a decision maker lacks, imitative behavior may be completely rational. Voters who know little about a political candidate, for example, might rationally interpret favorable early polls or fundraising totals to imply positive assessments of the candidate by others who know more.

People's reluctance to patronize a restaurant whose tables are mostly empty is another frequently cited example.[10] On any given evening, someone trying to choose between two completely unfamiliar restaurants can confidently assume that others must be at least as well informed about them as she is. Choosing the one that most others have chosen is thus likely to yield favorable results on balance, but not in all cases. For instance, poorly informed early arrivals might have chosen the lesser restaurant purely by chance, leading subsequent arrivals to follow suit. The lesser restaurant might then experience a significantly higher proportion of filled seats throughout the evening, despite its inferior offerings.

Studies have identified similar peer influences in a variety of other domains. The choice of how many children to have, for example, is heavily shaped by the fertility choices of other locals.[11] Decisions regarding the adoption of new technologies have also been shown to be strongly influenced by others' decisions.[12] Other commonly cited examples include riots, urban legends, economic bubbles, panics, speeding, body piercing, tattoos, and cosmetic surgery.[13] The likelihood that Norwegian workers take advantage of paternity leave provisions has also been shown to be subject to behavioral contagion.[14]

Behavioral contagion is also strongly implicated in illicit behavior. The economist Edward Glaeser and his coauthors, for example, have identified significant herd behavior in the propensity to commit crimes, showing that less than 30 percent of the variation in crime rates across cities could be accounted for by differences in the objective characteristics of the cities and their residents. They found that contagion effects were strongest for larceny and auto theft, and weakest for arson, murder, and rape.[15] The sociologist Colin Loftin found evidence of spatial clustering in support of the claim that episodes of violent assault constitute a contagious social process.[16]

One of the most powerful examples of herd behavior comes from stock markets. Those who own stock in a company essentially own a claim to a share of the company's current and future earnings. Economic theory thus implies that the price of a company's shares traded on public exchanges should move in proportion to the present value of its current and future profits. But because no one really knows exactly what the future profits of any company will be, investors are forced to rely on estimates. Those estimates often rest heavily on well-reasoned market analysis, but investors also know that a company's share prices sometimes respond to general waves of optimism and pessimism. As John Maynard Keynes once observed, the stock picker's challenge is not to identify the firms that she feels will perform best but rather to predict which ones other investors will identify as top performers.[17]

Investors also know that a company's stock price may be heavily influenced by information possessed by only a limited number of people. One of the most pressing concerns of active traders is thus to take every available step to uncover such information before it becomes public. The fear of missing out (FOMO) is one of the most powerful motives driving the behavior of these investors. And one of the most powerful triggers of FOMO is a sharp movement in the price of a company's shares that is unexplained by publicly available new information.

Such price changes may lead investors to conclude that somebody somewhere knows something that they themselves do not. So it's easy to see why some risk-averse investors might interpret a sudden unexplained decline in a company's stock price as possible evidence of insider knowledge of future earnings declines. And if that interpretation prompts some to sell their holdings, the stock price will decline further, motivating still other investors to sell their stakes, and so on. Because of such information cascades, it's really no mystery that stock prices are dramatically more volatile than the under-lying company profit streams on which they are based.

The social dimension of modern information theory also suggests plausible explanations for many seemingly strange positions taken by political leaders. Why, for example, would even those politicians who believe the death penalty to be both ineffective and morally offensive often support it vigorously in public? The outlines of an answer were laid out in a 1994 paper by the economist Glenn Loury,[18] who built on earlier work by the sociologist Erving Goffman.[19]

Politicians want to appear tough on crime, but voters have only imperfect information about what leaders' actual beliefs are. Voters may understand that public statements about the death penalty are an imperfect measure of whether politicians are tough on crime. But voters also believe, correctly, that politicians who are tough on crime are at least somewhat more likely than others to favor the death penalty. That's all it takes to launch the dynamic that Loury described.

Since being perceived as tough on crime is advantageous, some politicians who privately oppose the death penalty will publicly de-clare themselves in favor of it. The ones with the strongest incentive to take this step are those who really are toughest on crime and whose reservations about the death penalty are least serious. But when they speak out, the set of those who remain silent about the death penalty becomes smaller and even more heavily weighted toward those who really are lax on crime. In the end, the pressure to speak out in favor of the death penalty can become all but irresistible.

That's why we applaud the moral courage of those who speak out in similar circumstances. When Mario Cuomo was governor of New York, for example, he repeatedly vetoed death penalty bills that had passed by wide margins in the state legislature. Most voters forgave him because they recognized that his opposition was rooted not in an indifference to the costs of crime but rather in his well-known religious commitments.

Similarly, most voters were willing to embrace Richard Nixon's overtures to China because his anticommunist credentials were beyond challenge. If Hubert Humphrey had won the presidency, similar overtures would have met much stiffer resistance.

Although researchers have tended to focus on negative effects of behavioral contagion, as in the case of smoking, it can also have positive effects, as when people find it easier to exercise regularly if many of those around them also do so. But the asymmetry in emphasis by researchers appears to stem from an actual asymmetry in the effects of behavioral contagion. Thus, as the economists Philip Cook and Kristen Goss write, "Negative behaviors and beliefs, which are subject to social restraints, are more likely to produce contagions than are socially desirable behaviors, which people feel freer to choose independent of other people's choices."[20]

———

In noting that our choices are heavily shaped by the choices of others, I am not saying anything new or controversial. As sociologists and psychologists have long stressed, situational factors predict what people will do far more accurately than do traits of personality or character.

But as scholars in these fields have also stressed, public awareness of peer influences tends to underestimate their importance substantially. That has been especially true of my fellow economists. Apart from their recent interest in mechanisms of information transmission, most have ignored other dimensions of social influence entirely in their analyses of public policy. My central motive for writing this book is to explain why taking careful account of those influences can lead to substantially better policy choices.

Even those who fully appreciate the extent to which our own behavior is influenced by peers have tended to ignore the significance of causal arrows running in the opposite direction: what we ourselves do also influences the behavior of others. Individuals naturally pay little heed to that reverse link because any specific choice has only negligible influence on social environments overall. But the aggregate effects of our choices on those environments are of course anything but negligible. They shape the very essence of social forces that influence us. My claim, put simply, is that we could adopt simple incentives to choose in ways that would foster environments more likely to bring out the best in us.

The core of the argument is illustrated by reviewing how social considerations supplement conventional rationales for regulation in the smoking example already discussed. I will develop a related example in chapter 9, where I will describe evidence that purchases of sport utility vehicles (SUVs) are also socially contagious. In both instances, the standard case for regulation rests on John Stuart Mill's dictum that the government should not curtail people's right to do as they please except when necessary to prevent undue harm to others. If a consumer's choices about whether to smoke or which type of vehicle to buy had no adverse consequences for others, there would be no reason for policy concern. Of course, no one denies that both smoking and heavier vehicles cause harm to others. But since the same is true of many other things we do, that by itself is not a case for regulation.

If the benefit of an activity exceeds the harm it causes, its continuation would increase the overall surplus of benefits over costs, which is presumptively a good thing. Banning heavy vehicles, for example, would reduce harm by making it less likely that others would be injured or killed on the road. But if construction crews had to transport their equipment in family sedans, others would be harmed by steep increases in building costs. Similarly, banning smoking would make people less likely to die from various illnesses. But it would also gratuitously harm those who enjoy smoking and are able to do so in isolation from others. A coherent case for regulating an activity therefore must begin with a showing that its benefits fall short of the harm it causes.

In attempting to make this case in the two domains just mentioned, policy analysts have confined their attention to the direct physical harms to third parties that are associated with smoking and heavy vehicle use. This is logically coherent, since individual cost-benefit calculations about whether to engage in an activity generally ignore any costs it might impose on others and are therefore biased in its favor. Taxing cigarette purchases, or taxing vehicles by weight, is a simple way to reduce or eliminate this bias.

But as we saw earlier, the harm from secondhand smoke that is cited as justification for taxing cigarettes is just a small fraction of the harm caused by smoking itself, which increases sharply with the proportion of one's peers who smoke. By the same token, the harms cited as reasons for taxing heavier vehicles—most notably, greater contributions to road damage, congestion, and pollution, and greater risks of injury and death of innocent bystanders—were not serious problems when those vehicles were limited to the commercial uses for which they were best suited. The real harms caused by SUVs became significant only when peer influences led millions of other motorists to buy them.

Skeptics may object that it is not government's job to hold the negative effects of peer pressure in check. It is the responsibility of parents, they argue, to teach children to resist peer pressure when appropriate. But if there were a drug that would make children completely impervious to peer influences, parents would be well advised to avoid it. Because we are deeply social animals, trust and cohesion often become more difficult to maintain if values and opinions diverge too sharply within a group, and there is clear evidence that a desire to harmonize with others helps explain successful team performance. So beyond a certain point, resistance to peer pressure may well be maladaptive. At any rate, despite attempts by most parents to teach their children to resist peer pressure, evidence affirms its enduring power. As a purely practical matter, then, it may be easier to change the peer environment itself than to eliminate our tendency to be influenced by it.

How we might go about doing this will be my focus in the chapters in part IV. For now, I'll note only that if we can agree that an activity causes undue harm to others, it is difficult to see why taxing it could be considered illegitimate. Taxing a harmful activity reduces the incentive to engage in it, thereby reducing harm to innocent bystanders. Relative to a prohibition, taxing also shows greater respect for those who value the activity most highly. Truly committed smokers, for example, can pay the tax and continue to smoke. Others who either attach lower value to smoking or wish they had never started in the first place will be more likely to cut back or quit. Because taxation encourages greater adjustments from those who can change their behavior most easily, it commands approval from economists on efficiency grounds.

But taxation is also attractive on grounds of fairness. Because increased revenue from those who continue to engage in a harmful activity enables us to reduce other taxes, those who are harmed by the activity will enjoy a net reduction in tax liability, which constitutes at least partial compensation for whatever harm they continue to suffer.

Some may concede that taxes aimed at mitigating behavioral externalities might have certain desirable properties in practice, yet still oppose such taxes because they seem to legitimize the view that people aren't responsible for resisting peer pressure on their own. This objection merits the serious consideration I'll attempt to give it in chapter 10.

Paying taxes will of course always be unpopular. Yet society couldn't exist at all if we didn't tax anything. Government currently raises much of its revenue from taxes levied on beneficial activities. We tax business payrolls, for example, which weakens business incentives to hire additional workers. We also tax income, and since savings is a significant component of income, we are also discouraging valued savings.

Why not instead raise as much tax revenue as possible from levies on activities that cause undue harm to others? As we will see in later chapters, the scope for replacing taxes on useful activities with taxes on harmful ones grows considerably once we recognize the pervasiveness of behavioral externalities.

PART III

Cases

4

It Was, Until It Wasn't: The Dynamics of Behavioral Contagion

In 1989, the journalist Andrew Sullivan wrote an article in which he argued for the legalization of same-sex marriage by invoking the same conservative arguments traditionally offered in support of heterosexual marriage.[1] At the time, legalization was a heretical position, and few pollsters even attempted to measure public attitudes toward it. One exception was the General Social Survey conducted by the National Opinion Research Center at the University of Chicago, which found only 12 percent of those queried in favor.

Just over a quarter of a century later, however, the Supreme Court's 2015 *Obergefell v. Hodges* decision required that every state recognize same-sex marriage on the same terms and conditions as for opposite-sex couples. The 5–4 decision, written by Justice Anthony Kennedy, was grounded on many of the same arguments Sullivan had made in 1989.[2]

In the legal climate of 2015, the court was hardly breaking new ground, for by that time same-sex marriage had already won legal status in thirty-six states, plus the District of Columbia and Guam.[3]

But if the *Obergefell* decision didn't surprise experts familiar with legal trends and polling data in 2015, it would have been all but unimaginable to many of those who read Sullivan's article when it first appeared.

For example, as the data journalist Nate Silver described his experience as a closeted gay high school student during that era,

> I was raised in East Lansing, Michigan. It was a great place to grow up: a college town with good public schools, a beautiful campus, a modicum of diversity, and an active, walkable downtown. But I came along just a few years too soon (I was born in 1978) to really consider coming out as gay when growing up. There were no openly gay students in my high school. And there were few gay role models in American society: certainly not on television and in the movies, which invariably portrayed gay men as camp characters, or freaks, or AIDS victims. If coming out was hard to contemplate, however, the possibility of gay marriage was unthinkable.[4]

Almost three-quarters of Americans were opposed to same-sex marriage when Sullivan's article appeared, and as recently as 2008 even Barack Obama and Hillary Clinton were publicly on record against it. In January of 2009, even liberal California voters approved a referendum banning same-sex marriage.[5] Yet when *Obergefell* was decided, just six years later, more than 60 percent of Americans thought same-sex marriage should be made legal, and even traditionally conservative states like West Virginia and the Carolinas had already taken that step. By May of 2018, a Gallup poll revealed that more than two-thirds of all Americans believed that same-sex marriage should be permitted.[6]

By almost any standard, this is an extraordinarily rapid change in public attitudes on such an emotionally charged subject. It's also a change that offers useful lessons about the dynamics of behavioral contagion. Why did events unfold so rapidly?

Nate Silver estimates that opinion shifted in part because of generational turnover. For decades, support for same-sex marriage was consistently higher among younger voters, and as older cohorts died

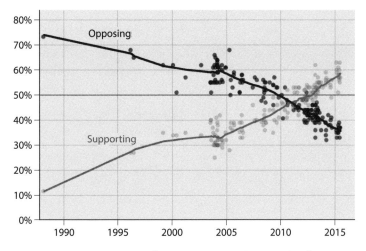

FIG. 4.1. Percentage opposing and supporting gay marriage in national, live-interviewer polls since 1988. Source: Roper Center, PollingReport.com, General Social Survey.

off, the composition of population opinion shifted accordingly. But an even bigger component of the increase in support appeared to stem from many people having changed their minds.

The dotted line in figure 4.2, for example, summarizes Silver's estimates of how much lower support for same-sex marriage would have been in 2014 if all respondents had continued to hold the same opinion they held a decade earlier.

But why did people change their minds? Silver suggests that part of the answer is that voters are more likely to support same-sex marriage if they are personally acquainted with a gay person. Statistics on changes in the proportion of gay people who are out are harder to come by, but there is little doubt that it is considerably higher than when Silver was in high school. In a 2013 Pew survey, for example, 77 percent of gay men and 71 percent of lesbian women said that all or most of the important people in their lives were aware of their sexual orientation.[7] Media portrayals of gay characters have also become both more common and much more sympathetic in the years since Sullivan's article appeared.

Although Republicans are only roughly half as likely as Democrats to support same-sex marriage,[8] the positions taken by prominent

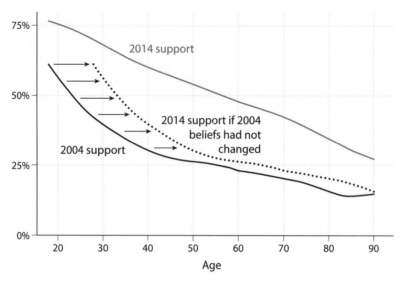

FIG. 4.2. Estimated support for gay marriage by age, 2004 and 2014. Source: General Social Survey and 538.com.

Republican leaders provide further support for the implied role of empathy in the growth of support for same-sex marriage. Senator Rob Portman (R-OH), for example, once opposed gay marriage legalization but has said that when his son Will came out to him, his position began to change. "It allowed me to think of this issue from a new perspective, and that's of a dad who loves his son a lot and wants him to have the same opportunities that his brother and sister would have, to have a relationship like Jane and I have had for over 26 years."[9] Former vice president Dick Cheney, whose daughter Mary has been with her partner, Heather Poe, since 1992, expressed his support for same-sex marriage legalization at the state level in a 2009 speech.[10] Mary Cheney and Ms. Poe were married in Washington, DC, in 2012.

To understand why public opinion on same-sex marriage changed so rapidly, we will also find it helpful to consider the related question of what it is considered safe to say publicly. As the essayist Paul Graham wrote in 2004, "It seems to be a constant throughout history: In every period, people believed things that were just ridiculous, and believed them so strongly that you would have gotten in terrible trouble for saying otherwise."[11]

Even today, the mere fact of being gay is still a crime punishable by imprisonment or death in many countries.[12] Antigay sentiment never ran that high in the United States, and even fifty years ago there were already substantial numbers of Americans who believed that same-sex marriage should be permissible. But most of them also understood that they would receive serious pushback if they stated that view publicly. Today, by contrast, most Americans seem to believe that it is safe to state publicly that same-sex marriage should be permitted.

International and intertemporal contrasts in attitudes abound regarding issues other than same-sex marriage. In the United States, today, for instance, few people think, and many fewer still would be willing to say publicly, that eating dogs would be a good thing. But dogs have long been staple menu items in Cambodia, China, Laos, South Korea, Thailand, the Philippines, and Vietnam.

Are the citizens of those countries morally wrong? Or are Americans the ones who are missing something? What seems true is that countries in which dogs are most commonly kept as pets are also the ones whose citizens are most likely to regard eating dogs as a moral violation. Taiwan, where keeping dogs as pets has become increasingly common, recently outlawed the practice.[13]

Is it morally wrong to eat the eggs of chickens raised in cages? Decades ago, few Americans would have given thought to the question. But today, a growing number of people are willing to purchase only the eggs of humanely raised chickens.

Belief patterns exhibit such striking variability over time and across geographic locations in part because we have limited capacity for reaching independent judgments on what it makes sense to believe about any given subject. Under the circumstances, it is perhaps inevitable that we exhibit such a strong tendency to be influenced by what our peers believe.

Taking cues from others is an adaptive strategy much of the time. Philosophers once engaged in vigorous debate about whether human slavery could be morally justified, but today few people give even a moment's thought to the details of that debate. That slavery is morally wrong is almost universally regarded as a settled question. Most people didn't arrive at that view after having carefully studied the arguments that led to the historical debate's resolution. We think it's a settled question simply because almost everyone we know regards it as one. The considerable energy we once devoted to this question can now be allocated to the long list of still-unanswered questions and other more useful pursuits.

Regardless of why others influence us so strongly, the simple fact that they do is the key to understanding why belief patterns are often so volatile across time and space. Such instability is an inevitable consequence of behavioral contagion.

If a family member, friend, or neighbor comes out, each member of that person's social network now knows one more gay person. In the process, each of the social networks of each of these people becomes marginally more sympathetic and generous in their attitudes toward gay people. And that, in turn, makes it less difficult for others to come out. The speed of the resulting changes in attitudes is impossible to predict without more knowledge about the specific magnitudes of these positive-feedback processes. But given what formal mathematical modelers know about the dynamics of such processes, the possibility of extremely rapid change should surprise no one.[14]

———

Positive-feedback processes foster not only rapid shifts in public opinion, but also ones that are extremely difficult to predict. For example, as the economist Timur Kuran described in his 1997 book, *Private Truths and Public Lies*, virtually no political experts foresaw the rapid breakup of the Soviet Union that began in the late 1980s (apart from a few who had predicted its collapse every year for many years). In Kuran's account, pundits overestimated the Soviet bloc's stability largely because most people who lived in member countries voiced consistent support for their leaders in public opinion polls.

But because speaking out against a regime in power entailed obvious risks, polling data were not a reliable measure.[15]

There's safety in numbers. The cost of speaking out depends in part on how many others are also speaking out. Some speak out no matter what, but others are willing to do so only if sufficiently many others join them. The upshot is that even seemingly minor provocations or small changes in the odds of punishment can unleash a prairie fire of unexpected public opposition—first, by inducing a few additional people to speak out, which then induces still others to do so, and often culminating in a near-complete reversal of public opinion. This kind of process explains why big changes sometimes happen so quickly and with so little forewarning.

The potential for explosive shifts in public support for a country's government can be seen clearly in the context of a simple numerical example. Imagine a population consisting of ten citizens—call them A, B, C, D, E, F, G, H, I, and J—who live under an authoritarian regime that they would oppose publicly if they thought it safe to do so. Each has a threshold indicating his or her willingness to speak out as a function of how many others are speaking out. A, for example, is a radical who's willing to speak out no matter what. B and C are only slightly more cautious, each willing to speak out if at least 20 percent of their fellow citizens are also speaking out. The remaining citizens have higher thresholds, as summarized in figure 4.3 (top). Citizen A, by assumption, will speak out irrespective of what others do. But A constitutes only 10 percent of the population, and that's below the threshold of each of the others, all of whom therefore remain silent. The stable outcome in this situation, indicated by the asterisk above the shaded entries, is thus that only one in 10 citizens speaks out. The regime survives.

But now suppose something causes B to become less cautious. Perhaps he is emboldened by news accounts of German dissidents who suffered no consequences when they dismantled the Berlin Wall. Or perhaps he or a family member has suffered in some unexpected way from an action by the regime. Whatever the cause, his threshold for speaking out falls from 20 percent to only 10 percent, as indicated in figure 4.3 (bottom). Since A is already speaking out,

	Individual	* A	B	C	D	E	F	G	H	I	J
1.	Threshold for speaking out	0%	20%	20%	30%	40%	50%	60%	70%	80%	90%

	Individual	A	B	C	D	E	F	G	H	I	* J
2.	Threshold for speaking out	0%	10%	20%	30%	40%	50%	60%	70%	80%	90%

FIG. 4.3

B's slightly lower new threshold is now met, so he too speaks out, in the process raising the percentage of citizens speaking out to 20. This makes citizen C willing to speak out as well, pushing the percentage to 30. Citizen E then starts speaking out, raising the percentage speaking out to 40, and so on.

In short order, a small change affecting only B causes the percentage of the population speaking out against the regime to rise from only 10 percent to 100 percent, again as indicated by the asterisk above the shaded entries. This time, the regime topples.

This skeletal example illustrates the concept of a tipping point, a term coined by the sociologist Everett Rogers, later developed by the economist Thomas Schelling, and popularized by the author Malcolm Gladwell.[16] In related work, the climate scientist Edward Lorenz described what came to be known as butterfly effects, cases in which even a tiny change in one part of an interconnected system can cause dramatic changes in the system's later behavior.[17] The term was inspired by the idea that the flapping of a single butterfly's wings in one location could unleash a cascade of events that would precipitate a tornado in a distant locale. Lorenz stumbled on this insight when he noted that even tiny changes in data-rounding procedures often produced dramatic changes in the forecasts of his mathematical climate models. Earlier versions of the same insight have been credited to the French mathematician Henri Poincaré and the American mathematician Norbert Wiener, whose models were later popularized by James Gleick.[18] And in an analysis richly informed by research across multiple disciplines, Cass Sunstein has explored contagion's role in political change.[19]

———

The Me Too movement is another important case study in the dynamics of behavioral contagion, one that highlights the internet's evolving role in shaping public opinion. The movement originated under that name in 2006 as a result of Harlem activist Tarana Burke's efforts to highlight public awareness of sexual assault in minority communities.[20] Yet despite evidence of widespread sexual misconduct in the workplace and beyond, the Me Too movement attracted little attention over the next decade.

The catalysts for the movement's meteoric takeoff in 2017 were several. One was an October 5, 2017, *New York Times* article by Jodi Kantor and Megan Twohey in which they described a long history of egregious sexual misconduct by the celebrated film producer Harvey Weinstein. Weinstein was then CEO of the Miramax Studio, whose releases included such critically acclaimed films as *Sex, Lies, and Videotape*, *The Crying Game*, *Pulp Fiction*, *The English Patient*, *Shakespeare in Love*, and *The King's Speech*.

Over a span of nearly three decades, the *Times* reporters wrote, "after being confronted with allegations including sexual harassment and unwanted physical contact, Mr. Weinstein has reached at least eight settlements with women, according to two company officials speaking on the condition of anonymity."[21] Among those cited as complaining about harassment by Weinstein were several prominent actors, including Ashley Judd and Rose McGowan.

The article by Kantor and Twohey was prompted in part by an internal staff memo by the Weinstein Company's Lauren O'Connor, who described a culture of widespread sexual harassment at the firm: "I am a 28 year old woman trying to make a living and a career. Harvey Weinstein is a 64 year old, world famous man and this is his company. The balance of power is me: 0, Harvey Weinstein: 10."[22]

Less than a week after the *Times* article ran, an even more explosive piece by Ronan Farrow appeared in the *New Yorker*'s online edition.[23] Farrow cited several more prominent actors, including some who accused Weinstein of rape.

Days after the Farrow article appeared, the actor Alyssa Milano sent this October 15, 2017, tweet:

> If you've been sexually harassed or assaulted write 'me too' as a reply to this tweet.
>   Me too.

> Suggested by a friend: "If all the women who have been sexually harassed or assaulted wrote 'Me too' as a status, we might give people a sense of the magnitude of the problem."

Several days later, the actors Gwyneth Paltrow, Angelina Jolie, and Kate Beckinsale reported that they too had been harassed by Weinstein. Those reports provoked a flood of additional #MeToo statements, including ones by Reese Witherspoon, Anna Paquin, Lady Gaga, Rachel Evan Wood, and Rosario Dawson, who described abuse by entertainment industry figures other than Weinstein.[24]

Less than two weeks later, according to Twitter records, there had been over 1.7 million tweets containing the Me Too hashtag—#MeToo—and eighty-five different countries in which at least one thousand such tweets had originated.[25]

The Milano tweet highlights one of the ways that the internet has dramatically altered the speed and power of behavioral contagion. Twitter's hashtag feature—a keyword preceded by a pound sign—succinctly identifies the subject of a tweet, thereby making it substantially easier for people interested in that subject to find and communicate with one another. In a matter of days, the Me Too movement garnered dramatically more attention than it had during the preceding eleven years.

But the internet has affected Me Too in a second, less obvious, way, by radically disrupting the historical business models of entertainment purveyors and the news organizations that report on them. When Weinstein launched his Miramax production company in 1980, roughly one hundred films were released to theaters each year. There were more than seven times that many films released in 2016, but still only about one hundred slated for wide release in theaters, which was Miramax's market niche. Expanding on the point made by Lauren O'Connor in her Weinstein Company internal staff memo, the technology analyst Ben Thompson wrote,

> Suppose there are five meaningful acting jobs per movie: that means there are only about 500 meaningful acting jobs a year. And Weinstein not only decided who filled many of those 500 roles, he had an outsized ability to affect who filled the rest by making or breaking reputations. Weinstein was a gatekeeper, presented with virtually unlimited supply while controlling limited distribution: those that wished to reach consumers had to accede to his demands, no matter how criminally perverse they may have been. . . . If he were to not select an actor, or purposely damaged their reputation through his extensive contacts with the press, they wouldn't have a chance in Hollywood. After all, there were many others to choose from, and no other routes to making movies.[26]

Thompson went on to argue that the internet has been rapidly weakening the power of gatekeepers like Harvey Weinstein, because talent and cachet are increasingly flowing away from movies toward distributors like Netflix and HBO, which go directly to consumers. Lest that seem merely the replacement of one set of gatekeepers by another, Thompson reminded us that only so much time is available for watching video entertainment and that YouTube showed over a billion hours of video each day in 2016. YouTube's minor-league superstars don't earn nearly as much as the best-known film actors, of course, but they are almost completely invulnerable to threats from gatekeepers like Harvey Weinstein.

Thompson noted that the internet has further weakened the power of gatekeepers by diminishing their capacity to punish media outlets that publish damaging stories about them. Among the most disturbing elements of the Weinstein revelations were complaints from reporters who had tried to publish articles about Weinstein's abuses many years earlier, only to see them quashed by editors fearful of losing substantial Miramax ad revenue. More recently, however, people have been getting much of their information from outlets like Twitter and Facebook. The upshot is that the kinds of stories that reach the public depend much more on the public's appetite for information than in the past, and much less on what would-be gate-keepers want people to see.

———

As one final example of how behavioral contagion can affect public attitudes, consider the evolution of views toward marijuana legalization. Over the past half century, surveys done by the Pew Research Center show a dramatic increase in the proportion of Americans who think that the use of marijuana should be made legal. But although the increase over that period is as great as the increase in support for same-sex marriage that has occurred since the 1980s, it follows a less uniform pattern. As seen in figure 4.4, support for marijuana legalization increased sharply during the counterculture revolution from 1969 through the late 1970s, then declined almost as sharply during the Reagan-era backlash, before resuming its upward trend in 1990.[27]

As in the case of same-sex marriage, support for legalization of marijuana has been consistently higher among younger cohorts, and those self-identifying as liberal are more likely to favor legalization than those who identify as conservatives. But whereas women were consistently more likely than men to favor the legalization of same-sex marriage, the reverse has been true for marijuana.

Will the recent momentum in favor of marijuana legalization persist? According to scholars who have studied the survey data closely, it is too soon to say. As William Galston and E. J. Dionne, Jr., wrote, for example, "But while it is true that the country is unlikely to return to overwhelming opposition to legalization, it is much less clear that opinion on marijuana will follow the exact trajectory of opinion on gay marriage."[28]

Behavioral contagion processes, once launched, are not always unstoppable. The continuation of growing support for marijuana legalization is uncertain in part because the arguments for and against

Do you think the use of marijuana should be made legal, or not? (%)

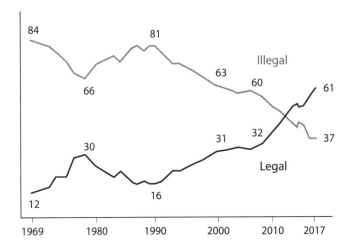

FIG. 4.4. Pew Research Center.

it embody much of the ambiguity that characterizes those for and against the legalization of other mind-altering drugs.

There is no dispute, for example, that alcohol consumption causes enormous harm not just to heavy drinkers themselves but also to innocent bystanders. The desire to limit such harm led to passage of the Eighteenth Amendment to the US Constitution, which prohibited the production, transport, and sale of alcohol in the country. Enforcement of this amendment began with passage of the Volstead Act in January of 1920. Prohibition was in effect for more than a decade, during which time many of the clearly documented harms from excessive alcohol consumption, including family abuse and deaths from cirrhosis of the liver, declined precipitously.

But in part because there were also numerous unintended negative side effects of Prohibition, and in part because of changing voter attitudes caused by the Great Depression, political support for Prohibition had declined significantly by the early 1930s. Passage of the Twenty-First Amendment officially repealed the Eighteenth Amendment in 1933.[29] But because the alcohol-related injuries that had led to Prohibition's original enactment have not gone away, many policy analysts continue to search for practical ways to limit those injuries without incurring the costs of outright prohibition. (More on this point in chapter 7.)

Although many studies suggest that marijuana poses fewer dangers for both users and bystanders than alcohol does, researchers remain concerned about the possibility of serious long-term side effects, especially for adolescents. As Galston and Dionne concluded,

> Here again, the lesson of Prohibition is helpful, though in the opposite direction. Prohibition lost public support because of its unintended consequences. The question this time will be whether legalization of marijuana achieves the ends that those who support it promise without an undue number of unanticipated negative side-effects. The kinds of regulatory regimes states establish will be an important part of the story. How the federal government deals with states that have legalized marijuana will also play a major role in whether these state experiments are seen as successes or failures. This, in turn, will determine whether the strong support for legalization among younger Americans endures and creates a new majority on behalf of a cause once supported by only a few.[30]

———

Additional insight into how behavioral contagion alters belief patterns is afforded by studying the world of fashion. As the essayist Paul Graham has observed, the forces that drive clothing styles are analogous to those that drive fashions in the domain of opinion more generally:

> Have you ever seen an old photo of yourself and been embarrassed at the way you looked? Did we actually dress like that? We did. And we had no idea how silly we looked. It's the nature of fashion to be invisible, in the same way the movement of the earth is invisible to all of us riding on it.[31]

That fashion shapes people's ideas about what to wear would strike few people as a matter of great public concern. Nothing of lasting importance, after all, hinges on how people answer the question

"How wide should my necktie be?" Nor are there clear criteria according to which a particular answer to that question could be judged correct.

But Graham argues that fashion shapes people's ideas about many other things, too. Like fashion's influence on clothing demand, some of those other influences are not matters of concern. It is not clear, for example, that anyone has suffered because of fashion's influence on tastes in art. But in many other cases, fashion's influence on our thinking can be costly indeed. As Graham writes,

> What scares me is that there are moral fashions too. They're just as arbitrary, and just as invisible to most people. But they're much more dangerous. Fashion is mistaken for good design; moral fashion is mistaken for good. Dressing oddly gets you laughed at. Violating moral fashions can get you fired, ostracized, imprisoned, or even killed.[32]

Moral fashions can be correct, as most of us believe current views about slavery and same-sex marriage to be. But because current beliefs about these subjects were once regarded as incorrect, there is of course no presumption that current moral fashions are correct just because most people embrace them.

From a public policy perspective, the cases of greatest interest share two properties: (1) What people believe affects the policies they support in ways that have significant impact on people's lives; and (2) there are cogent reasons for thinking that the currently prevailing beliefs are wrong. In such cases, a better understanding of behavioral contagion processes may offer useful guidance about how to change prevailing beliefs.

To illustrate, let's assume, uncontroversially, that beliefs about legalization of same-sex marriage have a profound impact on people's lives. And with acknowledgment that some will still disagree, let's also assume that most Americans' beliefs about the consequences of legalization were incorrect when Andrew Sullivan's article was published in 1989. How would what we know about behavioral contagion processes influence someone's strategy for trying to change people's beliefs on this subject? Examining the sequence of events by which beliefs actually did change offers some suggestions.

The core objective is to launch contagious conversations based on persuasive arguments against prevailing beliefs. Nate Silver argues that attitudes toward same-sex marriage changed in large part because of the strength and clarity of advocates' pro-legalization arguments.[33] In his 1989 article, for example, Sullivan wrote,

> Society has good reason to extend legal advantages to heterosexuals who choose the formal sanction of marriage over simply living together. They make a deeper commitment to one another and to society; in exchange, society extends certain benefits to them. Marriage provides an anchor, if an arbitrary and weak one, in the chaos of sex and relationships to which we are all prone. It provides a mechanism for emotional stability, economic security, and the healthy rearing of the next generation. We rig the law in its favor not because we disparage all forms of relationship other than the nuclear family, but because we recognize that not to promote marriage would be to ask too much of human virtue. In the context of the weakened family's effect upon the poor, it might also invite social disintegration. One of the worst products of the New Right's "family values" campaign is that its extremism and hatred of diversity has disguised this more measured and more convincing case for the importance of the marital bond.[34]

Sullivan pointed out that precisely the same arguments apply with equal force to same-sex marriage. He went on to argue that domestic partnership arrangements, then the most common alternative proposal for same-sex relationships, would "open a Pandora's box of litigation and subjective judicial decision-making about who qualifies." Many of the same arguments were offered by Justice Kennedy in his defense of the court's *Obergefell* decision.

Of course, even compelling arguments don't always prevail in the short run. But although progress is far from uniform, many have argued that better arguments tend to prevail in the long run. As Martin Luther King, Jr., once put it, "The arc of the moral universe is long but it bends toward justice."[35]

It's a view with a long history. Theodore Parker, a nineteenth-century Unitarian minister, was a passionate advocate of the abolition of slavery. A collection of his sermons published in 1853 included this passage:

> Look at the facts of the world. You see a continual and progressive triumph of the right. I do not pretend to understand the moral universe, the arc is a long one, my eye reaches but little ways. I cannot calculate the curve and complete the figure by the experience of sight; I can divine it by conscience. But from what I see I am sure it bends towards justice. . . . Things refuse to be mismanaged long. Jefferson trembled when he thought of slavery and remembered that God is just. Ere long all America will tremble.[36]

The Civil War broke out less than a decade later.

The difference in the public-opinion trajectories of support for same-sex marriage and marijuana legalization provides further support for the view that substantive arguments actually matter in the long run. Regarding same-sex marriage, opposition was grounded largely on the fact that same-sex couples had long been forbidden to marry. As the conservative philosopher and politician Edmund Burke would have argued, that fact alone places a significant burden of proof on those who advocate change. But opponents of change offered little else. In particular, they offered few carefully reasoned arguments about why same-sex marriage should have been forbidden. In contrast, proponents of same-sex marriage painstakingly attempted to explain why such marriages would not only pose no threat to community interests; they would actually contribute to many positive outcomes. Once people began to hear and discuss those arguments, they steadily gained traction.

It would be a mistake to paint too rosy a picture. The properties that make a meme effective often encourage the spread of ideas that are socially destructive. So in the short run, at least, there can be no presumption that competition in the marketplace for ideas promotes the common good. And as John Maynard Keynes observed, "In the long run, we are all dead."

In today's hyperpolarized political climate, the biggest challenge is simply to initiate productive conversations between people who don't agree to begin with. Studies have shown that those who deny the existence of human influence on the earth's climate tend to discount reports that temperatures are rising faster than scientists had expected, while embracing reports that temperatures are rising more slowly. By contrast, those who believe that human actions do contribute to climate change show the opposite pattern of reactions to the same scientific reports.[37]

The good news is that psychologists and others have made at least some progress in learning how to overcome such communication barriers. The lessons of that research will be our focus in chapter 13.

5

The Sexual Revolution Revisited

The year 2017 marked the fiftieth anniversary of the "Summer of Love," during which as many as one hundred thousand young people congregated in San Francisco's Haight-Ashbury neighborhood to proclaim their support for new social norms. According to contemporaneous accounts, that summer's celebration of "sex, drugs, and rock & roll" was a major inflection point in changing national attitudes toward the acceptability of premarital sex.[1]

Some have attributed the sexual revolution of the 1960s to the sudden availability of oral contraceptives, which gave women a more effective and less conspicuous means of controlling their risk of pregnancy.[2] But although the pill reduced some of the most important costs of engaging in premarital sex, its significance is overstated. After all, many millions of sexually active unmarried women did, and still do, rely on other, nonhormonal forms of contraception.

That the pill alone did not launch the sexual revolution is not a novel claim. As the historian Stuart Koehl wrote, for example,

> Many of the behaviors predisposed by the pill were already common, albeit covert, features of American life once the pill became available. The pill added fuel to a smoldering fire; it

didn't start the blaze, but it certainly accelerated it and ensured its spread.[3]

A tendency to overstate the pill's role is in part a reflection of economists' influence on how researchers think about human decision making. The cost-benefit model that guides economists' thinking is highly individualistic in nature. In this framework, the decision rule for whether to engage in premarital sex is the same as for any other action: if the benefits to someone of taking an action exceed the costs, she should take it; otherwise not. This approach emphasizes costs and benefits that apply directly to the decision maker herself. Any positive or negative side effects that an action might entail for others are typically given little or no weight by the decision maker. Broader influences from the social environment are sometimes acknowledged in the cost-benefit framework but seldom occupy center stage.

Here I will argue that social forces figured much more strongly in the sexual revolution than is generally acknowledged. Failure to appreciate their significance, I believe, has distorted the debate between those with opposing views about casual sex. A better understanding of the role of social forces in this domain won't settle any debates, but it may help opposing camps to better appreciate one another's point of view. And that, as we will see in chapter 13, is an important precondition for progress.

The pill did, of course, produce a significant reduction in the direct personal costs of engaging in premarital sex, especially for women, and for that reason alone led many more women to be willing to become sexually active. As the economic historian Claudia Goldin put it,

> The Pill was a great "enabler." With The Pill, large numbers of college women could embark on careers that involved long-term, up-front time commitments in education and training as physicians, lawyers, veterinarians, managers, and academics, among others. The Pill fostered women's careers by effectively lowering the costs of training. Sex was risky without a highly effective, female-controlled and easy to use contraceptive. A

pregnancy could derail a career, but The Pill enabled women to stay on track.[4]

All true. But the pill was not the only development that affected the direct costs and benefits of engaging in premarital sex, or even the most important one. A far more important predictor of the frequency with which people engaged in premarital sex in any era was the degree to which people believed that it was socially acceptable to do so. And in circular fashion, the degree to which people held that belief was itself strongly dependent on the proportion of people who were engaging in premarital sex. That proportion, in turn, was the result of many forces besides the pill.

Some of those forces altered individual cost-benefit calculations in ways analogous to the effects of the pill. As the economist Andrew Francis noted, for example, it was not until 1943 that penicillin was discovered to be effective against syphilis, which Francis called "the AIDS of the late 1930s and early 1940s."[5] In the space of a few years, penicillin eliminated what was then widely viewed as one of the biggest risks of engaging in premarital sex.

In a 2013 article, Francis argued that the era of modern sexuality originated not in the mid-1960s, but in the mid- to late 1950s. In support of his claim, he noted that measures of risky sexual behavior, such as teen pregnancy, out-of-wedlock births, and the incidence of less serious venereal diseases, rose sharply during the 1950s, in close correspondence with a decline in the incidence of syphilis infections to an all-time low. "Together," Francis concluded, "the findings supported the notion that the discovery of penicillin decreased the cost of syphilis and thereby played an important role in shaping modern sexuality."[6] The timing of events is at least consistent with Francis's argument: although the first legal birth control prescription in the United States was written in 1961, the pill was not legally available in many states until the Supreme Court's *Griswold* decision in 1965.

Other historians have pushed back against claims that technical innovations like the pill or penicillin hold the key to understanding more permissive attitudes toward premarital sex. Linda Gordon, for instance, notes that effective birth control methods became available to American women in the 1910s, followed by "a nationwide, massive birth control movement" in the aftermath of World War I.[7] These developments, in tandem with a shortage of young men in the years immediately following World War I, helped spawn the "Flapper Era" of the 1920s, described by many as a precursor to the sexual revolution of the 1960s. Family sizes shrank during those years as many states repealed laws against contraception, and extramarital sex also became more common.[8] The Kinsey Report, published in 1950, found that only 14 percent of women born before 1900 acknowledged having had premarital sex before the age of twenty-five, a figure that rose to 36 percent for women born after 1900.[9]

The historian Elaine Tyler May also argues that the role of pharmaceutical agents has been overstated as a cause of changing sexual attitudes. "Pharmaceutical products have a huge impact, but they're not causal agents," May wrote. "Sexual behaviors change more as a result of social changes than any kind of technological changes."[10]

According to the sociologist David John Frank, many of the social changes that helped spawn the sexual revolution are reflected in the repeal of laws against nonmarital or nonprocreative sex. As he put it, "I think it's the French Revolution that begins to break apart the monopoly of family thinking and begins to assert the primacy of individual thinking, and a shift from baby-making sex to individual-pleasure sex."[11] In Frank's view, penicillin and the pill magnified changes that were already well under way. He cited the example of oral sex, which became much more common during the middle of the twentieth century: "That's not because of the pill, or penicillin, or the condom," he said. "It's because we changed our way of thinking of sex."[12]

To agree with this statement is not to imply that technological innovations were unimportant. How we think about sex matters a great deal, of course, and technological innovations also played an important, if indirect, role in how we think about sex.

But at least some of the most important social forces that produced rapid changes in sexual attitudes were independent of technological innovations. Consider, for example, the sex-ratio imbalance in the implicit market for relationships during the mid-1960s, the very height of the sexual revolution often attributed to the pill. Because it had long been the custom for women to date men older than themselves, women reaching sexual maturity in the mid-1960s would normally have dated men born during World War II. But since birthrates were significantly depressed during the war, men born during those years were in short supply. Women who reached sexual maturity in the mid-1960s, who were born during the baby boom that began just after the war, were therefore significantly more numerous than men in the age group they would normally have dated.

Unless men and women then held substantially different attitudes about casual sex, this imbalance would have been expected to have little effect on courtship practices. But there is persuasive evidence that women's attitudes did differ from men's in the mid-1960s, and continued to do so for many years thereafter. Consider, for example, the economist Marina Adshade's description of an experiment done on university campuses in the late 1970s and early 1980s:

> This evidence may seem outdated, but in fact the timing was perfect; the sexual revolution was in full swing, and yet lovers were still blissfully unaware that right around the corner was a new disease, AIDS, that was about to change the way we think about casual sex. During the course of the study, moderately attractive men/women walked up to a woman/man on a university campus and said, "I have been noticing you around campus, I find you very attractive. Would you . . ." and then offered the unknowing participant one of three options: "have dinner with me tonight?"; "come to my apartment tonight?"; or "go to bed with me tonight?" Both the target men and women must have found the person attractive since more than 50 percent of each group said yes to dinner (56 percent of women and 50 percent of men). The interesting result, though, is that as the offers became more sexual the men increased, while the women decreased, their willingness to participate. Remarkably, 50 percent more men were willing to have sex with the random stranger than were willing to have dinner with her. And even those who said no (only 25 percent of the sample) expressed regret at having to do so. None of

the women in the sample agreed to have sex with the handsome random stranger. Not one. It isn't true that no women like sex with strangers—just as it isn't true that all men do—but there aren't enough to make [brothels for women], for example, profitable business ventures. After all, if women turn down offers of free sex, why should anyone think that they'd be willing to pay for it?[13]

Adshade went on to describe evidence that 42 percent of male respondents in a nationally representative survey said that they would like to have sex with multiple partners at the same time, compared with only 8 percent of female respondents.[14]

Let's assume, for the sake of discussion, that the traditional stereotype of men being more likely than women to favor premarital sex was roughly as strong during the mid-1960s as suggested by these survey findings. Given the shortage of eligible men in the dating pool during the mid-1960s (again, a shortage of men roughly two years older than the women who wanted to pair with them), did disagreements about premarital sex become more likely to be resolved in favor of the preferences of men?

To answer this question, we must first ask how big the sex-ratio imbalance actually was during 1967's Summer of Love and then look for evidence about whether an imbalance of that magnitude would have been likely to produce significant changes in courtship practices.

The general prediction of theoretical biologists is that the number of males in sexually reproducing species will tend toward equality with the number of females.[15] The logic underlying this prediction, articulated by R. A. Fisher, is straightforward. Suppose there were initially many more males in a population than females. A female born into this population would then be more likely than a male to be successful in finding a mate. People whose genes made them more likely to have female offspring would thus be expected to have more grandchildren than those who tended to have male offspring. And that difference, in turn, would cause the population's share of males to fall. The same argument proceeds in reverse for a population ini-

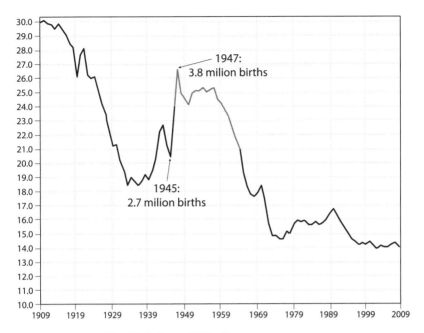

FIG. 5.1. Post–World War II baby boom, Wikipedia.

tially consisting disproportionately of females. The inevitable tendency, Fisher concluded, was for populations to end up with roughly equal numbers of males and females.

In human populations, there are actually slightly more males than females at birth.[16] But because mortality rates for males are slightly higher than for females, the male numerical advantage gradually gives way over time to a slight tilt in favor of females. For present purposes, I will assume, conservatively, that equal numbers of males and females born in the 1940s survived to young adulthood in the 1960s.

Figure 5.1 shows the dramatic increase in US birthrates that occurred following World War II. The US population in 1945 was approximately 132 million, so with a birthrate of about 20.4 per thousand for that year, there were roughly 2.7 million births in 1945. By 1947, the postwar baby boom was under way in earnest. The corresponding population and birthrate figures for that year were 143 million and 26.6, which translate to slightly more than 3.8 million births in 1947.[17]

The average male-female age difference at first marriage in 1967 was 2.5 years.[18] Given the sizes of the birth cohorts in 1945 and 1947, and assuming that equal numbers of males and females from those cohorts survived to adulthood, the implication is that for every one hundred twenty-year-old women seeking a male partner in 1967, there were fewer than seventy-one twenty-two-year-old men.

Is a sex-ratio imbalance of that magnitude large enough to matter? The evidence that bears most directly on this question comes from a 2011 study by the sociologists Jeremy Uecker and Mark Regnerus. The authors employed a nationally representative sample of college women to investigate dating practices and attitudes at American colleges and universities with a range of different sex ratios, many of them more heavily tilted toward women than the one for young Americans overall in 1967.

The authors began by describing the change in college dating practices that has occurred since the 1960s:

> The formal dating script that calls for men to ask women out on—and pay for—dates is no longer the primary heterosexual relationship script on campus. . . . Instead, men and women often meet at parties and engage in "hookups"—an ambiguous term describing casual physical encounters that range in intimacy from kissing to intercourse—which sometimes, but often do not, lead to a romantic relationship. Dating is not dead, but it seems increasingly understood as commencing after an exclusive (and perhaps even sexual) relationship is formed.[19]

The aim of this study was to explore how an important change in the composition of campus student bodies might be implicated in the observed change in dating practices. Whereas in the 1950s there were more men than women studying in American colleges and universities, by the early 2000s there were only seventy-five males for every one hundred females.[20] As the authors summarized their findings,

> Our results suggest that women on campuses where they comprise a higher proportion of the student body give more negative

appraisals of campus men and relationships, go on fewer traditional dates, are less likely to have had a college boyfriend, and are more likely to be sexually active.[21]

The authors report that women in their sample who have never been in a committed relationship are more likely to have had sex with a male classmate on campuses where men are underrepresented in the student body. For example, women who report never having had a college boyfriend have a 46 percent chance of having had sex when 60 percent of their classmates are women, but only a 31 percent chance of having had sex when only 47 percent of their fellow students are women.

The authors also find a similar experience gap for woman in their sample who report having had one or more serious campus relationships. On campuses where men outnumber women, 45 percent of these women said they had never had sex. But on those where women outnumber men, only 30 percent offered that response. The authors found a similar gap even for women with a current campus boyfriend: 30 percent of these women said they had never had sex on campuses where men outnumber women, versus only 17 percent on campuses where women outnumber men.

Regnerus and Uecker also reported that the frequency of casual sex was higher on campuses where women outnumber men. On such campuses, 27 percent of women who reported having had a boyfriend in the past but were not currently in a committed relationship had had sex during the preceding month, versus only 20 percent on campuses where men outnumber women.

In short, the authors found that historical dating patterns are less likely to persist on campuses where women outnumber men. They describe two different mechanisms that, alone or in combination, might have produced this pattern. Under what they call the "dyadic power thesis,"[22] a surplus of women gives men more power in romantic and sexual relationships, "which translates into lower levels of commitment and less favorable treatment of women on the part of men and a more sexually permissive climate."[23] A second mechanism they call the "demographic opportunity thesis," according to which "the gender imbalance on university campuses may simply mean there are fewer men available with whom women can pair; women's relationship searches will be less successful because there is a diminished supply of potential partners."[24]

The authors concluded that although both mechanisms appeared to be at work, their survey results strongly favored the dyadic power thesis. Traditional dating would of course be less common in environments in which women encounter fewer potential partners, but Uecker and Regnerus found far less traditional dating than the shortage of potential partners would suggest. A 1 percent decrease in the proportion of female students, for example, was associated with a 3.3 percent increase in the likelihood that a woman had had six or more traditional dates.[25]

A concern when interpreting the findings of studies like this is the possibility that the observed differences in behavior might stem not from differences in sex ratios but rather from systematic differences in the types of people who choose different types of schools. For example, if women with more permissive attitudes toward casual sex were attracted disproportionately to campuses whose cultures were more sexually permissive, the observed sex-ratio pattern would be an effect, rather than a cause, of the observed behavioral differences.

Uecker and Regnerus investigated this possibility by exploring whether women's views about committed relationships are correlated with campus sex ratios. Responses to their survey questions revealed no such correlation. As the authors put it, "Women on campuses with different sex ratios hold similar views about sexual morality, and they are neither more nor less likely to agree that they are not ready to be serious about romantic relationships, that being married is a very important goal, or that they would like to meet their husband in college. We find no support for the notion that women are attracted to campuses with different sex ratios based on their attitudes toward sex, commitment, and marriage."[26]

In a book published shortly after their study appeared, Regnerus and Uecker reported that more women on female-majority campuses also described participating in sex acts they disliked, and that others said they were having sex more often than they preferred.[27] On balance, the portrait that emerges from this work is strongly consistent with the view that women's bargaining power in campus sexual relationships is diminished when they inhabit dating pools in which they significantly outnumber men.

The median campus sex ratio in the Uecker-Regnerus study was 53.2 percent women, while their 90th-percentile campus had 59.6 percent women. In 1967, the pool of twenty-year-old women and twenty-two-year-old men consisted of 58.5 percent women, well above the median campus and almost as high as the 90th-percentile campus in the Uecker-Regnerus study.

A divergent sex ratio on a college campus is likely to have a smaller impact on the balance of sexual bargaining power than the same divergent ratio in the overall dating pool. A college student, after all, has the option of seeking partners in the broader community. But when the sex ratio is imbalanced for the dating pool as a whole, there is no similar recourse. So if sex-ratio imbalances on college campuses affected dating practices in the ways described, the effect of the actual imbalance in the overall dating population of 1967 was likely to have been even larger.

It seems reasonable to conclude, then, that the sex ratio in the overall dating pool of mid-1960s America was sufficiently imbalanced to have given men greater bargaining power in sexual relationships. Again, this is not to deny the influence of the pill and other technological innovations on changing patterns of sexual behavior. My point is only that social forces are likely to have influenced behavior far more than has been generally recognized.

Another feature of explanations that stress peer influences is their explicit acknowledgment of positive feedback effects. In contrast, explanations based on technological innovations are often purely static. One of the strongest forces inhibiting premarital sex in earlier eras was a widespread belief that it was morally wrong, that engaging in it would be damaging to one's reputation. But as we saw in chapter 4, beliefs about morality are often highly elastic. Once sufficiently many people came to believe that same-sex marriage was not a moral violation, for example, it became steadily more difficult for others to continue to believe that it was wrong. And as we have seen, rapid change is often a hallmark of social processes that entail positive feedback effects of this kind.[28]

Although the economists' cost-benefit approach often omits any consideration of concerns about the opinions of others, there is nothing inherent in the framework that requires this omission. By reducing many of the more narrowly material costs of premarital sex, the pill undoubtedly caused many individual cost-benefit tests to tilt in favor of engaging in it. But cost-benefit calculations can also incorporate anything else that people care about, including their concerns about morality and about what others think of them. So, in inducing some unmarried people to become sexually active by reducing the direct material costs of sex, the pill must also have had the indirect effect of reducing people's concerns about their reputations. That the pill was so widely discussed is also likely to have contributed to a loosening of the taboos surrounding premarital sexuality.

It seems fair to conclude, then, that although the pill undoubtedly helped accelerate the sexual revolution, it may well not have been the primary cause of it.

Once restraints on premarital sex have relaxed beyond a certain point, do the social forces thus unleashed continue to push in the direction of ever-diminishing restraint? As discussed in chapter 4, opinion shifts are not always unidirectional. As with views about marijuana legalization, attitudes about premarital sex do not appear completely settled. But just as we are unlikely to see a return to the former strong consensus in favor of marijuana criminalization, we may also be unlikely to again embrace Victorian moral codes regarding premarital sex.

Even so, opinion is likely to remain sharply divided about many aspects of the current hookup culture. As the journalist Kate Taylor wrote in a widely quoted *New York Times* article, "Until recently, those who studied the rise of hookup culture had generally assumed that it was driven by men, and that women were reluctant participants, more interested in romance than in casual sexual encounters. But there is an increasing realization that young women are propelling it, too."[29]

Taylor went on to describe interviews with female students at the University of Pennsylvania who saw their main priority as building their résumés, not finding someone to marry. "They envisioned their 20s as a period of unencumbered striving, when they might work at a bank in Hong Kong one year, then go to business school, then move to a corporate job in New York. The idea of lugging a relationship through all those transitions was hard for many to imagine."[30]

The journalist Hanna Rosin went even further in portraying the hookup culture as actively pro-women:

> To put it crudely, feminist progress right now largely depends on the existence of the hookup culture. And to a surprising degree, it is women—not men—who are perpetuating the culture, especially in school, cannily manipulating it to make space for their success, always keeping their own ends in mind. For college girls these days, an overly serious suitor fills the same role an accidental pregnancy did in the 19th century: a danger to be avoided at all costs, lest it get in the way of a promising future.[31]

But this view of current dating practices is not universally shared. During her senior year at Middlebury College, for example, Leah Fessler published a long essay in which she described the hookup culture's injurious effects on her and many of her classmates. Much of her essay was impressionistic, but she also conducted a series of interviews and surveys to probe attitudes more systematically. Although committed relationships during her years on campus were rare, Fessler found that 100 percent of female interviewees and 75 percent of female survey respondents stated a clear preference for such relationships. Only 8 percent of female respondents who were currently involved in hookup relationships reported being happy with their situation. The women she interviewed "were eager to build connections, intimacy and trust with their sexual partners.

Instead, almost all of them found themselves going along with hook-ups that induced overwhelming self-doubt, emotional instability and loneliness." She described one classmate who

> reported trying "traditional" hookup culture after a relationship ended, sleeping with various guys as liberated experimentation. "I had this façade of wanting to hook up with people," she explained, "but I don't think that was ever the entire motive. . . . And the fact that most of these guys wouldn't even make *eye contact* with me after having sex or would run away from me at a party is one of the most hurtful things I've ever felt."[32]

With debates about sexual morality having persisted throughout recorded human history, a robust consensus on this issue doesn't appear imminent. But a clearer understanding of the social forces that govern sexual behavior and attitudes may help us better understand why others might hold views that differ from our own, and why many might prefer at least some degree of sexual restraint to a complete absence of it. More important, an appreciation of the strength of peer effects might help us better understand why many feel their interests threatened by the behavior of people they will never meet.

Just as most parents want their children to grow up to be non-smokers, most want their children to grow up able to enjoy satisfying personal relationships as adults. Virtually no one questions either the legitimacy or the sincerity of these parental aspirations. But pursuit of them inevitably creates conflicts with those who are pursuing other legitimate goals of their own. The proportion of smokers among their children's peers affects parents' ability to achieve the first goal, and the sexual behavior of their children's peers affects their ability to achieve the second.

Notwithstanding that most smokers wish they had never started, some report that they continue to experience smoking as pleasurable. Their desire to continue smoking is not evidence of a desire to harm others. But smoking does harm others, and we regulate it out of a desire to limit this harm. There is reason to believe that if smokers understood more clearly how others were harmed by their behavior, they would be more sympathetic toward steps aimed at discouraging smoking. Similarly, recognizing the legitimacy of some people's desire to smoke encourages us to regulate in ways that, insofar as is possible, preserve their right to do so.

Similar issues arise in the domain of sexual behavior. Some years ago, a colleague's middle school daughter brought home a notice advising parents that some students had been engaging in oral sex during morning school-bus trips. That he was distressed by this news did not brand him as a busybody. As a psychologist, he was concerned simply because he understood how profoundly the social environment affects the range of options that maturing children feel free to consider. It was not unreasonable for him to have wanted his pubescent daughter to grow up in an environment in which she wouldn't feel coerced to have sex with the first boy who hit on her.

How should such concerns inform our views on public policy? Many parents oppose sex education in public schools, for example, out of concern that their children will interpret those programs as a signal that society approves of teenage sex. Some have gone on to demand that schools abandon sex education in favor of programs that stress strict sexual abstinence. An unsympathetic observer might interpret such demands as a gratuitous desire by those parents to impose their own moral vision on others who do not share it. But a more charitable interpretation is possible. These parents may simply understand that the options available to their own children depend heavily on the relationship choices made by the children of others. And if they believe that conventional sex education programs increase the likelihood that children will become sexually active, they might reasonably also believe that such programs threaten their interests.

But to recognize a parent's goal as legitimate is not to endorse any and all policy demands that might be motivated by it. The United States has higher rates of teen pregnancy and sexually transmitted diseases than any other developed nation. Abstinence-only sex education programs were adopted in many jurisdictions because their supporters believed they would reduce those rates. Persuasive evidence suggests, however, that these programs have in fact been counterproductive.[33] Studies also show that exposure to conventional sex education programs increases the age at which adolescents become sexually active.[34] That abstinence-only programs may have been prompted by the legitimate aspirations of some parents does not mean that the children of others should be forced to suffer the adverse consequences of those programs.

———

Behavioral contagion has a life of its own. There is no invisible hand that harnesses social forces to promote society's well-being. In the domain of sexual behavior, as in the domain of smoking, there is no presumption that social forces will mold beliefs and practices that are optimal in any socially meaningful sense.

Societies throughout history have been reluctant to embrace unlimited freedom in the domain of sexual behavior. Earlier restrictions were motivated in part by a desire to prevent injuries that can now be prevented by modern contraception and other pharmacological innovations. But that does not necessarily imply that most parents now want to raise their children in environments that are completely free of sexual restraint.

As we will see in the chapters in part IV, a clearer understanding of the power of behavioral contagion offers useful suggestions about how to balance competing public policy interests in many domains. Although compromise has proved especially difficult in the domain of sexual behavior, even here recognizing the importance of behavioral contagion can help us better understand what motivates those whose positions differ from our own. And as we will see in chapter 13, when people better appreciate why their opponents hold the views they do, attempts at finding common ground become more likely to succeed.

6

Trust

If there were no possibility of being detected and punished, would cheating be inevitable? It's a timeless question. In book 2 of the *Republic*, Plato explored it by introducing the Ring of Gyges, an artifact that enables its possessor to become invisible at will. In the text, Plato's brother Glaucon invokes the ring's corrupting influence to argue that people do not value justice for its own sake. As he puts it, "no man can be imagined to be of such an iron nature that he would stand fast in justice. No man would keep his hands off what was not his own when he could safely take what he liked out of the market, or go into houses and lie with any one at his pleasure, or kill or release from prison whom he would, and in all respects be like a god among men." The apparent conclusion, according to Glaucon: "A man is just, not willingly or because he thinks that justice is any good to him individually, but of necessity, for wherever any one thinks that he can safely be unjust, there he is unjust."[1]

Many share Glaucon's view that when individual interests conflict with those of society more broadly, narrow self-interest inevitably triumphs. Yet there are plentiful counterexamples, large and small.

A small one: Consider a traveler's decision of whether to tip in a distant restaurant he will never visit again. As the American custom has evolved, the tip is meant to compensate for the extra effort that good service requires, whose value to the diner generally exceeds the cost of the tip. From society's perspective, it would be better to leave the customary gratuity. Yet a truly selfish diner would always refrain from tipping while on the road. The tip comes at the end of the meal, after all, so the server cannot alter the level of service already provided. Nor can servers credibly threaten to retaliate by withholding good service in the future, since in most cases the offending diners won't be coming back. A vocal complaint from an untipped server is also unlikely, since it would serve only to risk being fired.

The apparent upshot is that if diners routinely failed to tip on the road, servers in restaurants patronized mostly by travelers would eventually cease providing good service. Yet courteous service persists even in such restaurants, where observed tipping rates are essentially the same as in other restaurants.[2]

Tipping on the road is just one of a long list of behaviors that challenge Glaucon's skepticism about morality. Many people donate anonymously to charity; they return lost wallets to their owners with the cash intact; they vote in presidential elections, even in the face of long lines and inclement weather, and even though no presidential contest in any state has ever been decided by a single vote. Some examples of unselfish behavior come at great cost indeed, as when people risk their lives to save strangers in peril. For those who adopt Glaucon's view, such actions are completely unexpected.

In purely descriptive terms, personal sacrifice for the common good often seems motivated by moral sentiments such as empathy, or by a desire to affirm one's identity as an honorable person. When asked why they leave tips even after dining at restaurants they expect never to visit again, for example, people often say they don't want to feel responsible for the server's disappointment at not having received the expected reward for good service.

That people are often guided by moral sentiments is of course a good thing from the perspective of society as a whole. But it also poses interesting questions, not just for Glaucon's position, but also for Charles Darwin's framework of evolution by natural selection.

According to Darwin, the selection pressures that shaped our nervous systems are much like those that molded eyes and opposable thumbs: unless a specific feature assists in the struggle to acquire the resources needed to survive and rear offspring, it will not be favored. In purely Darwinian terms, then, people would not be expected to pass up opportunities to cheat in situations in which punishment is impossible, or even sufficiently unlikely.

I spent much of my early academic career grappling with these apparent contradictions. As I will try to explain, an examination of the social cues by which people influence one another can help to reconcile them. Under a set of perfectly plausible conditions, genuinely principled behavior can indeed emerge in even the most intensely competitive environments.

But if Glaucon's skepticism about genuine morality was not fully justified, opportunities to cheat can nonetheless become all but impossible to resist when one's peers are actively seizing them. As we will see, cheating is sometimes driven by even more powerful impulses than greed: *rule followers in a world without effective enforcement would often fail to earn even a minimally fair return on their talents and efforts.*

The logic behind these claims emerges clearly in the context of some simple examples. Consider first a competition between two types of people, those willing to promote the common good at personal expense, and those who are self-interested in the narrowest sense. In the Darwinian framework, the growth rate of each type in a population increases with its ability to acquire material resources. One cannot eat moral sentiments, after all, or feed them to one's offspring. Satisfaction from doing the right thing counts in the evolutionary struggle only insofar as it fosters resource acquisition.

By definition, however, doing the right thing entails avoidable costs. (Otherwise, we would call it "doing the prudent thing.") It thus seems to follow that people who were intrinsically motivated to do the right thing would inevitably be crowded out by opportunists.

Yet that hasn't occurred. How might an impulse to do the right thing generate additional material benefits that could compensate for the avoidable costs that it leads people to incur?

To see how this could happen, imagine yourself the owner of a successful local business. You are confident that a branch outlet of your enterprise would thrive in a similar city located two hundred miles away, but you cannot manage it yourself, and limitations on your ability to monitor a hired manager would prevent you from knowing whether she or he had cheated you. You could pay an honest manager a premium salary and still expect to earn a healthy profit. But a dishonest manager could reap an even larger gain by cheating you, in the process causing you to lose money on the venture. You would have no recourse, since there are many reasons besides dishonest management that a business might fail. You would have no way to know, much less prove, that your manager had cheated. Would you open the branch outlet?

A manager hired into this situation would confront what I call a *golden opportunity*—an opportunity to cheat with no possibility of detection and punishment. The economists' traditional self-interest model assumes that people who confront golden opportunities will cheat. If you find that assumption plausible, you would predict that opening the branch outlet would be a losing proposition. And for that reason, you would reluctantly decide against it. Note that this decision results in a worse outcome for both you and the manager than if you had opened the outlet and the manager had run it honestly.

This situation confronts you and potential managers with what the economist Tom Schelling called a *commitment problem*. If an applicant for your managerial position could somehow commit herself to manage honestly, she would want to. But merely declaring an intention to manage honestly would seem insufficient, since even a dishonest manager would have an incentive to say that under the circumstances.

What kinds of signals might lead you to predict that someone would manage honestly? The following thought experiment suggests a framework for thinking about this question:

> Imagine that you have just returned from a crowded concert to discover that you have lost $10,000 in cash. The money had been

in an envelope with your name and address on it that apparently fell from your coat pocket when you were leaving the concert. Do you know anyone not related to you by blood or marriage who you feel certain would return your cash?

When I've confronted students with this question, almost all respond affirmatively. In most cases, the person they have in mind is a close friend, someone they have known for a long time.

What makes them feel so confident? Since they almost certainly have never lost such a large sum in the past, they can't invoke similar experiences with the friend in support of their prediction. When pressed, most respond in terms that Adam Smith, David Hume, and other early moral philosophers would have approved: they say they know their friend well enough to feel certain that she would feel terrible at the mere thought of keeping their money.

In effect, they are invoking what those early writers called the moral sentiment of sympathy, a term that corresponds more closely to empathy in current usage. Note that for empathy to solve the branch-outlet commitment problem, it need not literally tie the manager's hands. If the gain from hiring an honest manager were sufficiently high, your expected payoff from opening the branch outlet could be positive even if there were some chance your assessment of the manager was incorrect.

If your own intuitions are in accord with those expressed by most of my students, you accept the essential premise required for moral sentiments to be sustainable in competitive settings. Because certain profitable exchanges are possible only when people can trust one another, trustworthiness becomes, in effect, a valuable economic asset. A trustworthy manager incurs avoidable costs by not cheating when there is no possibility of detection, yes. But if others can identify that person as trustworthy, she can command a premium salary that can compensate for those costs.

A moral sentiment that moves people to be trustworthy can thus be favored by natural selection for its capacity to help solve commitment problems like the one just described. To serve this purpose, the sentiment must satisfy two requirements: those who experience

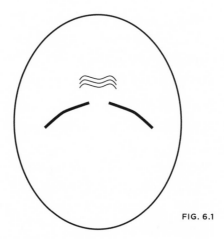

FIG. 6.1

it must be willing to subordinate narrow self-interest in the service of a higher goal; and at least some people must be able to make statistically reliable assessments of the extent to which a prospective trading partner is predisposed to behave in this way.

In the specific case of empathy, abundant evidence suggests that these requirements are met.[3] Darwin, for example, wrote of the hardwired link between emotional states in the brain and various details of involuntary facial expression and body language.[4] The crude drawing in figure 6.1, for example, shows only a few details, yet people in every culture recognize it as an expression conveying sadness, empathy, or some other closely related emotion. The expression requires specific contractions of the pyramidal muscles at the bridge of the nose and the corrugator muscles at the center of the brow. Most people cannot produce it on command.[5] (Sit in front of a mirror and try it!) Yet the relevant muscles display the expression spontaneously when the corresponding emotion is experienced.[6] Suppose you stub your toe painfully, leading an acquaintance who witnesses your injury to manifest that expression immediately. Seeing that happen would boost your estimate of the likelihood that your acquaintance would be a trustworthy trading partner. Someone who reacted to the same incident without expression would seem less likely to reward your trust.

Simple facial expressions are of course not the only clues on which we rely, or even the most important ones. Typically, we construct character judgments over extended periods on the basis of a host of other subtle signals, many of which enter awareness only subconsciously.[7] On the basis of these impressions, we choose among potential trading partners those we feel are most likely to weigh not just their own interests when deciding what to do, but our interests as well.[8] When two people enjoy a strong sympathetic bond with one another, they seem to realize it. And they are likely to behave cooperatively toward one another, even though they could earn more by behaving noncooperatively in situations that entail no chance of detection and punishment.

An obvious difficulty for this account is that dishonest people would have powerful incentives to mimic whatever signals others might use to identify someone as trustworthy. Skeptics object that such mimicry would always prevent the emergence of credible signals of honesty.

Notwithstanding this objection, the claim that specific emotions are accompanied by characteristic observable signals is well established. Numerous investigators have confirmed Darwin's claim that emotional states within the brain produce characteristic suites of autonomic nervous system responses that are visible to external observers.[9] And substantial evidence suggests that people rely on such cues when they interact with others in social dilemmas.[10]

If you believe you could confidently identify someone who would return your lost envelope in the earlier thought experiment, then you accept the fundamental premise necessary for genuine moral sentiments to emerge, even in bitterly competitive environments. But there is also experimental evidence that people can predict what others will do in situations that test their trustworthiness.

For example, my Cornell colleagues Tom Gilovich, Dennis Regan, and I found that subjects were surprisingly accurate at predicting who would cheat in a game in which cheating was impossible to detect.[11] Traditional self-interest models predict that everyone will cheat under these conditions. In our experiments, however, 74 percent of subjects behaved honestly, and only 26 percent cheated.[12] The focus of this experiment was not on the rate of cheating, but rather on whether subjects could predict which of their partners would cheat.

A stopped watch tells the correct time twice a day. Since 26 percent of subjects had cheated their partners, a random prediction of cheating would be accurate 26 percent of the time. Yet 57 percent of partners who were predicted to cheat actually did so. The likelihood of such high accuracy occurring by chance is less than one in one thousand.

Subjects in this experiment were strangers at the outset and interacted with one another for only thirty minutes before making their predictions. Predictions would almost surely be more accurate for people who had known one another for a longer time.

If signals that identify potential trading partners as trustworthy could be observed without cost and were completely reliable, people would be willing to do business only with people identified by those signals as trustworthy. Under these conditions, only trustworthy people would survive in the long run. In the evolutionary struggle, the lower payoffs characteristic of interactions plagued by mutual cheating would eventually consign dishonest people to extinction.

But that's of course not the world we live in. Signals that enable us to predict the behavior of others are not only imperfect; they also take time and effort to observe and evaluate. If a population consisted entirely of trustworthy individuals, it would be wasteful to expend that effort, just as it would be wasteful to install an expensive home security system if you lived in a community that had never experienced a burglary.

The implication is that an environment initially consisting only of trustworthy individuals would offer ripe pickings for dishonest mutants. Since most people wouldn't expend the effort needed to scrutinize potential trading partners, these mutants would enjoy ready access to trusting victims. In the process, they would acquire resources at a premium rate, causing their share of the population to grow. Once dishonest types became sufficiently numerous, however, it would pay honest types to take greater care in screening potential trading partners.

A similar dynamic would unfold in reverse if we began with a population consisting only of dishonest individuals. A small band of honest mutants that happened to find themselves in such a population would be exceptionally vigilant in their scrutiny of potential trading partners. By taking care to interact only with others they could confidently identify as trustworthy, they would garner higher payoffs than dishonest types, who would receive the low payoffs associated with mutual cheating.

The inevitable result in evolutionary models of this sort is a population composed of an uneasy mix of honest and dishonest types—in short, one like almost all human populations observed in practice. In mixed populations of this sort, behavioral contagion becomes exceedingly important.

That's because person-specific cues, such as a potential partner's reputation and your assessment of whether he seems to like you and feel concern about your interests, are rarely foolproof. Whether to trust someone should therefore depend not only on cues specific to that person, but also on what you know about the trustworthiness of people more generally. For any given set of person-specific cues, you would thus be more likely to judge someone trustworthy if your prior experience had shown 80 percent of the population to be trustworthy than if the corresponding figure had been only 30 percent.

That simple observation helps explain why rules and enforcement are so important. People who can be trusted when confronted with golden opportunities are chosen as trading partners only if others can identify them as such with sufficient accuracy. So even though genuine trustworthiness can emerge in a world without rules, its actual prevalence in any population will depend strongly on how strictly laws and norms are enforced.

To see why, note first that effective enforcement means that cheating doesn't often pay, leading people to behave honestly for prudential reasons, much as Glaucon argued. Yet many people also behave honestly even when faced with golden opportunities, or opportunities to cheat with no possibility of detection. As Aristotle realized, the moral sentiments that motivate such restraint do not arise out of thin air. Rather, they are nurtured by force of habit.[13] As the philosopher Will Durant paraphrased Aristotle, "we are what we repeatedly do. Excellence, then, is not an act but a habit."[14]

Enforcement is important because those who are induced by the threat of punishment to behave honestly in most circumstances become more likely to develop an inclination to behave honestly even when confronted with golden opportunities. The proportion of a population that is trustworthy even when confronted with golden opportunities will therefore be significantly higher in societies in which laws and norms are strictly enforced.

The prodigious power of behavioral contagion in the domain of trust should now be apparent. Any change in the environment that reduces the proportion of trustworthy people in a population—such as a relaxation of enforcement—will set in motion a feedback process that causes still further reductions. Each new reduction, in turn, will cause a further decline in the material rewards that come from being chosen as a trustworthy trading partner, leading to still further declines in the actual proportion of trustworthy people, and so on.

In short, although Glaucon was almost surely wrong about the possibility of genuine trustworthiness in the absence of strict enforcement, it would be a mistake to conclude that enforcement is unimportant. On the contrary, even though genuine morality can evolve spontaneously, it would be dramatically less common if laws and social pressure did not strongly reinforce it.

A second dimension of the power of behavioral contagion in the moral domain is the resentment people feel when they see rule-breakers gain at their expense. This is evident in the case of restaurant servers, who receive much of their compensation in the form of cash tips. Income in that form is difficult for the tax authorities to monitor. (In fact, tax authorities in most jurisdictions attempt to monitor tips and similar cash payments, so it would be more accurate to say that such payments are underestimated rather than not counted at all. But to simplify the discussion, I'll assume that tips cannot be monitored by the tax authorities at all.)

Imagine that your choices were to work in a factory for a pretax salary of $1,000 a week, or to wait tables for a weekly pretax salary of $500 a week plus weekly tips of the same amount. You consider the two jobs equally attractive apart from the matter of pay, and because you are honest, you expect to pay tax at the rate of 20 percent on income you earn from any source. Your after-tax pay would then be $800 a week no matter which job you took, and you would be indifferent between the two.

But now suppose that many factory workers shared your views about the two jobs except for one thing: they would feel no qualms about failing to declare tips that tax authorities could not monitor. These workers would want to switch to waiting tables because they could avoid tax on half their weekly income. Their after-tax pay as servers would thus be $100 a week higher than what they were earning in the factory.

The result would be an excess supply of people wanting to wait tables and a shortage of those wanting factory work. The inevitable response would be for wages to adjust until supply and demand in both labor markets were again in balance. If we assume for simplicity that foreign competition won't permit higher wages in factory work, the entire adjustment would fall on table servers. In the likely event that restaurants could fill every available server position with people willing to evade taxes on tips, the new wage for table servers would then decline until their after-tax income became equal to the $800 after-tax income of factory workers. This would require a server's salary to fall from $500 to $375 weekly.[15]

The difficulty confronting an honest waiter is immediately apparent. If he pays tax on the $500 a week he receives in tips, his weekly after-tax salary will be only $700, or $100 a week less than he would have taken home as a factory worker. And since he could have taken home $800 a week as a fully tax-compliant factory worker, he might reasonably conclude that paying taxes on his tips would be unfair.

This example, which I call *the waiter's dilemma*, illustrates why pressures to cheat are even stronger than those that would arise in social isolation. We see many examples in which people resist the temptation to plunder even when confronted with golden opportunities. But such opportunities become dramatically more difficult to resist when one's peers are seizing them without punishment. Indeed, it is easy to see why a waiter might consider it unjust to declare untraceable cash income that would cause him to be underpaid.

There is perhaps no policy arena in which behavioral contagion and traditional economic incentives reinforce one another more strongly than the domain of tax compliance. Traditional economic models of the extent to which people obey their country's tax laws focus almost exclusively on narrow material incentives.[16] Enforcement is important even in the context of such models, but to a far lesser extent than when we also allow for the effects of behavioral contagion.

Economists have begun to recognize that social forces play an important role in this domain.[17] James Andreoni and coauthors, for example, present evidence that tax compliance is also influenced by norms and social interactions, a position supported experimentally by James Alm and coauthors.[18] Brian Erard and Jonathan Feinstein suggest that moral sentiments like guilt and shame are also important determinants of tax compliance.[19] Michael Spicer and L. A. Becker offer experimental evidence that tax evasion is more likely when subjects believe they are being taxed unfairly.[20]

A creative study by the economists Jörg Paetzold and Hannes Winner sheds light on the extent to which tax evasion is influenced by peer behavior.[21] It employs data from Austria, where the government allows workers to deduct commuting expenses from their incomes for tax purposes. Under this allowance, workers self-report their total commuting distances, and it is then their employers' responsibility to certify the accuracy of their reports. But because many employers devote few resources to the verification step, misreporting entails little risk of punishment. Combining detailed tax data with employer and worker location data, Paetzold and Winner were able to verify that the claiming of excessive commuting expense deductions was in fact widespread.

By itself, that result is hardly surprising. For present purposes, the far more interesting part of the study was the authors' examination of the extent to which exaggerated deduction claims were influenced by peer behavior. To estimate that magnitude, they focused only on workers who had moved to new workplaces during the current tax year. Those who were now employed by a firm in which tax evasion was either the same or less common than in their previous workplaces showed no change in their own rates of tax evasion. But the pattern was strikingly different for workers who had moved to a new job in which tax evasion was more common: for these workers, tax evasion grew by an even larger proportion than the one by which their new colleagues' tax evasion exceeded that of their former colleagues.

Employers implicitly realize that if tax evasion entails little risk of punishment, they won't have to pay as much to attract the employees they need. One consequence is that employees who know that their coworkers are cheating on their taxes confront a version of the waiter's dilemma discussed earlier. In such cases, employees who are scrupulously honest on their taxes might reasonably view themselves as being unfairly underpaid. So even in Austria, which would normally be regarded as a rule-abiding country, citizens are not magically immune from peer influences.

Countries in which tax compliance is low operate at a significant disadvantage, often unable to sustain the infrastructure investments needed to support broad economic and social prosperity. In contrast, countries with high tax compliance have historically enjoyed an enormous edge. The United States was once firmly in the latter group. In a 2004 study that ranked thirty industrial countries on a 6-point tax-compliance scale, for example, it was in seventh place with a score of 4.47.[22] Highest on the list was Singapore at 5.05, followed by New Zealand (5.00), Australia (4.58), the United Kingdom (4.67), Hong Kong (4.56), and Switzerland (4.49). Last among the thirty nations studied was Italy, with a score of 1.77.

High levels of tax compliance are relatively easy to maintain if most citizens believe that others are behaving honestly. But that belief becomes more fragile once we allow for behavioral contagion. Traditional models, which ignore peer effects, suggest that tax evasion will increase if a reduction in tax enforcement causes people to believe themselves less likely to be punished for cheating. But because few taxpayers relish feeling like chumps, the indirect effects of reduced enforcement are likely to swamp the direct effects. Once people realize that others are getting away with cheating on their taxes, explosive feedback processes quickly ignite.

Since 2011, Republicans in Congress have been enacting steep cuts in the IRS budget that have led to reductions in the agency's enforcement activities. Nationwide in 2017, the criminal division of the IRS brought only 795 cases in which tax fraud was the primary crime, almost 25 percent fewer than it had brought only seven years earlier.[23] The agency audited only 1 in every 161 individual returns in 2017, compared to 1 in 90 in 2011. Only 1 in 101 corporate returns were audited in 2017, down from 1 in 61 in 2012.[24]

Relative reductions in audit probabilities have been even steeper for individuals and corporations at the top of the economic pyramid. Only 4.4 percent of people with over $1 million in annual income were audited in 2017, compared to 12.5 percent in 2011. For corporations with assets over $10 million, the audit rate fell from 17.8 percent in 2012 to only 7.9 percent in 2017.[25]

These moves have been ill-timed, coming as they have in conjunction with the passage of a complex and extensive change in the nation's tax laws in December of 2017. That legislation creates new distinctions between different types of income that are taxed at different rates, creating powerful new incentives to game the system by recharacterizing income. As Emily Horton of the Center on Budget and Policy Priorities wrote,

> If the IRS can't prevent this type of gaming, the tax cuts could be both costlier and more tilted to the wealthy than official estimates now show. But despite the new tax law's once-in-a-generation enforcement challenge, the 2018 government funding bill funded enforcement at roughly last year's level. The combination of new gaming opportunities and an underfunded, overworked IRS may well encourage the wealthy to push the boundaries of the new law.[26]

The top 0.5 percent of income earners were already accounting for a fifth of all unreported income, according to a study completed before the IRS budget cuts began.[27] The new enforcement environment clearly puts the American tradition of high tax compliance even further at risk. As IRS commissioner John Koskinen wrote in 2015, for example,

We estimate the drop in audit and collection case closures this year will translate into a loss for the government of at least $2 billion in revenue that otherwise would have been collected. Essentially, the government is forgoing billions to achieve budget savings of a few hundred million dollars, since we estimate that every $1 invested in the IRS budget produces $4 in revenue. The cumulative effect of the cuts in enforcement personnel since Fiscal 2010 is an estimated $7–8 billion a year in lost revenue for the government.[28]

The figures cited by Koskinen refer only to the direct effects of IRS budget cuts on lost revenue from obligations owed on current incomes. But the far more serious threat posed by reduced enforcement is that future revenue shortfalls will grow substantially larger as a result of behavioral contagion. The long-run cost of each $1 reduction in the IRS budget is thus likely to be far higher than the $4 revenue loss reported by Koskinen.

Some people's tax cheating is never discovered, even by the peers closest to them. But at least some proportion of tax cheating becomes known to others and, in a small number of cases, is made public for the entire world to see. According to a fourteen-thousand-word investigative report published by the *New York Times* in 2018, for example, most of the several hundred million dollars that Donald Trump inherited from his father was the fruit of "dubious tax schemes during the 1990s, including instances of outright fraud."[29] Revelations of this sort inevitably weaken the population's inclination to play by the rules.

———

Many of Adam Smith's modern disciples celebrate his theory of the Invisible Hand, which, in their telling, holds that market forces harness selfish individuals to serve the broader interests of society. As Smith wrote in *The Wealth of Nations* (bk. 2, chap. 2), "It is not from the benevolence of the butcher, the brewer, or the baker that we expect our dinner, but from their regard to their own interest."

Yet Smith was far more circumspect than many of his modern disciples about the power of the Invisible Hand. He understood that self-interest alone wouldn't lead to the greatest good for the greatest number. And he believed that markets could not function adequately in the absence of an elaborate foundation of laws and ethical norms.

George Akerlof and Robert Shiller, both Nobel laureates in economics, have argued that the same incentives that lead sellers to introduce quality improvements and cost-saving innovations in Adam Smith's Invisible Hand narrative also ensure that no profitable opportunity to cheat consumers will remain unexploited.[30]

Under even the most optimistic assumptions about human nature, such opportunities will remain abundant. Because of behavioral contagion, the social cost of each successful act of cheating is a multiple of its direct private cost. Resources invested in efforts to thwart cheating thus yield far higher returns than generally supposed.

The only people who stand to lose from such investments are precisely those we should most want to see lose.

7

Smoking, Eating, and Drinking

"Example, whether it be good or bad, has a powerful influence," wrote George Washington in a March 5, 1780, letter to Lord Stirling, one of his revolutionary war generals.[1]

We have long known that human behavior is heavily shaped by situational factors, especially by the behavior of peers. But many of those factors are themselves a consequence, in the aggregate, of our own actions. That the causal arrows also run in that second direction has received relatively little attention. That ought not to seem surprising, since the influence of any single individual's behavior on the overall environment is usually negligible.

Chapter 1 made these points in the context of the decision of whether to become a smoker. As considerable evidence suggests, the most important predictor of whether someone will smoke is the proportion of his or her peers who do so. Yet we can be sure that few people who are considering whether to smoke seriously consider that doing so might encourage others to take up smoking.

To the delight of public health advocates, smoking rates in the United States and many other industrial nations have declined sharply in recent decades, in large part because of higher cigarette taxes and other regulations aimed at discouraging smoking. But regulators did not invoke behavioral contagion as a rationale for these measures. Instead, they insisted that regulations were needed to protect nonsmokers from harms caused by secondhand smoke, or to protect taxpayers from having to subsidize the medical expenses of smokers. Those harms, however, are orders of magnitude smaller than the harms experienced by smokers themselves. The objection that government has no obligation to protect people from the consequences of their own actions loses force once we recognize that the harm smokers cause to themselves is far smaller than the harm they cause by making others more likely to take up smoking.

If social environments heavily influence our behavior, sometimes for the better but often for worse, it follows that the public has a legitimate interest in shaping individual behavior with an eye toward its impact on those environments.

In this chapter, I will explore in greater detail what researchers have learned about peer influences in the domain of smoking. I will also consider the extent to which obesity and excessive alcohol consumption are significantly affected by peer behavior.

Estimating the strength of peer influences on a specific behavior such as smoking might seem like a straightforward matter: just examine how the likelihood that someone with given personal characteristics will smoke varies with the proportion of his or her peers who smoke. And as researchers have long demonstrated, the correlations found in survey data are invariably large and positive. When the psychologist Laurie Chassin and coauthors queried almost four thousand students ranging from grades 6 to 11 about their smoking behavior in successive years, for example, they found that nonsmokers in the first survey were significantly more likely to have started smoking by the second survey if more of their friends were smokers.[2]

But simple correlations in survey data don't answer the question of greatest interest to policy makers, which is how someone would respond to changes in the behavior of peers. As the economist Charles Manski explained in an influential 1993 paper, any observed correlation could plausibly result from causes other than direct peer influence.[3] For example, if there were a high rate of smoking in a community, and teens were influenced to smoke primarily by whether their parents smoked, there would be a correlation between any given teen's likelihood of smoking and the proportion of his or her peers who smoke. But if parental influence had been the sole source of that correlation, policies aimed at reducing the smoking rate of peers would not make any particular teen less likely to smoke.

Similarly, even when the likelihood that a given person will smoke depends on peer smoking rates, it almost certainly depends on a host of other genetic and environmental influences as well. And because peer group membership is not randomly assigned in most cases, there will often be a tendency for people with similar genetic and environmental backgrounds to choose one another as friends. Here, too, we would observe a correlation between an individual's likelihood of smoking and the proportion of his or her peers who smoke. But that correlation would not be evidence that someone's decision to smoke would make peers more likely to do so. A tax on cigarettes would still make smoking less attractive to each individual peer group member, but the resulting lower smoking rate of others would not make it any more likely that a given individual would refrain from smoking.

To estimate the direct peer influences that are of greatest interest to policy makers, then, researchers must find ways to control for two potentially important confounding effects: that external causal factors other than the direct influence of peers often matter; and that peers typically select one another, rather than being assigned to group membership at random.

In the domain of adolescent smoking behavior, one study in particular stands out for the care with which the authors attempted to control for these potential sources of bias.[4] Using a large, nationally representative longitudinal sample of adolescents, the economists Mir Ali and Debra Dwyer estimated a multivariate statistical model in which they controlled for a variety of common environmental factors and peer-selection mechanisms. Their peer-group measures included not just people named as close friends, but also other classmates. Peer-group smoking rates were based on subjects' reports of their own cigarette consumption.

Ali and Dwyer estimated that even after they controlled for potential confounding variables, the direct causal influence of peer behavior was substantial. For their sample, a 10-percentage-point increase in the proportion of classmates who smoke raised the probability that a given adolescent would smoke by 3 percentage points. They also reported that peer effects are even stronger among groups of friends. If the proportion of smokers among close friends rose by 10 percentage points, for example, that adolescent's probability of smoking would rise by 5 percentage points.

A simple numerical example illustrates how dramatically the harm caused by peer influence overshadows the harm caused by exposure to secondhand smoke.

Consider a group of one hundred adolescent friends in which the number of smokers rises from ten to twenty, an increase in the group's smoking rate of 10 percentage points (from the initial rate of 10 percent to the new rate of 20 percent). According to Ali and Dwyer, the direct peer effect of this change is to raise the likelihood of each group member becoming (or remaining) a smoker by 5 percentage points. And since the group has one hundred members, that implies an expected increase of five smokers.

But the story doesn't end there. These five additional smokers raise the total number of smokers in the group from twenty to twenty-five, an additional increase in the group's smoking rate of 5 percentage points. The expected result of this second-round effect would be 2.5 more smokers—increasing the group's initial smoking rate by an additional 2.5 percentage points—which in turn would imply an additional 1.25 smokers, and so on. Effects of subsequent rounds would of course quickly become negligible. But when the process plays out, the final increase in the number of smokers in this group of one hundred would be twice as large as the original ten-person increase.

Many teens would of course have fewer than one hundred friends. I started with a group that large only because it makes the example simpler to describe. Examples involving smaller groups would yield the same conclusion. Consider, for instance, a group of five friends in which the number of smokers initially rose from one to two, an increase of 20 percentage points. According to the estimates of Ali and Dwyer, this would cause each member of the group to become 10 percent more likely to become or remain a smoker, which, in a group of five, translates to an additional increase in the expected number of smokers by 0.5 persons. That's a further increase of 10 percentage points in the proportion of smokers, which, in turn, would cause a further increase in the number of smokers, and so on. The ultimate effect of the initial one-person increase in the number of smokers would thus be $1 + 0.5 + 0.25 + 0.125 + 0.0625 + \ldots = 2.0$. The size of the peer group chosen thus doesn't alter the central conclusion that peer influence within a group effectively doubles the effect of an individual's decision to become a smoker.

Yet the examples I've just described actually understate the magnitude of peer influences on teen smoking. That's because they omit an important set of peer transmission channels that take place outside the boundaries of the original peer group. The original group of one hundred that I considered was constructed from the perspective of a specific individual member of it. In practice, many of its other ninety-nine members would include some of the group's members in their own personal peer groups, but those groups would also include many outsiders. So when new members of the original peer group take up smoking, the smoking rate in each of those other groups would rise as well, causing additional outsiders to become smokers, and so on.

Where this process would ultimately lead would obviously depend on many additional features of the environment, most critically on the degree of overlap between individual peer group memberships. But suppose we ignore those additional transmission channels and focus only on effects within the original peer group. The Ali and Dwyer estimates imply that if one additional person starts smoking in a group of adolescent friends of any size, direct peer influences within that group alone will result in one other teen taking up smoking as well.

Government policy makers, hoping perhaps to parry libertarian objections to cigarette taxes and regulations, have emphasized that measures to discourage smoking are not paternalistic, not intended to protect people from harming themselves. Rather, they are meant to limit the harm caused to innocent bystanders by secondhand smoke. Exposure to secondhand smoke does indeed cause real harm, but, as noted, that harm is extremely small in comparison to the health consequences of being a smoker. By far the greater harm caused when someone becomes a smoker is that he or she "causes" someone else to start smoking—someone who otherwise wouldn't have.

Yes, as opponents of regulation insist, people influenced in this way by peers are not forced to take up smoking. They have agency, and many do in fact resist. Yet for large populations, it becomes a statistical near certainty that an additional smoker in a group of friends will cause another person in that group to become or remain a smoker. So those who smoke are in fact causing harm to others vastly greater than any damage associated with exposure to second-hand smoke. With effort, many will succeed in avoiding that harm. But many others, such as parents who do not want their children to become smokers, simply have no recourse.

Largely because the smoking rate in the United States today is less than a third of what it was when I was a teen, none of my four adult sons has become a smoker. The stringent regulations that produced this outcome would be difficult to defend if their only purpose had been to prevent harm from secondhand smoke. But those regulations have clearly prevented harm on a vastly greater scale. With significant population groups continuing to smoke at high rates, peer pressure continues to cause enormous harm. If we adopted substantially tougher measures that caused smoking rates to fall still further over the next generation, would anyone look back at that step as having been misguided?

———

Behavioral contagion has also been shown to have influenced steep rates of growth in the incidence of obesity, both in the United States and in other parts of the world.

The condition is generally defined as an excess of body weight in relation to height. People are formally classified as obese if their Body Mass Index (BMI), calculated as weight in kilograms divided by the square of height in meters, takes a value of 30 or higher. Those with BMI values between 25 and 30 are classified as "overweight."[5]

Obesity is associated with increased risk of contracting a variety of health problems, including depression, type 2 diabetes, cardiovascular disease, certain cancers, as well as overall mortality from all other causes.[6] Some researchers, however, have argued that these risks have been overstated. In any event, there is broad agreement that they are less serious than those associated with smoking.[7]

But the risks are significant, and there is little question that obesity is on the rise. The proportion of American adults in the overweight category hovered around 31 percent between 1960 and 1994, but obesity rates climbed sharply during those same years, rising from 13 percent to 23 percent. By 1994, significantly more than half of all American adults were either overweight or obese.[8] The proportion of obese adults had risen to 32 percent by 2004 and in surveys completed in 2016 had reached almost 40 percent.[9] Rates for some groups are significantly higher, such as Hispanics (43 percent) and non-Hispanic blacks (48 percent).[10] There are also significant sex differences in extreme obesity (BMI values greater than 35), with many more women than men in that category.[11]

That peer influences are significantly implicated in the rise of obesity was introduced to the scientific community in a pathbreaking study by Nicholas Christakis and James Fowler published in the *New England Journal of Medicine* in 2007.[12] The authors studied a densely interconnected social network of more than twelve thousand people who were medically assessed at regular intervals between 1971 and 2003 as part of the renowned Framingham Heart Study. Each evaluation recorded not only the individual's BMI, but also a variety of other data that made it possible to examine how his or her weight gain was related to weight gains by friends, siblings, spouse, and neighbors.

Christakis and Fowler introduced their report with a brief summary of what had led them initially to believe that behavioral contagion might be a contributing factor in the spread of obesity:

To the extent that obesity is a product of voluntary choices or behaviors, the fact that people are embedded in social networks and are influenced by the evident appearance and behaviors of those around them suggests that weight gain in one person might influence weight gain in others. Having obese social contacts might change a person's tolerance for being obese or might influence his or her adoption of specific behaviors (e.g., smoking, eating, and exercising). In addition to such strictly social mechanisms, it is plausible that physiological imitation might occur; areas of the brain that correspond to actions such as eating food may be stimulated if these actions are observed in others. Even infectious causes of obesity are conceivable.[13]

Christakis and Fowler observed clusters of obese people among participants in the Framingham study at every point in time. If person A identified person B as a friend, for instance, and neither A nor B was initially obese, the likelihood that A would become obese increased by 57 percent if B became obese. That effect was greatly amplified when the friendship was mutual. Thus if B also identified A as a friend, A's probability of becoming obese increased by 171 percent if B became obese.

The strength of such links depends powerfully on gender. In male-male friendships, for example, a man's probability of becoming obese rose by 100 percent if a male friend became obese, but a female's probability of becoming obese did not rise significantly if a female friend became obese. Weight gains were also uncorrelated across friendships of people of the opposite sex.

Among adult brothers, a man's probability of becoming obese rose by 44 percent if his brother became obese. The corresponding estimate for adult sisters was 67 percent. But there was no statistically significant relationship for opposite-sex siblings. Among married couples, a husband becoming obese was associated with a 44 percent increase in the probability of his wife becoming obese. A wife becoming obese had almost the same effect, a 37 percent increase in the probability of her husband becoming obese.

As in the case of smoking, such correlations are not by themselves evidence of behavioral contagion, since they could be the result of selection effects or other common causal factors shared by study participants. Christakis and Fowler considered three separate explanations for obesity clusters: first, that people might choose to associate with similar others ("homophily"); second, that people might share attributes or be influenced by unobserved contemporaneous events that produce simultaneous changes in their weight ("confounding"); and third, that people might exert social influence on one another ("induction").

The astonishingly rich detail of the Framingham Study data permitted Christakis and Fowler to disentangle these competing explanations for obesity clusters. That a person's weight gain was not affected by the weight gain of immediate neighbors, and that geographic distance did not modify the effect for friends or siblings, helped to rule out common exposure to local environmental factors as an explanation for clustering. The authors also controlled for people's previous weight status, which helped to account for confounding factors that are stable over time, like childhood experiences or genetic endowments. Also, by controlling for previous weight status, they were able to account for a possible tendency for obese people to form ties among themselves.

The authors' findings regarding the directional nature of friendship effects suggested that obesity correlations among friends are not a result of contemporaneous exposure to unobserved environmental factors (because if friends became obese at the same time, the effect of such influences would not have differed with the directionality of the friendship tie). The authors also note, finally, that the stronger obesity correlations observed for same-sex friends and siblings further support the contagion hypothesis, on the plausible assumption that people are more likely to be influenced by people they resemble more closely.[14]

Again, although the risks to health and well-being posed by obesity are less serious than those associated with smoking, they remain significant. Obesity has been shown to be the leading risk factor for the development of type 2 diabetes, which in turn is a leading risk factor for heart and kidney disease.[15]

Obesity not only is associated with significant threats to physical health but also is a well-documented cause of social stigmatization.[16] Both costs, moreover, are poised to grow dramatically worse.

Detailed simulation models published in the *Lancet* in 2011 estimated that roughly 50 percent of American adults would be classified as obese by 2030.[17]

Further evidence that obesity is socially contagious comes from a natural experiment involving the transfer of military personnel to new geographic locations. Relative to those assigned to counties with average levels of obesity, those assigned to a county whose obesity rate was 1 percent higher than average were 5 percent more likely to be classified as overweight or obese during the course of their new assignments.[18] Consistent with the contagion hypothesis, the likelihood of becoming obese rose with the length of stay at such locations, and was higher for those who lived in the community than for those who lived on base.

The obesity epidemic shows no signs of curing itself spontaneously. Nor is it likely to be curbed by putting additional pressure on people to lose weight. On the contrary, researchers have shown that obesity stigma has actually undermined public health efforts to slow the epidemic.[19] Achieving permanent weight reduction is a difficult challenge, and stigmatization appears to deplete important psychological resources for confronting it.

There are, however, public health interventions that have shown promise in changing individual eating choices. What is clear, in any event, is that because behavioral contagion is so strongly implicated as a factor behind the current obesity epidemic, any policy changes that lead individuals to lose weight will trigger positive feedback effects that multiply the impact of those changes.

I'll return to this point in chapter 11, where I'll consider the kinds of measures that hold greatest promise for mitigating undesirable consequences of behavioral contagion.

———

Around the world, most people who consume alcohol do so in moderation. For example, someone who drinks a single glass of wine with dinner each evening would rank among the top 30 percent of all Americans in terms of per capita alcohol consumption. Two glasses each evening would put someone in the top 20 percent. But those in the top 10 percent of drinkers consume an average of two bottles of wine each evening. People in this group consume an average of more than seventy-four alcoholic drinks per week. Together, they account for more than half the alcohol consumed in the country each year.[20]

Researchers continue to debate whether moderate alcohol consumption entails any significant risks to health, and some studies suggest that it may even confer modest health benefits.[21] But there is no doubt that the top 10 percent of drinkers are doing themselves serious bodily harm. According to the National Institutes of Health, for example, almost ninety thousand Americans die each year from alcohol-related injuries and illnesses, making alcohol the third leading cause of preventable deaths, after smoking and poor diet/inactivity.[22]

Heavy drinkers cause harm not only to themselves but also to others. In 2014, for example, there were 9,967 alcohol-impaired driving fatalities in the United States, only a minority of which were the impaired drivers themselves.[23] Globally, more than 10 percent of children live with a problem-drinking parent.[24] And a 2012 survey in New Zealand estimated that harms caused by drinkers were 50 percent more likely to befall people other than the drinkers themselves.[25]

In the domain of smoking, the direct harms to others caused by exposure to secondhand smoke have been the primary justification for regulations aimed at curbing smoking. So, too, in the domain of alcohol consumption, where the harms that heavy drinkers inflict on others have been the primary justification invoked for collective measures to limit excessive drinking. But as with smoking, direct harm to others is only part of the problem, for here too there is compelling evidence that drinking is socially contagious.

Researchers faced with the task of identifying peer influences on alcohol consumption encounter the same methodological hurdles that confronted smoking and obesity researchers. That a person becomes more likely to drink when a larger proportion of his or her peers drink would not by itself imply a causal link. It might be, for example, that a common set of external causal factors was responsible for the correlation. And it is almost surely also true that people with a high propensity to drink are more likely to select other drinkers as friends.

A study by the economists Michael Kremer and Dan Levy takes advantage of a natural experiment to help isolate direct peer influences from other causal factors.[26] The authors examined the behavior of students at a large state university that employed a lottery system to assign first-year roommates. Because freshmen were assigned at random to a roommate, any association between subsequent changes in their own behavior and their roommate's prior drinking behavior cannot have resulted from a self-selection effect. By comparing students who had the same observable characteristics but were randomly assigned to different types of roommates, the authors could estimate whether a roommate's prior drinking history had an observable impact on the student assigned to live with him.

The authors measured precollege drinking behavior from responses on entering-student questionnaires administered during freshman orientation week. Students were asked the extent to which they had engaged in a variety of activities, to which they could answer either "frequently," "occasionally," or "never." Included among the activities were two that pertained specifically to drinking: "Drank beer," and "Drank wine or liquor."

In the authors' classification scheme, frequent drinkers were the 15 percent of students who answered "frequently" to at least one of the two drinking questions. The 53 percent of students who answered "occasionally" to at least one of these questions but not "frequently" to either were classified as occasional drinkers. The 32 percent of students who answered "never" to both drinking questions were classified as nondrinkers.

Kremer and Levy did not have data on how much alcohol students in their sample consumed after arriving on campus. So instead they estimated the impact of a student's precollege drinking behavior on his or her roommate's subsequent academic achievement, as measured by grade point averages at the end of the freshman and sophomore years.

When both males and females were considered as a single group, the impact of having a roommate classified as a frequent or occasional precollege drinker was to reduce a student's end-of-year GPA by more than a tenth of a point on a four-point scale. But the effect was dramatically larger for males than for females. Relative to males whose roommates were nondrinkers, those whose roommates were frequent precollege drinkers had end-of-year GPAs that were 0.28 lower; for those whose roommates were occasional drinkers, the corresponding deficit was almost as great, 0.26 lower. These effects are comparable to the effect of a student's own high school GPA being lower by half a point, or to having scored fifty points lower on the Scholastic Aptitude Test.[27]

By far the most dramatic impact observed in this study was for males who were themselves frequent precollege drinkers and were randomly assigned to a roommate who was also a frequent precollege drinker. Relative to the overall sample GPA, these males had end-of-year GPAs that were almost a full point lower.[28]

Because Kremer and Levy did not have data on student drinking while in college, their inference that these reductions in GPA were a consequence of peer-induced alcohol consumption is circumstantial. But they took pains to rule out other plausible causes. They reviewed a comprehensive literature, for example, that concluded that prior academic achievement measures and other individual roommate characteristics have little impact on the academic achievement of the students they live with. The authors' own data set also enabled them to control directly for the potential influence of a rich set of student characteristics, such as frequency of television watching or degree of socializing, none of which were systematically related to changes in a roommate's end-of-year GPA.

Kremer and Levy went on to note that the link between frequent high school drinking and larger GPA deficits for students paired with roommates who were also frequent drinkers is also consistent with the behavioral contagion hypothesis: "Those who have some predisposition to alcohol use are most vulnerable to the cues and social acceptability provided by a drinking roommate, while those who do not want to use alcohol anyway are less affected."[29]

Finally, the authors noted that the persistence of the correlations they observed also supports the hypothesis of a direct causal link. Only 17 percent of students lived with their freshman year roommate during their sophomore year. So if disruptive behavior by a drinking roommate was the cause of reduced academic performance, rather than an induced preference for more frequent drinking, that would have applied to only a small minority of students during their second year. Yet male students whose roommates were frequent drinkers in high school had a GPA deficit of 0.43 points in their second year, as compared to a deficit of only 0.18 points in their first year.[30]

Unlike the study by Kremer and Levy, many other studies of peer effects on drinking employ data on actual changes in alcohol consumption. These studies typically report that individual consumption levels are strongly positively correlated with the consumption levels of peers.[31] But here, too, the challenge is to discover the extent to which these correlations imply causation.

In response to this challenge, the economists Mir Ali and Debra Dwyer applied the same strategy they used in their teen smoking study cited earlier.[32] In this case, they employed data for some ninety thousand adolescents from the National Longitudinal Study of Adolescent Health (Add Health). Students came from 132 schools between grades 7 and 12. More than twenty thousand of the original subjects were interviewed in their homes several years after the initial survey, by which time most of them had left high school. Those second-round interviews report detailed information on parental characteristics, and the authors were also able to construct measures of peer drinking from information provided by classmates included in the sample.

The Add Health interviewers asked participants the following specific question about their drinking: "During the last 12 months, on how many days did you drink alcohol?" Ali and Dwyer used responses to this question to classify students on a six-point scale: 0 = never drinks, 1 = drank once in the last year, 2 = drinks once a month, 3 = drinks 2–3 times a month, 4 = drinks 1–2 times a week, and 5 = drinks 3 or more times a week. The authors measured the drinking of a student's classmates in two ways: first, as the average of their drinking scores thus defined; and second, as the percentage of class-mates who participated in drinking in the past twelve months.

In versions of their study in which they controlled only for back-ground demographic characteristics, they found that positive as-sociations between individual drinking and friends' drinking grew stronger with the intensity of friends' drinking. They also found a positive association between individual drinking and classmates' drinking, but this link did not depend on the intensity of classmates' drinking.

But for present purposes, the estimate of greatest interest from their study is the one for which they controlled for both background characteristics and peer-selection effects in an effort to isolate the direct effect of peer influence. As Ali and Dwyer summarize their findings, a 10-percentage-point increase in classmates' drinking rate increases both the likelihood and the intensity of individual drinking by slightly more than 4 percentage points.[33]

———

The research discussed in this chapter persuasively demonstrates the central role of behavioral contagion in three important public health arenas—smoking, obesity, and problem drinking. These find-ings reinforce the case for helping individuals alter the behaviors that contribute to these problems, because those behaviors harm not just people who engage in them, but also many others.

But the same findings have a second implication, which is that successful efforts to change any individual's behavior in these do-mains will generate substantial multiplier effects. Behavior modifica-tion programs that provide peer support, for example, are known to be more successful than those that do not.[34] I'll return to this point in the chapters of part IV, which focus more closely on the policy implications of behavioral contagion.

8

Expenditure Cascades

Behavioral contagion contributes to smoking, excessive drinking, unhealthful eating, low tax compliance, and a host of other problems. But harms in these areas pale in comparison to those that can reasonably be attributed to peer influence on spending patterns. Losses that result from wasteful spending patterns almost surely exceed $2 trillion annually in the United States alone.

As free-market enthusiasts like to say, people spend their own money more carefully than any government bureaucrat would. For the sake of discussion, let's grant that private spending decisions are largely rational from the perspective of the individual. But individual rationality need not imply collective rationality, as when all stand to get a better view, only to see no more clearly than if all had remained comfortably seated. Individual and collective rationality exhibit a similar tension in spending decisions. Peer effects ignite a cascade of mutually offsetting expenditures in certain areas, while at the same time starving other areas of much-needed resources. Policies that could reduce these distortions would yield enormous benefits.

The simplest illustration of the source of the problem is the familiar military arms race. When one of two rival nations adds to its stock of weaponry, the other feels compelled to respond in kind, lest the balance of power be upset. Uncertainty about how much a rival has spent will often make it seem prudent to increase one's own spending just a little further, provoking further escalations, and so on.

Each nation, of course, would prefer to devote those same funds to schools, hospitals, roads, houses, and other goods that would improve living standards at home. Yet each knows that to fall behind a military adversary could entail serious existential risk. From each individual nation's perspective, then, it is prudent to respond in kind to a rival's arms buildup.

Arms races do not proceed without limit, since expenditures on weaponry cannot exceed national income. But even when an uneasy equilibrium is reached, the resulting composition of each side's total spending is profoundly wasteful. From the collective vantage point, after all, mutual spending on arms does nothing to enhance either nation's security. On the contrary, greater firepower on each side would make serious damage more likely if hostilities were to erupt. But unlike escalations of military spending, investments in public infrastructure are not mutually offsetting. Increasing these investments would benefit everyone.

The logic of the arms-race narrative is completely uncontroversial. Indeed, most observers regard widespread attempts to negotiate enforceable arms-control agreements as clear evidence that it would be a good thing for rival nations to spend less on weapons and more on other things. It is much less widely understood, however, that exactly analogous forces have created enormous waste in our private consumption patterns. The steps by which this happens are suggested by two simple thought experiments:

1. WHICH WORLD WOULD YOU CHOOSE?

World A: You and your family live in a neighborhood with 4,000-square-foot houses, and all other neighborhoods have 6,000-square-foot houses;

or

World B: You and your family live in a neighborhood with 3,000-square-foot houses, and all other neighborhoods have 2,000-square-foot houses.

Standard economic models, which assume that the satisfaction provided by a house depends only on its absolute features, say that World A is the unambiguously better choice. Yet most people don't seem to see things that way. And after careful thought, significantly more than half of respondents choose World B. Some of the minority who choose World A seem to do so out of concern that they *shouldn't* care about others' houses. Even so, few among them seem puzzled that others might choose differently.

My point is not that World B is the uniquely correct choice here. For the moment, I note only that most people say they would choose it. (John Bates Clark, Richard Ely, Thorstein Veblen, and other economists born in the nineteenth century would not have been surprised by the preference for World B. But the views of those authors have long since disappeared from modern economics textbooks.)

Now consider a second thought experiment, one with exactly the same structure:

2. WHICH WORLD WOULD YOU CHOOSE?

World A: You have a 2 in 100,000 chance of dying on the job this year, and others have a 1 in 100,000 chance;

or

World B: You have a 4 in 100,000 chance of dying, and others have a 6 in 100,000 chance.

As in the first thought experiment, here too the choice is between absolute advantage (World A) and relative advantage (World B). Over a span of many years, I've put this question to hundreds of people of different ages, sexes, and nationalities, and not once has anyone indicated a preference for World B. In the domain of safety, everyone opts for absolute advantage. But when people face a similar choice in the domain of housing, most opt for relative advantage.

The late British economist Fred Hirsch coined the term *positional good* to describe things that derive their value primarily from their scarcity rather than from their absolute characteristics. "The value of my education," he wrote, "depends on how much education the man ahead of me in the job line has."[1] In what follows, I will use Hirsch's term to mean a good whose value depends relatively heavily on how it compares with other goods in the same category. For people who chose relative over absolute advantage in the first thought experiment, housing would thus be a positional good.

Similarly, I will use the term *nonpositional good* to describe one whose value depends relatively little on how it compares with other goods in the same category. For people who chose absolute advantage in the second thought experiment, workplace safety would be a nonpositional good.

To call housing positional is not to say that only the relative attributes of a house matter. Someone who chose World B in the first thought experiment, for example, might well have preferred to live in a world in which her neighborhood had 3,500-square-foot houses and others had houses of 3,000 square feet.

Similarly, choosing a world with high absolute safety doesn't mean that relative safety levels are of no concern. Most people choosing World A would almost certainly notice that their jobs were much more dangerous than others'. But if their only recourse were to move to World B, where their own absolute risk of death would double, they would decline.

Caring more about relative consumption in some domains than in others distorts people's spending decisions. It leads to what I call *positional arms races*—patterns of escalating expenditure focused on positional goods. The resulting dynamic is exactly analogous to the one that drives military arms races. In both cases, wasteful spending occurs only because some categories of expenditure are more context-sensitive than others.

Military arms races occur only because relative differences in spending on weapons have more important consequences than relative differences in nonmilitary spending. If, to the contrary, spending less than a rival nation spent on toasters and television sets had more serious consequences than spending less on bombs, we would expect expenditure imbalances of precisely the opposite sort: countries would spend ever less on armaments in a quest to gain relative advantage in the domain of nonmilitary spending. That is of course not what we see. Military arms races are a consequence, pure and simple, of relative spending on armaments being more important—because it contributes so heavily to the outcome of military conflict.

In the domain of domestic consumption spending, an exactly parallel distortion occurs. Because relative spending matters more, by definition, for positional goods than for nonpositional goods, people end up spending too much on the former and too little on the latter. To see how the dynamic unfolds, consider a worker's choice between two jobs that offer different levels of risk to safety. Both because safety devices are costly, and because workers prefer safe jobs to risky ones, employers who want to attract workers to riskier jobs must pay higher wages. Choosing additional safety on the job therefore comes at the expense of having less income to spend on other things. Choosing a riskier job would enable a worker to buy a nicer house. If she has children, that option might look doubly attractive since she knows that in almost every jurisdiction, better schools are those located in more expensive neighborhoods.

So let's imagine that she chooses the higher-paying but riskier job. The same logic would also lead similarly situated workers to make the same choice. And if they too chose riskier jobs to be able to afford houses in better school districts, their increased bidding would serve only to bid up the prices of those houses. Half of all children would still attend bottom-half schools, the same as if no one had sacrificed safety for higher wages. All will have sold their safety in pursuit of a goal that none achieves.

Since Adam Smith's day, classical economic theory has held that well-informed workers in competitive markets will sensibly navigate this trade-off between income and safety. They will accept additional risk in return for higher pay only if the satisfaction from having what they can buy with the extra income is greater than the corresponding loss in satisfaction from reduced safety. According to proponents of this view, regulations that mandate higher safety levels harm workers by forcing them to buy safety they value at less than its cost.

But why, then, does virtually every country in the world regulate workplace safety?[2] (Even the poorest countries have at least rudimentary safety requirements.) Classical economic theory doesn't have a good answer. It portrays such regulations as either anomalous or else needed because workers are uninformed, or because markets aren't competitive enough. Yet we regulate many safety risks that workers clearly understand. Most coal miners, for example, know their work entails risk of black lung disease since their fathers and grandfathers died of it.

Nor is imperfect competition the problem. Most safety regulations, after all, have their greatest impact in precisely those markets that most closely approximate the competitive ideal. They have little effect on engineers in Silicon Valley or on investment bankers on Wall Street, whose conditions of employment are substantially safer than required by the Occupational Health and Safety Administration. It's the employers who compete most fiercely with one another to attract the workers they need, such as fast-food restaurants and manufacturing firms that employ unskilled labor, that seldom go long without a visit from a safety inspector.

Individually rational decisions regarding workplace safety produce unattractive outcomes for the same reason that individually rational decisions lead to wasteful military arms races. Countries spend too much on arms not because they are stupid, but because falling behind a military rival is so costly. By the same token, workers take excessive risks on the job not because they are ill-informed, or because markets are insufficiently competitive, but because earning less than your peers consigns your children to schools of lower quality. Even with full knowledge and ample self-discipline, no worker can solve that problem individually, just as no nation can end a military arms race unilaterally. Restraint requires collective action. In short, the most parsimonious explanation for ubiquitous safety regulation is the same logic that explains military arms-control treaties.

That same logic also plays out in microcosm in the rules that govern athletic competition. The economist Tom Schelling once observed, for example, that when hockey players were permitted to play without helmets, few players wore them.[3] Yet players strongly supported the adoption of rules requiring helmets. If helmets are a good thing, Schelling asked, why don't players just wear them voluntarily? Why do they need a rule?

His answer was that skating helmetless confers a competitive advantage, enabling players to see and hear a little better. A bareheaded skater's willingness to accept extra risk may also help to intimidate rivals. The resulting competitive advantage, moreover, occurs immediately and with certainty, whereas the increased risk of injury comes only with uncertainty and delay. The rub, of course, is that if one side skates without helmets, opponents will feel compelled to respond in kind. In the end, no team gains a competitive advantage, and all players face greater risk of injury. Hence the powerful attraction of helmet rules.

Schelling's analysis of the logic of helmet rules highlights my central theme in this book, which is that society has a legitimate public policy interest in altering individual incentives to promote social environments that bring out the best in us. Much of what we do affects others profoundly, sometimes for good, but often for ill. Sometimes the best response will be to urge people just to mind their own business. But not always. For as we will see in chapter 11, people's incentives can often be altered in relatively unintrusive ways.

Schelling's analysis also sheds light on the misuse of terms like "freedom" and "liberty" in contemporary political discourse. Just as Milton Friedman objected that safety regulation robs workers of the freedom to decide for themselves how to weigh trade-offs between income and safety, others have objected that helmet rules similarly deprive players of their liberty. But those objections are like complaining that military arms-control agreements deprive nations of their freedom to build as many weapons as they choose. Well, yes. But that's precisely their point!

Nations that sign military arms-control agreements do so because they understand that if they are free to make arms decisions individually, they will end up spending far too much on weaponry. By the same token, hockey players know that if they are free to make helmet decisions individually, they will end up incurring greater risk for no purpose. The same is true with workplace safety regulation. To enshrine the right to make workplace decisions individually is to deny the right of workers to support laws that enable them to make those same decisions collectively. Accordingly, it is instructive to think of regulations of this sort as *positional arms control agreements*.

––––––

More than three decades ago, I published my first academic paper about how people influence one another's spending decisions.[4] The Norwegian-born economist Thorstein Veblen had written about this subject at great length almost a century earlier, as had many others in the interim, including James Duesenberry, Harvey Leibenstein, Richard Easterlin, Richard Layard, and the aforementioned Fred Hirsch.[5] And in the years since I began thinking about this issue, many other capable scholars have taken up this subject.[6]

Yet it is safe to say that none of us has had any significant impact on how mainstream economists think about consumption decisions. To this day, it remains standard practice to assume that spending decisions depend only on incomes and relative prices. People's assessments of their needs and wants are assumed to be completely independent of the spending of others around them. But how could that be true if, as all evidence affirms, virtually every human evaluation is profoundly dependent on local context?

Why have economists consistently ignored this evidence? One possibility is that many of them believe that peer influences are rooted in base emotions such as envy and jealousy, and that it would be an ethical misstep to craft public policies that take such emotions into account. As the economist Donald Boudreaux once put it, for example,

> I agree that people are concerned about their relative standing in society. But I don't believe that such a concern should necessarily be embodied in government policy. (I also agree with those who point out that people naturally are biased against foreigners— prejudiced against others whose appearance and language and

customs are very different from what is familiar—but I don't want to elevate this natural tribal impulse into government policy.)[7]

In a similar spirit, John Maynard Keynes, widely regarded as the most brilliant economist of the twentieth century, described two classes of human desires, those that "are absolute in the sense that we feel them whatever the situation of our fellow human beings may be, and those which are relative in the sense that we feel them only if their satisfaction lifts us above, makes us feel superior to, our fellows."[8]

Few of us look kindly on those driven by a desire to feel superior to others. On the contrary, we do our best to avoid such people, and our relative success in doing so seems to imply that they cannot be too common. If concerns about relative position are viewed as resulting from a desire to outdo one's friends and neighbors, and if few of us are aware of having any such desire ourselves, it is perhaps not surprising that economists might have felt justified in ignoring positional concerns.

Yet such concerns would powerfully shape human behavior even in a world in which envy, jealousy, and one-upmanship were completely absent. That's because the ability to achieve basic goals in life often depends strongly on relative purchasing power. The housing market again provides the clearest illustration of the validity of this claim.

Before Massachusetts senator Elizabeth Warren went into politics, she and her daughter, Amelia Warren Tyagi, coauthored a book in which they asked why most one-earner couples could live comfortably within their budgets in the 1950s, yet the two-earner couples that had become the norm by the 1990s often struggled to make ends meet.[9] Their answer was that the second paycheck went largely to fuel a bidding war for houses in better school districts.

Even in the 1950s, one of the highest priorities of most parents was to send their children to the best possible schools. Because the labor market has grown more competitive during the ensuing years, this goal now looms even larger. It was thus no surprise, Warren and Tyagi argued, that two-income families would choose to spend much of their extra income on better education for their children. And because the best schools are almost always located in the most expensive neighborhoods, the imperative was clear: to gain access to the best possible public school, you had to purchase the most expensive house you could afford.

In the 1950s, strict credit limits held the bidding for houses in better school districts tightly in check. Lenders typically required down payments of 20 percent or more and would not issue loans for more than three times a borrower's annual income.

In a well-intentioned but ultimately misguided move to help more families enter the housing market, borrowing restrictions were relaxed during the intervening decades. Down payment requirements fell steadily, and in the years leading up to the 2008 financial crisis, many houses were bought with no money down. Adjustable-rate mortgages and balloon payments further boosted families' ability to bid for housing.

The result was a painful dilemma for any family determined not to borrow beyond its means. It would be difficult to fault a middle-income family for aspiring to send its children to schools of at least average quality. (Indeed, many would think ill of any family that aspired to less.) Yet any family that stood by while others exploited more liberal credit terms would consign its children to below-average schools. So even financially conservative families might have reluctantly concluded that their best option was to borrow up.

Those who condemned such families saw a different picture. They saw undisciplined spendthrifts overcome by their lust for cathedral ceilings and granite countertops, families that needed to be taught a lesson. The late Senator John McCain, for example, argued that "it is not the duty of government to bail out and reward those who act irresponsibly, whether they are big banks or small borrowers."[10]

Yet millions of families got into financial trouble simply because they understood that life is graded on the curve. The best jobs go to graduates from the best colleges, and because only the best-prepared students are accepted to those colleges, it is quixotic to expect parents to bypass an opportunity to send their children to the best elementary and secondary schools they can. The financial deregulation that enabled them to bid ever-larger amounts for houses in the best school districts essentially guaranteed a housing bubble that would leave millions of families dangerously overextended.

Many people who have written about peer effects in consumption describe them as a manifestation of the familiar notion of "keeping up with the Joneses." The first advice I offer a junior colleague who wants to work in this area is never to use this expression. It conjures the image of insecure people who are putting on airs, trying to seem as if they're more than they are. But although there surely are such people, this is fundamentally not what drives the consumption behavior we're considering.

Placement counselors, for example, stress the importance of looking good when a client goes for a job interview. But looking good is also a relative concept. It means looking better than the other candidates for the same job. If you're a soon-to-graduate MBA looking for a position in investment banking, the competition is steep. You and your rivals are likely to be roughly equally qualified on paper. If you show up for your interview in a $300 off-the-rack suit while they show up in custom-tailored suits costing ten times that amount, you're unlikely to get a callback. For reasons discussed in chapter 2, such cues typically operate outside of conscious awareness. Most interviewers couldn't report even the color of a suit worn by a job candidate, much less estimate how much it cost. Yet they somehow remember which candidates looked the part.

Quite apart from the link between relative spending and the ability to achieve basic goals, the influence of context on evaluation affects spending decisions in a host of less concrete ways that have nothing to do with keeping up with the Joneses. Even someone who lived alone on an island, for example, would take pleasure in driving a car that seemed special, one that was faster and handled better than expected. But special is also an inescapably relative concept. I'm a lifelong car enthusiast, and the most thrilling driving experience in my memory bank occurred decades ago, when a high school friend let me take the wheel of his 1955 Ford Thunderbird. The car's brilliant handling and neck-snapping acceleration left me in awe. But no sports car enthusiast today would react that way to a '55 T-Bird. The car's 0–60 time was 11.5 seconds, positively tortoise-like by current standards.[11] The family-friendly Honda Accord Touring sedan does the 0–60 sprint in 5.6 seconds. The Porsche 918 Spyder? Only 2.2 seconds.[12]

Sometimes, a cigar is just a cigar. In a preponderance of cases, base emotions like envy and jealousy have nothing to do with spending decisions. Nor does enjoying a special-seeming consumption experience imply a desire to feel superior to others. It is simply about enjoying something that seems special.

But even if base emotions were an important source of positional concerns, that would hardly justify ignoring them in the design of public policy. The base emotion of avarice, for example, undoubtedly motivates some people to commit larceny. Would anyone view that as an argument against policies to discourage theft?

———

The dynamic by which positional concerns distort spending patterns suggests that waste will be exacerbated by rising income and wealth inequality. Recent experience offers an opportunity to test that hypothesis.

During the three decades after World War II in the United States, incomes of rich, middle-income, and poor families grew at about the same rate—almost 3 percent a year. But since then almost all gains have gone to people at the top. Those gains have been truly spectacular. The top 1 percent of earners, who received less than 9 percent of total income in 1973, saw their share rise to 22 percent by 2015. Gains grow ever larger as we move up the economic ladder. The top one-tenth of 1 percent of earners, for instance, saw their share of total income rise more than sixfold during those same years. Members of this group had an average income of $6.75 million in 2015. Earnings of the CEOs of the largest American companies have grown even more rapidly. In 2016 they earned 347 times as much as the average worker, up from 42 times as much in 1980.[13]

Extra income leads people at all income levels to spend more, and the rich are no exception. In 2016, private equity magnate Daren Metropoulos paid $100 million for Hugh Hefner's Playboy Mansion in Holmby Hills, then the highest price ever paid for a house in Los Angeles.[14]

But the Playboy Mansion's record price is likely to be ephemeral. At this writing, the largest and most expensive property on the American market is a Los Angeles mansion named The One, a 100,000-square-foot dwelling on a Bel Air hilltop with an asking price of $500 million.

The property is well equipped. It has twenty bedrooms, the largest a 5,500-square-foot master suite with its own office, pool, and kitchen. The mansion also has six other pools, a nightclub, a commercial-sized beauty salon, and five elevators.[15]

The One's asking price is $200 million more than the $300 million that Saudi Crown Prince Mohammed bin Salman paid in 2015 for the Chateau Louis XIV in Louveciennes, France—at the time the highest price ever paid for a private residence.[16] But even if The One fetches its full asking price, it is unlikely to remain the world's most expensive dwelling for long. Also on the market is The Mountain of Beverly Hills, a 157-acre site with spectacular panoramic views of the city and ocean below. No structures have yet been built on the property, but zoning laws authorize a compound whose buildings total up to 1.5 million square feet. The asking price for the site alone? $1 billion.[17] Worldwide, there are hundreds of potential buyers who could afford to pay cash.

Of course, The One and The Mountain of Beverly Hills may not fetch their asking prices. The Playboy Mansion, for example, had originally been listed at $200 million but sold for only half that. But no matter. The point is that outsized income gains have been leading top earners to spend unprecedented sums for houses. And not only for houses. In addition to buying the $300-million Chateau Louis XIV, for example, the Saudi crown prince recently bought a $500-million yacht and a $450-million Leonardo da Vinci painting.[18]

Many have castigated the world's rich for their over-the-top spending. From the perspective of a middle-income family struggling to make ends meet, that's hardly puzzling. Yet the criticism overlooks something important, which is that radically different local frames of reference shape the choices of people in different income strata. As a young man just out of college, for example, I lived in a two-room house with no electricity or running water during my two years as a Peace Corps Volunteer teacher in a remote village in Nepal. At no time did that house feel unsatisfactory in any way. It was in fact nicer than the houses of my fellow teachers. Yet that same house would seem grossly unsatisfactory in any wealthy industrial country.

My current house in Ithaca, New York, is much larger and better appointed than my house in Nepal. If my Nepali friends were to see it, they would wonder why anyone would need such a grand estate. Why so many bathrooms, they would wonder. But middle-income colleagues here don't react to it that way at all. They see it as the sort of old house that many professors live in. To be astonished by the mansions of the ultrarich is to fail to recognize that the local context in which they travel is simply different from our own.

In any event, there is little evidence that middle-income Americans resent the superrich. On the contrary, they display a brisk appetite for pictures and video footage of the new megamansions. Those structures, however, have changed the frames of reference that shape the housing choices of the near rich, who travel in the same social circles. To entertain in the manner now expected of them, they feel they, too, must build bigger. An expenditure cascade ensues, resulting in larger houses for families up and down the income ladder. The median new house built in the United States grew from fifteen hundred square feet in 1973 to more than twenty-five hundred square feet today.[19] And since the median house now has fewer occupants than before, living space per person is nearly twice what it was in 1973.

Part of this growth was caused by the lax credit terms described earlier. But the credit market can't account for the expenditure cascades we've seen in other domains. We're buying heavier, more expensive cars and bigger boats. And we're staging ever more elaborate wedding, anniversary, and birthday celebrations. Standard economic models assume that higher spending by top earners won't affect what middle-income families spend. But if context shapes people's evaluations in the ways we've seen, that can't be true. Higher spending at the top has shifted the frames of reference that define adequate for those just below the top, and so on, all the way down the income ladder.

Why does the average American wedding now cost over $35,000, more than three times as much in real terms as in 1980?[20] Like a good school, a special celebration is a relative concept. It must stand out from what people expect. But when everyone spends more, the effect is merely to raise the bar that defines special. Spending on weddings has tripled, yet the total amount of special remains essentially the same as before.

Are couples who marry today any happier because their weddings cost so much more? The reverse may in fact be true. In one large sample of women, for instance, the annual probability of divorce among those whose weddings cost more than $20,000 was more than three times that of those whose weddings cost between $5,000 and $10,000.[21]

Yet it is difficult to second-guess parents' desire to host a wedding whose guests will feel that they have celebrated the occasion properly. Someone who is especially creative might organize a party that meets that goal on half of what most others spend. But since half of all people are in the bottom half of the creativity distribution, that's not an option available to everyone.

One way to test the hypothesis that rising inequality fuels expenditure cascades is to investigate whether geographic variations in inequality occur in tandem with signs of increasing financial distress. Census data do in fact reveal a strong connection of this sort. One of the most direct statistical measures of financial distress is the rate at which people file for bankruptcy. Between the census years of 1990 and 2000, income inequality grew in each of the country's one hundred largest counties, but there was substantial variation across those counties. And those that experienced the largest increases in income inequality were also the counties experiencing the largest increases in bankruptcy filings.[22]

A less direct measure of financial distress is the rate at which couples file for divorce. Marriage therapists report that they rarely counsel couples for whom financial hardship is not high on their list of problems. Here, too, the same counties that saw the largest increases in inequality were also the ones that reported the steepest increases in divorce rates.[23]

One way that financially struggling families try to make ends meet is to move to more distant residential areas, where housing is cheaper. The rub, of course, is that commutes from such locations are longer and more stressful. And once more, we see inequality's footprints. The counties that experienced the biggest increases in automobile commutes longer than one hour were also those in which income inequality had increased most.[24]

Rising inequality may not have been the only cause of the expenditure cascades we have witnessed. But one thing is certain: they haven't been happening because median earners have become more prosperous. The median hourly wage of American men, adjusted for inflation, is actually lower now than it was in 1980.[25]

How severe are the financial hardships spawned by expenditure cascades? Figure 8.1 shows the toil index, a simple measure I constructed to track one important cost of the expenditure cascade in housing for middle-income families. Because of the strong link between house prices and perceived school quality, median earners must buy the median-priced home in their area to achieve even the modest goal of sending their children to a school of average quality. The toil index plots the number of hours the median earner must work each month to earn enough to achieve that goal.[26]

When incomes were growing at roughly the same rate for all income classes during the post–World War II decades, the toil index was almost completely stable. The median earner had to work slightly more than a week to earn a month's rent for the median-priced house. But income inequality began rising sharply after 1970, just as median wages began to stagnate. Since then, the toil index has risen in tandem. By the early 2000s, the median earner had to work

Hours per month

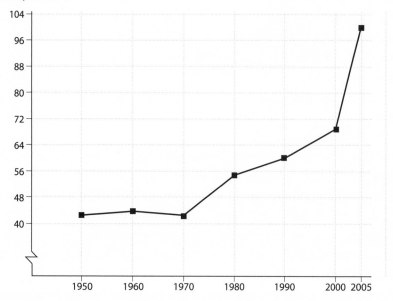

FIG. 8.1. The toil index.

approximately one hundred hours a month to be able to afford that median home, up from only forty-two hours in 1970. Little wonder that Warren and Tyagi found that a second income had become necessary simply to make ends meet.

———

Behavioral scientists have good reason to believe that even a doubling of the size of every mansion in the country would not produce a measurable increase in human well-being. In part, this belief is grounded on evidence that, beyond a certain point, it is relative, not absolute, mansion size that matters.

But having a larger mansion would also be unlikely to produce a durable increase in the happiness even of someone who lived in complete isolation from others. That's because of the human nervous system's remarkable powers of adaptation. It spans the range of biological functioning, all the way down to molecular changes at the cellular level. Without even a trace of conscious effort, for example, neural changes in the visual cortex of the brain operate in concert with autonomic changes in pupil dilation and photochemical changes in the retina that enable us to see, more or less normally, in environments whose actual luminosity varies by a factor of more than one million.[27] Our capacity to adapt to different material living standards is no less remarkable. Even in a Robinson Crusoe setting, then, having a larger mansion would quickly become the new normal.

This observation suggests what might seem a compelling objection to my earlier claim that positional arms races are harmful. If adaptation helps explain why extra spending on positional goods doesn't make people happier, doesn't it also imply that reduced spending on nonpositional goods won't diminish long-run happiness? Why wouldn't people just adapt to any shortfall of nonpositional goods?

Adaptation is of course not the only reason that higher spending on positional goods tends to disappoint. As in a military arms race, such spending also serves the implicit aim of gaining competitive advantage. Across-the-board increases in spending on positional goods disappoint not just because of adaptation but also because they don't affect competitive balance. As noted, when all spend more on interview suits, no one becomes more attractive relative to rival candidates. And when all buy bigger houses, no one's relative house size changes.

But competitive advantage plays a much-diminished role for nonpositional goods. If fewer resources were devoted to safety, for example, people might be sensitive in the short term to the environment's having become more dangerous. But over time, adaptation might be expected to cause them to view the new conditions as normal.

Yet even if adaptation drove concern about higher risk levels completely out of conscious awareness, that would not imply that increased risk does not matter. Suppose, for example, that someone faced a simplified version of the second thought experiment discussed earlier, one where the choice was between two worlds that were identical except that the risk of death by injury was twice as high in one than in the other. No one could argue with a straight face that the level of risk wouldn't matter for such a choice.

In fact, our capacity to adapt varies considerably across domains. There are some stimuli, such as environmental noise, to which we adapt quickly at a conscious level, yet to which our bodies continue to respond in measurable ways even after decades of exposure. There are some stimuli, including various allergens, to which we not only do not adapt over time, but actually become more sensitive.[28]

If our ability to adapt is different for different kinds of purchases, and if similar differences exist with respect to their importance for competitive outcomes, it is easy to see how rearranging our spending patterns might result in durable increases in well-being. A convenient way to summarize some of the evidence that bears on this possibility is again to imagine once-and-for-all choices between environments in which the composition of total spending differs. In each case, imagine that people in Society A live in 6,000-square-foot houses while those in Society B live in 4,000-square-foot houses, and that in each case spending in a second category differs in the ways described in table 8.1.

In each of the examples shown, the citizens of Society B use the resources saved by building smaller houses in an attempt to improve some other aspect of their living conditions. Available evidence provides no reason to believe that citizens of a society in which all live in 4,000-square-foot houses would experience lower subjective well-being than if all lived in 6,000-square-foot houses, even if all other conditions in the two societies were the same. Someone who moved to a society with larger houses would probably be pleased at first with the additional living space. But over time the larger house would simply become the norm. Nor is there any evidence that a society in which citizens occupy 6,000-square-foot houses would enjoy greater longevity or freedom from illness than their counterparts in a society with somewhat smaller houses. In short, there is no reason to believe that the assumed difference in house size would affect well-being in any significant way.

Yet it takes substantially more real resources to build 6,000-square-foot houses instead of 4,000-square-foot houses. A society

TABLE 8.1

Society A	Society B
All citizens live in 6,000-square-foot houses and have one-hour commutes to work by car each way through heavy traffic.	All citizens live in 4,000-square-foot houses and have 15-minute one-way commutes to work by rapid transit.
All citizens live in 6,000-square-foot houses and have no free time for exercise each day.	All citizens live in 4,000-square-foot houses and have an hour of free time for exercise each day.
All citizens live in 6,000-square-foot houses and have time to get together with friends one evening each month.	All citizens live in 4,000-square-foot houses and have time to get together with friends four evenings each month.
All citizens live in 6,000-square-foot houses and have one week of vacation time each year.	All citizens live in 4,000-square-foot houses and have four weeks of vacation time each year.
All citizens live in 6,000-square-foot houses and have relatively low levels of personal autonomy in the workplace.	All citizens live in 4,000-square-foot houses and have relatively high levels of personal autonomy in the workplace.

that instead produced the smaller houses would thus have additional resources with which to produce the things described in the Society B examples. Elsewhere I have summarized voluminous evidence that each of the specific shifts described would produce large, reliably measured, and durable improvements in personal well-being.[29]

The examples just discussed constitute only a small proportion of the expenditure shifts that have been shown to promote human flourishing. As many studies have demonstrated, for example, money spent on experiences results in larger and more durable increases in well-being than the same amounts spent on goods. The psychologists Tom Gilovich and Leaf Van Boven, who have done much of the pioneering work in this area, argue that the difference occurs in part because experiences are far less susceptible to adaptation than material goods.[30] People quickly get accustomed to the greater clarity of a 4K TV image, for instance, but spend years recalling memories of a vacation with friends.

Gilovich and his collaborators also note that relative comparisons matter less for experiences than for goods.[31] Here they cite survey evidence from the economists Sara Solnick and David Hemenway that echoes the patterns seen in the thought experiments discussed earlier:[32] although people sometimes hesitate when faced with a choice between absolute and relative income, the same uncertainty doesn't seem to apply to experiential goods like vacations. Most people say they would strongly prefer a world in which they got four weeks of vacation and peers got eight to one in which they got two weeks and peers only one.

Using consumer expenditure data, the economist Ori Heffetz has demonstrated that goods that are easily observed are more likely than others to be positional.[33] This is as one would expect, perhaps, since it is difficult to be influenced by environmental features that cannot be seen. An important implication is that personal savings, which are typically invisible to outsiders, may be one of the most important of all nonpositional budget categories. This would be consistent with evidence that most consumers save far less than what rational life-cycle spending plans would require.[34]

In short, behavioral scientists have identified a host of ways in which society has failed to glean maximal advantage from its available resources. If practical policies could be found to rearrange spending patterns in the ways suggested by the findings of these researchers, virtually everyone could lead healthier and more satisfying lives.

———

Even as positional concerns have been steering a growing share of national income toward luxury consumption, they have also been making it more difficult for national, state, and local governments to maintain our decaying infrastructure. Public goods are fundamentally different from private goods. When some people spend more on houses or wedding celebrations, for example, others feel pressure to follow suit, but the same dynamic does not occur for public goods, which are available on essentially equal terms to all citizens. Because public goods do not lend themselves to interpersonal comparisons, they are nonpositional almost by definition.[35]

In any event, it is a truism that greater spending on positional goods leaves fewer resources available for public investment. And there is little question that levels of public investment have not kept pace in recent decades. More than 20 percent of the nation's roadways, for example, were classified as being in substandard condition in 2015, meaning that they were significantly overdue for maintenance. Preventable damage to vehicles from potholes and other road-surface irregularities is also rising. The resulting repairs cost motorists more than $120 billion in 2015, an average of $533 per driver. Budget shortfalls have led at least twenty-seven states to downgrade low-traffic rural roadways from asphalt to gravel.[36]

In 2016, more than 9 percent of the nation's 614,387 bridges were rated by engineers as structurally deficient, and the backlog of bridge-rehabilitation funding stood at more than $120 billion.[37] In 2015 there were more than 15,000 dams in the United States that received engineers' "high hazard" rating, used to denote those for which failure would result in loss of life. This was a 50 percent increase over the corresponding estimate in 2005. Among the high-hazard dams, the number rated as deficient was also growing, reaching more than 2,100 in 2016.[38] Engineers also report long-standing maintenance backlogs in the nation's airports, schools, drinking water, and sewage systems.

In the face of these backlogs, proposals to launch significant new infrastructure initiatives, such as high-speed rail service or a smart electric grid, have consistently failed in Congress. Much more troubling, we have not yet launched the investments required to confront the climate crisis, by far the biggest challenge facing the planet. (More on this point in the next chapter.)

Although many factors have contributed to America's failure to invest in the public sphere, one in particular stands out: citizens' demands for government services have outstripped government tax revenue. That phenomenon, in turn, has many causes, among them the sharply rising costs of health care and pensions associated with our aging population. But an additional contributing factor has been the long-term decline in the nation's top marginal tax rate, summarized in table 8.2.

TABLE 8.2 MAXIMUM MARGINAL TAX RATES ON INDIVIDUAL
INCOME IN THE UNITED STATES

Year	Top Tax Rate
1966	70%
1982	50%
1987	38%
1995	39.6%
2018	37%

Source: Tax Policy Center, "Historical Highest Marginal Income Tax
Rates," March 22, 2017, https://www.taxpolicycenter.org/statistics
/historical-highest-marginal-income-tax-rates.

Many tax cuts were adopted in the hope that they would stimulate economic growth by enough to prevent a decline in overall tax revenues. That hope proved wishful thinking. The nonpartisan Congressional Budget Office estimated that the George W. Bush tax cuts reduced federal revenue by $2.9 trillion between 2001 and 2011. And in a widely cited *New York Times* article, Bruce Bartlett, a senior economic adviser in the Ronald Reagan and George H. W. Bush administrations, argued that the actual revenue shortfall caused by the Bush tax cuts was considerably larger.[39]

Proponents of the Tax Cuts and Jobs Act passed by Congress in December 2017 also predicted that the legislation would increase economic growth, boosting tax receipts by more than enough to offset the rate reductions. That forecast also failed. Revenues in the wake of the act's passage declined sharply, just as most economists had warned. Even the White House's Office of Management and Budget, whose director was one of the strongest proponents of the Trump tax cuts, has increased its earlier forecast of the national debt by more than $1 trillion over the next decade.[40]

———

Many economists celebrate the theory of revealed preference, which holds that we can learn much more about people's true preferences by watching what they buy than by listening to what they say. It's a useful theory in many settings, but it breaks down when individual motives and collective motives are in conflict, as they are in positional arms races. In such cases, we often learn more about what people value by listening to what voters say than by watching what they buy. Regulations are data.

An economist armed only with revealed preference theory would conclude that if a worker accepted a riskier job at a higher wage, he or she must view the additional income as more than adequate compensation for the greater risk exposure. That would be a reasonable inference if workers cared only about absolute income. But once we acknowledge the importance of relative income, the conclusion no longer follows. That virtually every society tries to limit the extent of risk exposure in the workplace is thus powerful indirect evidence in favor of the expenditure cascades narrative.

Consider, too, the quintessential nonpositional budget category, personal savings. A rational lifetime consumption plan would require spending significantly less than one's income during the working years, then using savings to maintain roughly the same standard of living in retirement. But apart from the wealthy, few people manage to execute such plans on their own. Widespread inadequacy of retirement incomes has led the governments of most countries to intervene. In the United States, for example, the government imposes a payroll tax of 12.4 percent, which it then uses to support Social Security payments to retirees.

Milton Friedman and other free-market enthusiasts object that such interventions deprive workers of the freedom to decide for themselves how much and in what forms to save. Embracing such criticism, the administration of President George W. Bush attempted to privatize Social Security. But if individual and collective savings decisions are squarely in conflict, as they are in the expenditure cascades narrative, it's easy to see why privatization proved so unpopular.

People who rely exclusively on private savings would always have the option of drawing down savings to bid for a house in a better school district. Some would undoubtedly do so. Others would then face pressure to follow suit, since the alternative would be to send their children to substandard schools. The Social Security system effectively prevents people from diverting a significant share of retirement income into such fruitless bidding wars. Here, too, revealed preference theory has difficulty explaining the support for government regulation of retirement savings—an intervention that is predicted by the expenditure cascades narrative.

Similar conclusions apply to ways in which societies attempt to regulate hours of work. The Fair Labor Standards Act, for example, mandates overtime pay premiums and other incentives for employers to limit the length of the workweek. Free market enthusiasts object that such measures limit the freedom of workers and employers to negotiate mutually attractive labor contracts. Indeed they do. But if relative income matters as much as evidence suggests, it's easy to see why workers might embrace such restraints. Working fifty hours a week instead of forty would significantly reduce a worker's leisure time in relative terms, but would also increase that worker's income in relative terms. From any individual's perspective, this would count as a net gain, since survey evidence reveals relative leisure to be less important than relative income.[41] But others could of course follow suit, causing that advantage to prove ephemeral.

Further support for this interpretation comes from survey evidence regarding the preferences of professional workers, who are not subject to the overtime provisions of the Fair Labor Standards Act. The economists Renée Landers, James Rebitzer, and Lowell Taylor asked associates in large law firms which they would prefer: their current situation, or an otherwise similar one with an across-the-board cut of 10 percent in both hours and pay.[42] By an overwhelming margin, respondents chose the latter. But they were not willing to choose that option unless their colleagues also did so.

Concerns about relative position also appear to affect labor force participation by much more than traditional economic factors. The economists David Neumark and Andrew Postlewaite, for example, investigated the labor force status of three thousand pairs of full sisters, one of whom in each pair did not work outside the home. Their aim was to discover what determined whether the other sister in each pair would seek paid employment. None of the usual economic suspects mattered much—not the local unemployment, vacancy, and wage rates, not the other sister's education and experience. A single variable in their study explained far more of the variance in labor force participation rates than any other: a woman whose sister's husband earned more than her own husband was 16 to 25 percent more likely than others to seek paid employment.[43] As the essayist H. L. Mencken observed, "A wealthy man is one who earns $100 a year more than his wife's sister's husband."

In sum, although the expenditure-cascades narrative trumps the revealed-preference narrative in domain after domain, economists and policy analysts doggedly continue to assume that people's assessments of their options are completely independent of the contexts in which they find themselves. Abandonment of that assumption is long overdue.

———

How large are the losses that result from positional arms races? At this chapter's outset, I suggested that they dwarf the total harm associated with the behavioral contagion processes discussed in earlier chapters. Given the limitations of available data and the primitive state of behavioral models, a precise estimate of the total loss from expenditure cascades lies well beyond reach. But if we're willing to make a few reasonable assumptions, we can get at least a rough idea of its scale.

Start with the observation that behavioral scientists who study human well-being cannot say with any confidence that Americans were happier in 2018 than they were in 2012, even though the inflation-adjusted total value of the nation's goods and services was more than $2 trillion higher in 2018. Now imagine that someone had possessed a magic wand that could have rearranged our 2012 spending patterns in favor of nonpositional goods. The nation's largest houses could be reduced in size, for example, wealthy motorists could all buy slightly less expensive cars, and families could spend less on weddings. The resulting savings could then be spent to shorten the workweek by a few hours and provide an additional two weeks of vacation time for everyone. And a bit more could be spent on infrastructure.

Existing evidence leaves little doubt that expenditure shifts of this sort would have caused clear gains in well-being for 2012 Americans, gains that would enable us to say that Americans living in this rearranged version of 2012 would have been happier than actual Americans in 2018, even though those in the first group were $2 trillion poorer. Unless we are willing to deny the validity of that evidence, the clear implication is that our current spending patterns are wasting at least $2 trillion annually. That's a lot more than the harm caused by behavioral contagion in all other domains.

Of course, no one has a magic wand that could rearrange spending patterns in the ways just described. As I take pains to emphasize to my students, merely demonstrating the existence of a market failure provides no assurance that government intervention would improve matters. And unfortunately, many interventions have actually made matters worse.

The practical question, then, is whether our existing arsenal of imperfect economic and social policy tools might enable us to rearrange our spending patterns at acceptable cost. I'll return to this question in the chapters in part IV.

9

The Climate Crisis

Some political leaders have long denied that our planet is getting warmer. Others acknowledge a warming trend, but deny that human activity has had anything to do with it. Because even the mere possibility of significant climate change has sweeping policy implications, Congress created a government agency to study the issue. The Global Change Research Act of 1990 requires a report to Congress and the president at least once every four years that analyzes, among other things, "current trends in global change, both human-induced and natural, and projects major trends for the subsequent 25 to 100 years."[1]

NCA4, the fourth such report, was delivered in the fall of 2018. Its first sentence could hardly be less equivocal: "Earth's climate is now changing faster than at any point in the history of modern civilization, primarily as a result of human activities."[2]

Climate change is caused largely by the discharge of carbon dioxide and other greenhouse gases into the atmosphere. Unintended by-products of many production and consumption activities, these gases slow the rate at which heat absorbed from the sun radiates back into space, gradually causing the temperature of the atmosphere and oceans to rise. Economists who study climate change consider the problem a standard environmental externality, a view that also enjoys nearly unanimous support in the broader scientific community.

But there is also an important social dimension to the problem. Behavioral contagion influences a variety of choices that affect greenhouse gas emissions—such as the kinds of houses we live in, the vehicles we drive, and the foods we eat.

It is also heavily implicated in a host of other climate-related choices. Google has attempted to spur solar panel adoption, for example, by creating Project Sunroof, a website that enables homeowners to discover which of their neighbors have already adopted them. That so many people visit this website is clear evidence of people's interest in what their neighbors are doing to save energy. Note the striking degree of clustering in the aerial photo reproduced in figure 9.1, where the houses designated by white dots represent those with solar panels. Rare is the house with solar panels that is not adjacent to at least one other house that also has them.

Among the effects of behavioral contagion discussed so far, the monetary value of the losses associated with expenditure cascades are larger than all others combined (as discussed in chapter 8). But the threat posed by climate change portends losses on a far grander scale.

The precise magnitude of this threat remains uncertain. In 2009, the global climate simulation model constructed by researchers at the Massachusetts Institute of Technology estimated that in the absence of policies to limit greenhouse gases, the median surface temperature on Earth by the last decade of this century will be 5.1°C (or 9.2°F) higher than during the preindustrial era.[3] Just six years earlier, the same MIT model had predicted a late-century median temperature rise of "only" 2.4°C (4.3°F).

The 2009 version of the model also projected a range of possible temperature increases and their corresponding probabilities. That year, climatologists estimated that we faced a 10 percent chance of a temperature increase greater than 7°C (12.6°F) by the last decade of this century. Warming on that scale would alter life on Earth in ways that are difficult to comprehend. Smaller temperature increases

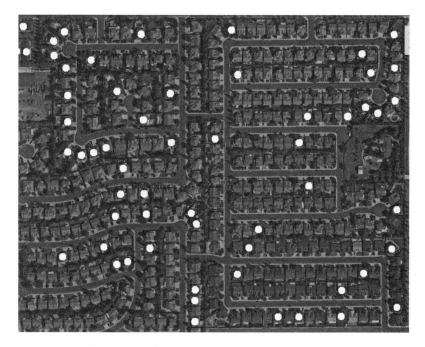

FIG. 9.1. Source: Project Sunroof Data Explorer (November 2018).

would be less catastrophic, but even the most optimistic projections implied enormous costs.

In the years since those estimates were published, temperatures have been rising more rapidly and polar ice has been melting much faster than had been projected. According to the most recent comprehensive assessment from the United Nations Intergovernmental Panel on Climate Change (IPCC), released in October 2018, Earth's median temperature is now on course to be 1.5°C (2.7°F) above preindustrial levels by 2040, several decades sooner than had been forecast earlier.[4] Average temperature has already risen by about 1°C (1.8°F).

Although it is difficult to associate any specific extreme weather event with global climate change, climatologists now believe that recent increases in the severity of storms and droughts are directly linked to the warming trend. At minimum, a 1.5°C temperature rise by 2040 would thus imply inundation of heavily populated coastal areas and still more intense and frequent floods and droughts.[5]

FIG. 9.2. Senator James Inhofe. C-SPAN.

One of the most formidable cognitive hurdles preventing earlier acknowledgment of the importance of climate change was that warming does not take place uniformly. In addition to more frequent episodes of intense heat, we have also been experiencing periods of unusually intense cold.

The month of March, for example, is generally the start of spring weather in Washington, DC, and in some years the city's fabled cherry blossoms are poised to bloom even in late February. But 2015 was an exception. In late February of that year, the nation's capital experienced a cold snap accompanied by several significant snowfalls. Senator James Inhofe (R-OK), a longtime climate-change skeptic, seized the opportunity to bring a snowball onto the Senate floor, which he offered as proof that global warming is a myth.

Senator Inhofe is also the author of *The Greatest Hoax*, in which he portrays climate scientists as perpetrators of a grand conspiracy to increase government's control over people's lives.[6]

As noted in chapter 4, people sometimes believe things that are false for extended periods. But we also saw that once evidence against a claim becomes sufficiently compelling, support for it can unravel quickly. That describes what currently appears to be happening to Senator Inhofe's claim that global warming is a hoax. Public figures

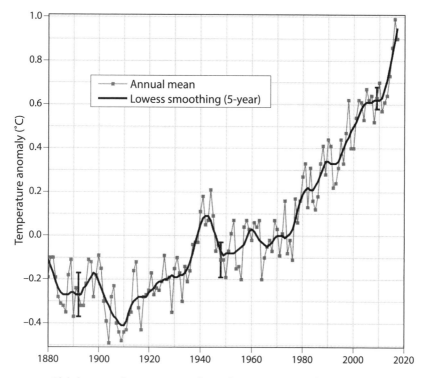

FIG. 9.3. Global mean surface temperature change from 1880 to 2017, relative to the 1951–1980 mean. GISTEMP Team, 2018: GISS Surface Temperature Analysis, NASA Goddard Institute for Space Studies.

once felt emboldened to state that claim in public forums with confidence. But doing so today entails a nontrivial risk of public ridicule. A cautious prediction: within the next two years, almost all public figures will find it prohibitively costly to challenge the validity of climate science in public.

And little wonder, given the accumulating weight of the relevant evidence. Although average temperatures vary from year to year, often substantially, figure 9.3 portrays the dramatic upward trend in average temperature deviations of the oceans and the atmosphere during the twentieth century. February of 1985 was the last month with an average temperature lower than the average temperature for the same month during the twentieth century. Two of my sons, both now over thirty, have never experienced a single month that is cooler than the average temperature for that month before they were born.

Data reported by multiple authoritative sources have identified 2016 as the hottest year ever recorded since the systematic collection of weather data began in the 1880s.[7] The four hottest years yet recorded were 2015, 2016, 2017, and 2018; eighteen of the nineteen hottest years have taken place in the first nineteen years of the twenty-first century.[8] Estimates based on climate proxies suggest that these same years may also have been the hottest during the past several centuries or even millennia.[9]

If we accept that global climate change is real and portends potentially catastrophic consequences, what should we do about it? The economist's diagnosis of the problem is that people and firms discharge greenhouse gases into the atmosphere because they can do so without penalty and because alternative production and consumption options are either more costly or for some other reason less attractive. This framework suggests that the natural solution is to make the discharge of greenhouse gases more expensive by taxing them. As we will see in chapter 11, the functional equivalent of this approach proved spectacularly successful when Congress mandated a market for tradable sulfur dioxide emissions permits as a solution to the acid rain problem in the 1990s.

But price remedies are often more likely to be effective when reinforced by social forces. Energy use patterns are in fact powerfully shaped not just by prices, but also by behavioral contagion, and typically in ways that reinforce one another.

Perhaps the most significant single example involves house size. As discussed in chapter 8, most income gains in recent decades have accrued to top earners, leading them to spend more in all categories of consumption, including houses. The larger houses they build alter the frames of reference that shape housing demands of those in the next income tier, and so on, all the way down the income ladder. Largely because of this expenditure cascade, the median new house built in the United States now has almost twice as many square feet per occupant as its counterpart from 1973.

Larger houses of course require more energy to heat, light, and cool. But they also require more materials to build, which themselves require substantial energy to produce. Larger houses require more maintenance as well, further increasing energy demands.

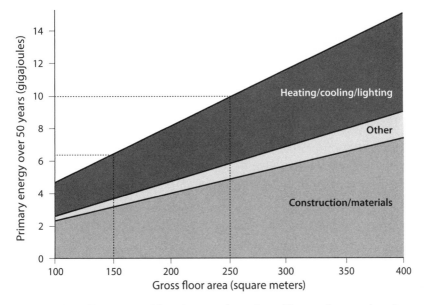

FIG. 9.4. Effect of house size on life-cycle energy demand over fifty years, by use. Adapted from André Stephan and Robert H. Crawford, "The Relationship between House Size and Life-Cycle Energy Demand: Implications for Energy Efficiency Regulations for Buildings," *Energy* 116 (2016): 1158–1171.

Using a diverse sample of houses in Melbourne, Australia, the architects André Stephan and Robert Crawford have estimated the relationship between house size and energy use over a fifty-year life cycle. According to their findings, summarized in figure 9.4, a house of 250 square meters (about 2,700 square feet) consumes more than 50 percent more energy than a house of 150 square meters (about 1,600 square feet).[10]

As discussed in chapter 8, because better schools in most jurisdictions are in more expensive neighborhoods, middle-income families face a difficult choice: they must either roughly match peers' spending on housing, or else send their children to schools of lower quality. Most pick the former option, and because average income has grown little in recent decades, many of these families are finding it increasingly difficult to make ends meet. Many have therefore opted to commute to work from more distant locations, where land prices are lower. The average private-vehicle commute distance in the United States, which was 9.6 miles in 1977, had risen to 12.7 miles by 2017.[11] So here, too, behavioral contagion has contributed to greater energy use.

One of the clearest examples of behavioral contagion's effect on energy consumption has been the sport utility vehicle, whose explosive growth in market share is difficult to understand without reference to emulative behavior.

The Chevrolet Suburban (or, as the humorist Dave Barry called it, the Chevrolet Subdivision)[12] has been produced since 1935, but it and other similar vehicles were originally used almost exclusively for commercial purposes. Before the appearance of the Jeep Wagoneer in 1963 and the Ford Bronco in 1966, the family SUV segment essentially did not exist. As recently as 1975, it accounted for only 2 percent of total vehicle sales.

In the 1990s, however, it became perhaps the biggest success story in automotive history. From a base of only 750,000 units in 1990, annual SUV sales reached almost 3 million by 2000. In 2003, 23 percent of vehicles sold in the United States were in that segment.[13] By 2014, SUVs and crossovers had become the highest-selling passenger vehicle category in the United States, with a market share of 36.5 percent.[14] SUV sales have continued to grow rapidly in the interim, while car sales have continued to decline.[15]

The conventional determinants of consumer demand cannot explain this astonishing trajectory. Cheap fuel was a contributing factor, but clearly not an adequate explanation, because fuel had also been cheap in earlier decades. Similarly, rising average incomes cannot have been decisive, because the pre-SUV decades had experienced even more rapid income growth.

In any case, it is not obvious why people with higher incomes would want to switch from cars to SUVs. Many engineers who helped design these vehicles expressed wonder that they have sold in such numbers. Early ads, coupled with names like Blazer and Pathfinder, touted the vehicles' off-road capabilities. But as one engineer quipped, the only time most SUVs actually go off the road is when inebriated owners miss their driveways.

Nor can safety concerns explain the success of SUVs. As Keith Bradsher explained in his 2002 book *High and Mighty,* their weight confers some advantage in head-on collisions with smaller vehicles (at the expense of occupants of those vehicles), but their poor handling, higher propensity to roll over, and longer stopping distances combine to make them more dangerous, on balance, than cars.[16]

Nor, finally, is the greater cargo capacity of SUVs enough to explain their popularity, since minivans and station wagons offer similar capacity without the handling and mileage penalties.

To understand the explosive growth of SUV sales, we must look first to changes in demand caused by new patterns of income growth and then to how others responded to them. An important catalyst occurred when the post-1970 concentration of income gains among top earners helped persuade Land Rover, then a British-owned company, to bring its premium Range Rover SUV to the United States in 1987, at the then astonishingly high base price of $31,375.[17] Although Range Rover initially had the luxury SUV market to itself, and top earners could easily afford one, its early sales were modest.

That began to change, however, with the vehicle's appearance in the 1992 Robert Altman film *The Player*. The film's lead character, the studio executive Griffin Mill (played by Tim Robbins), could have bought any vehicle he pleased. His choice was a Range Rover with a fax machine in the dashboard.

An important feature of the herd instinct is that people are more likely to emulate others with higher incomes. Seeing a wealthy studio executive behind the wheel of a Range Rover instantly certified it as a player's vehicle of choice. As more and more high-income buyers purchased them, their allure grew. When other automakers began offering similar vehicles at lower prices, SUV sales took off. And with each driver who bought an SUV instead of a car, gasoline consumption and greenhouse gas emissions increased further.

But slowing the growth of SUV sales won't be nearly enough to hold climate change at bay. According to the United Nations' most recent IPCC report, greenhouse gas emissions must be reduced relative to 2010 levels by 45 percent within the next twelve years, and by 100 percent by 2050 if we are to have any hope of averting the most dire consequences of climate change.[18] Because the transportation sector accounts for the largest share of greenhouse gas emissions in many countries, it will be virtually impossible to meet those targets unless passenger vehicles and public transportation fleets move from internal combustion engines to electrification.[19] And for that to happen, behavioral contagion will have to play a decisive role.

Another important source of greenhouse gas emissions is the food industry. The growing, transporting, processing, and handling of food in the United States, for example, accounts for fully 10 percent of the nation's energy consumption.[20] That food consumption is strongly subject to behavioral contagion has long been evident from the popularity of fad diets like Atkins, gluten-free, ketogenic, macrobiotic, master cleanse, Mediterranean, paleo, Pritikin, South Beach, and others. And as we saw in chapter 7, behavioral contagion is also implicated in the obesity epidemic.

In figure 9.5, obesity researcher Stephan Guyenet plots the growth in food energy intake (in kilocalories per person) with the time trends in the proportions of obese (BMI > 30) and very obese (BMI > 40) American adults. The incidence of obesity has more than doubled since 1970, and the time trajectory of its growth closely tracks the increase in per capita calorie consumption during the same period.[21] The increase over the period shown, roughly four hundred calories per person, has boosted total US energy consumption by almost 2 percent.

Numerous other energy uses are also subject to behavioral contagion. Decades ago, most couples planning to marry would not have even known what a destination wedding was. Today, one in four American weddings is a destination wedding, often in an exotic locale far from home.[22] A subset of guests are increasingly expected to attend destination bachelor parties and bachelorette parties. One result has been a significant increase in air travel, a growing source of greenhouse gas emissions.

Further evidence of the importance of behavioral contagion in the energy domain comes from experiments that examine how people respond to information about neighbors' energy use decisions. The psychologist Robert Cialdini, for instance, led an experiment

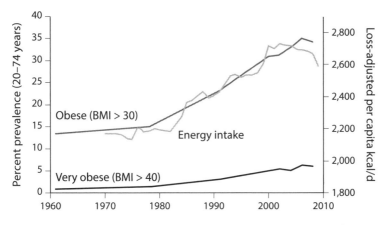

FIG. 9.5. Obesity and energy intake in the United States, 1961–2009. Adapted from CDC NHES and NHANES 1960–2008.

in which canvassers distributed four types of energy-conservation messages to homes in a San Diego suburb each week for a month.[23] One group of homes received weekly messages urging energy conservation for the environment's sake. A second group got messages urging conservation for the benefit of future generations. A third group was reminded that they could save money by conserving energy. The fourth group got the messages Cialdini thought would work best, which said, "The majority of your neighbors are undertaking energy-saving choices every day." (The statement was true, since an earlier survey had revealed that most neighbors were, in fact, taking at least minor steps to conserve energy.)

At month's end, canvassers collected data on electricity use for the four groups of homes. And sure enough, residents who had been told of neighbors' conservation efforts showed by far the biggest reductions in electricity use levels.[24] Discussing this experiment with the *New York Times*, Cialdini echoed a principal theme of this book: "We think of ourselves as freestanding entities: 'Oh, I'm independent of the influence of those around me. I'm an individual.' In fact, we are swept by that information in ways we don't recognize."[25]

In an experiment inspired by Cialdini's work, the economist Hunt Allcott designed a letter to electric utility customers living in comparison groups consisting of approximately one hundred houses with similar characteristics.[26] The letter conveyed two messages. One was a list of concrete suggestions the homeowner could follow to reduce electricity consumption. The second message was a "social comparison module" that gave the household one of three ratings based on a comparison of its electricity use with the usage of other homes in the same group. Those who used less electricity than the average of the most efficient quintile of homes received a rating of "Great." Those who used less than the average for all homes in the group got a rating of "Good," while those who used more than the group average got a rating of "Below Average."

Under this scheme, all homes in the highest decile of a group's electricity consumption would of course receive a rating of "Below Average." Relative to their own preexperiment baselines, people living in these homes reduced their consumption by 6.3 percent. By contrast, homes in a group's lowest-usage decile all received a rating of "Great." Usage went down even in these homes, but perhaps because residents were already taking advantage of the most effective conservation strategies, consumption in this group fell only 0.3 percent.[27]

As noted earlier, behavioral contagion is evident in decisions to adopt photovoltaic solar panels. The marketing professor Bryan Bollinger and the economist Kenneth Gillingham employed statistical methods like the ones discussed in chapter 7 to assess whether peer effects influenced solar panel adoption in a large sample of houses in California. After controlling for a variety of potentially important confounding influences, they estimated an even larger impact than earlier researchers had found for tobacco and alcohol use: a 1 percent increase in a zip code's installed base of solar panels led to a slightly greater than 1 percent increase in the solar-panel adoption rate.[28]

In a similar study, Gillingham and the economist Marcello Graziano employed detailed data on solar installations in Connecticut. Here, too, adoption patterns exhibited considerable clustering that did not simply reflect causal influences like income. The probability that a homeowner in their sample would install solar panels was strongly influenced by the number of previously installed systems in the immediate vicinity. Consistent with the hypothesis of a contagion conveyed through social interaction and visibility, the authors found that the influence of nearby installations diminished with both distance and time.[29]

The transportation industry is like virtually every other industry in that the adoption of new technologies exhibits strong behavioral contagion.[30] The explosive recent proliferation of micromobility vehicles is thus a hopeful sign that contagion can also foster significant reductions in greenhouse gas emissions in this industry. "Micromobility" is the term used to describe nonpolluting urban transport vehicles weighing less than five hundred kilograms, a category that includes bicycles, electric bicycles, electric scooters, and small electric cars.

In cities around the world, bike-sharing services are expanding at a rapid clip.[31] Sharing markets for electric scooters are growing even faster.[32] Sharing markets for electric bikes are also growing rapidly, as is private ownership.[33] The share of electric cars in the US fleet remains small (only 2.1 percent of all vehicles sold in 2018), but it too is growing rapidly (81 percent higher than in 2017).[34] And because adoption decisions in this domain are highly contagious, it is realistic to expect continued strong growth. Plug-in electric cars have already achieved high market shares in some countries, accounting for almost one-third of new passenger cars sold in Norway during 2018. If Norwegian purchases of hybrid cars are included, that share rose to almost half.[35]

As a final example of a behavioral contagion process that leads people to curtail energy use, consider the increasing popularity of walkable neighborhoods. Franklin Schneider offered this description of changing lifestyle tastes in Washington, DC, one of the walkability trend's epicenters:

> Now that walkability is universally recognized as the single most important quality for a prospective home, it's hard to imagine

that it was ever any other way. I mean, it just seems so *obvious*—
why wouldn't you want to live ten minutes from bars and restaurants and your job? Why would you ever voluntarily live any-
where that required you to drive every day? And yet, it wasn't so
long ago that the very people who are shelling out $2 million to
live at 14th and P coveted the no-sidewalks, McMansion-on-a-
huge-lot, ninety-minute-commute suburban lifestyle.[36]

Walk Score, a private company launched in 2007, can assign a
walkability score to any address in the country. The firm's one-
hundred-point scale is based on a proprietary algorithm applied to
the walking distances to a variety of amenities, such as schools, retail
shops, restaurants, bars, and coffee shops. The closer a dwelling is
to such amenities, the higher its Walk Score index. Real estate web-
sites like Zillow and Redfin now report walkability scores for their
listings.[37]

Perhaps the clearest evidence of the strengthening demand for
walkability is that homes with high walkability scores command
large and growing price premiums. A 2011 study found that a one-
point increase in walkability score led to a 0.1 percent increase in a
dwelling's value.[38] But just five years later, a second study estimated
that the same one-point increase commanded a price premium of
0.9 percent, which translated into an average price difference of
$3,250.[39]

As further evidence of the growing fashionableness of walkability,
the price increase associated with a one-point increase in walkability
score rises sharply at the upper reaches of the scale. A rise in walkability from 39 to 40, for instance, is associated with an average premium of only $1,704, whereas a move from 79 to 80 commands an
increase of $7,031.[40]

Moving from the suburbs to a walkable neighborhood reduces
energy consumption beyond the obvious savings from being able to
do errands on foot. Houses in more densely populated neighborhoods tend to be smaller, for example, and therefore require less
energy to heat and cool. Their greater proximity to public transportation also means fewer automobile commutes to work. An added

benefit is that people who live in walkable neighborhoods are significantly less likely to become obese.[41]

———

There is evidence that public concern about climate change is growing. According to the most recent of a series of national polls by Yale
University and George Mason University, for example, 69 percent
of Americans are "somewhat worried" about climate change and 29
percent are "very worried," the highest values for both categories
since the surveys began in 2008. The *New York Times* columnist
David Leonhardt argues that the extreme volatility of recent weather
patterns may thus have been a blessing in disguise. It has gotten
people's attention.[42]

Wildfires caused unprecedented damage in the western United
States in late 2018, and months later record flooding inundated the
Midwest. But these were just the latest in a cascade of weather-
related disasters. Figure 9.6, for example, plots the frequency of such
events in the United Stated that resulted in at least $1 billion in
inflation-adjusted damage.[43] In decades past, such events were much
less frequent, and there were even years in which none occurred.
But no longer.

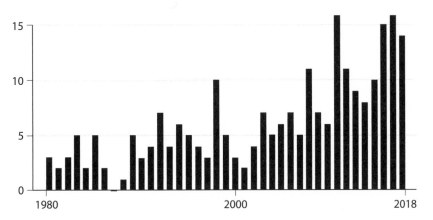

FIG. 9.6. Billion-dollar weather disasters on the rise. Note: Costs are adjusted for
inflation. Adapted from NOAA National Centers for Environmental Information.

FIG. 9.7. May 2018 flooding in Ellicott City, Maryland. Libby Solomon/ *The Baltimore Sun* via AP.

A *thousand-year rainfall* is defined as one so extreme that it is expected to occur only once in a thousand years. Ellicott City, Maryland, had one in 2016, then had another one only two years later.[44] (Video footage of the floodwaters that ravaged Ellicott, which are widely available online, must be seen to be believed.)[45]

Hurricanes of unprecedented force and duration are occurring with increasing frequency. Flooding and droughts have become far more common. For many, the vividness of these episodes appears to have shattered a complacency that ruled when the consequences of climate change were thought to lie one hundred years in the future. Growing numbers of voters are now more skeptical of the arguments of climate change deniers. And as those arguments have drawn closer scrutiny, their logical flaws have become glaringly apparent.

Some have claimed, for example, that because the forecasts of climate scientists are highly uncertain, spending large sums to reduce greenhouse gases might be a waste of money. Climate scientists themselves are of course quick to acknowledge the uncertainty of their estimates. But uncertainty is a two-edged sword. Temperatures might not rise by as much as predicted, yes, but they also might rise by substantially more. In other domains, uncertainty counsels a cautious approach. No one would recommend disbanding the military because we're uncertain that an adversary would attack. We spend a lot on the military because a successful attack would be devastating. The same logic applies to spending to mitigate climate change.

In any event, much of the uncertainty invoked by opponents of climate countermeasures has already been resolved. Increasingly severe storms and droughts linked to climate change are causing enormous damage even today. The only remaining uncertainty is how much worse things will get.[46]

———

Climate forecasts have grown significantly more pessimistic since the 2009 MIT climate simulation model estimated a 10 percent chance that temperatures would rise by more than 7°C (12.6°F) by century's end. A new study, for example, estimates that Earth's glaciers are now melting 18 percent faster than climatologists had estimated as recently as 2013. They are currently losing 369 billion tons of snow and ice annually, more than half of that in North America alone.[47] Even more troubling, a 2019 study published in *Nature Geoscience* demonstrated that increased concentrations of greenhouse gases could eventually result in the complete disappearance of clouds in the earth's atmosphere.[48] If that were to happen, the authors estimated, the effect would be to add a further 8°C (14.4°F) of warming beyond that attributable to other known greenhouse gas effects. Because even an increase far short of that magnitude could end life on Earth as we know it, it seems hardly an overstatement to call global climate change the most serious threat we have ever faced.

It would have been easier to parry this threat if we had acted much earlier. But we did not. Urging people to adopt more environmentally friendly consumption habits will help, but won't be nearly enough to stabilize our climate. To succeed, we must now marshal every resource at our disposal, including robust changes in public policy.

Of central importance will be high levels of public investment in technology. A recent MIT study reports that the cost of solar photovoltaic modules has fallen by 99 percent over the past four decades, primarily as a result of continuing research and development efforts.[49] And although the potential for direct carbon capture technology remains uncertain, Harvard physicist David Keith and his collaborators have published details of a prototype technology that could soon have the capacity to remove carbon from the atmosphere at a cost of less than $100 a ton.[50] With continued innovation, that cost will surely decline, even if not as dramatically as the decline we saw in solar.

But even without further cost reductions, David Wallace-Wells estimates that Keith's technology could neutralize our current thirty-two gigatons of annual global carbon dioxide emissions for an outlay of about $3 trillion a year. That's a hefty sum, but as Wallace-Wells points out, "estimates for the total global fossil fuel subsidies paid out each year run as high as $5 trillion."[51]

It might seem a manageable challenge to persuade voters to embrace a plan to divert fossil fuel subsidies to support carbon capture. Yet the American experience of recent years is that it's next to impossible to get any significant climate legislation passed in the face of determined and well-funded opposition. As the climate journalist David Roberts has argued, politics as usual, "a vague word salad invoking bipartisanship, centrism, and 'common sense' (i.e., DC conventional wisdom), is not a theory of change at all. There is no story to tell about how, if the basic power relationships of US federal politics remain in place, modest, incremental climate policies can pass."[52]

The only alternative, Roberts believes, is to build a broad-based social movement with the power to demand bigger changes, not just on climate policy but also on policies for dealing with income inequality: "Enacting sweeping reform, in the face of a US political system heavily weighted in favor of the status quo, requires a groundswell. A popular mandate. And that in turn requires an agenda that can spark the public imagination and pull in apathetic and infrequent voters. Policy that is designed not to bother anyone won't do that."[53]

Critics charge that ambitious proposals like the Green New Deal may stand little chance of success, to which proponents counter that incrementalism will almost certainly continue to enshrine the status quo.

A deeper appreciation of the power of behavioral contagion strengthens both the economic and the political arguments for the Green New Deal. As we saw in chapter 8, contagion affects our spending patterns in ways that waste trillions of dollars annually in the United States alone. A more steeply progressive income tax, or, better still, an even more steeply progressive consumption tax, would sharply reduce economic inequality while simultaneously generating vast sums for investment in green technology. (More on this point in chapter 11.) And as we'll see, neither of those policies, nor the imposition of a revenue-neutral carbon tax, would require painful sacrifices from anyone. Only the wealthiest would see their taxes rise, and since taxes don't affect relative bidding power, their ability to buy what they want would be virtually unaffected. A serious assault on economic inequality should therefore be viewed not as a competitor for the economic or political resources needed to battle climate change, but rather as a source of them. In this instance, the best policies for attacking each problem separately turn out to be mutually reinforcing.

PART IV

Policy

10

Should Regulators Ignore Behavioral Contagion?

In chapter 1, I argued that behavioral contagion is a far more compelling reason to regulate smoking than is the conventional rationale of protecting innocent bystanders from the dangers of secondhand smoke. Compared to the direct harm experienced by smokers themselves, harm from secondhand smoke is trivial. And because smoking is highly socially contagious, by far the greatest harm caused by smokers is the injury suffered by others who become more likely to smoke.

In my conversations with others about this proposition, the most consistent pushback I've received is that although each premise of my argument might be true empirically, there remains a deep difference between injuries from secondhand smoke and those suffered by people who smoke because of peer influences. The former is a proper basis for government intervention, critics argue, because the victims of secondhand smoke have little recourse. In contrast, people have agency over whether they become smokers. They may be more likely to smoke if peers do, as all evidence suggests, but it's still their decision in the end. My critics worry that if regulators were to acknowledge that it is legitimate for the state to protect us from the negative consequences of peer influences, the result would be to diminish efforts to take responsibility for our own actions.

This objection has obvious rhetorical force. The fundamental attribution error—our failure to recognize that people's actions are shaped more by circumstance than by traits of personality and character—does indeed raise difficult questions about individual responsibility. My aim in this chapter is to consider these questions seriously. But as I will attempt to explain, the case for taking behavioral contagion into account in regulatory decisions remains strong on balance.

Critics' concerns are supported in part by evidence from experiments that probe how behavior changes when people are led to question the concept of free will. The concept is important because many of the laws and institutions of modern societies are grounded on the implicit or explicit premise that people are responsible for their choices and actions.

In most countries, for example, people who are found to have committed serious crimes are deprived of their liberty for extended periods, a step that many would find hard to defend if people lack free will. The importance of free will is further underscored by the circumstances under which we exempt people from responsibility for acts that cause harm to others. Under extreme conditions—for example, when there is clear evidence of profound mental illness—the law explicitly refuses to hold even murderers accountable for their actions.

Yet scientists and philosophers continue to debate whether people have free will in any meaningful sense. The consensus among researchers has been moving slowly but steadily against free will in favor of the view that behavior is determined by genetic and environmental forces largely outside of individual control.[1] It's not yet a settled issue, but if the anti-free-will position wins this debate in the end, many worry about the consequences for society.

It's not an idle fear, for there is at least some evidence that believing in free will promotes a host of beneficial behaviors. As the psychologists Jasmine Carey and Delroy Paulhus have found, for example, those with stronger beliefs in free will also hold themselves and others to stricter moral standards.[2]

The psychologists Kathleen Vohs and Jonathan Schooler have shown experimentally that priming subjects to question free will makes them more likely to steal money and more likely to cheat on a math test.[3] The psychologist Roy Baumeister and his coauthors have shown that similar priming provokes a variety of other undesirable behavioral changes.[4] It makes people less creative, less willing to learn from their mistakes, and less grateful toward one another. Irrespective of whether people's actions are in fact predetermined, then, at least some positive effects appear to accrue from believing that they are not. (Some of these findings, however, have failed to replicate in a recent study.)[5]

It is clear, in any event, that situational factors affect our choices. Individual traits of personality and character matter, too, but such traits are themselves shaped largely by genetic and environmental factors beyond individual control. These observations would appear to imply at least some limits on the extent to which it is reasonable to hold individuals accountable for their actions.

In short, the deepest worry of those who oppose regulation based on behavioral contagion is that it would undercut people's sense of responsibility for their own actions. Additional threats to belief in free will, they argue, would make it more difficult to hold people accountable for harming others. If people's actions are predetermined, how could we blame them for robbing a bank?

Although this concern is widespread, its logical basis is shaky. To deny free will, or to acknowledge that our behavior is influenced by external factors, is not to deny that we are responsible for our actions. It simply means that all actions are the result of causes. When thinking about whether to rob a bank, a potential criminal weighs his lust for the money he hopes to obtain against not only whatever allegiance he feels toward norms against theft, but also the prospect of being caught and punished. If there were no penalty for robbing banks, many more people would rob them.

That's why every sensible society would maintain sanctions against robbing banks, even if none of its citizens believed in free will as conventionally defined. Free-will skeptics believe that every choice is caused by factors that exist prior to the moment of choice. As we saw in chapter 6, fear that one will be punished for violating laws or norms is simply one of those causal factors.

Some free-will skeptics acknowledge the possibility that questioning free will may make it more difficult for some people to resist temptation, but go on to argue that it also promises benefits. The philosopher Sam Harris, for example, notes that questioning free will encourages a more open-minded assessment of the environmental causes of behaviors that society wants to discourage. And this, he argues, may lead to more effective ways of discouraging those behaviors.[6]

In the case of smoking, at least, it is difficult to see how regulatory acknowledgment of the importance of peer influences would make it more difficult for nonsmokers to refrain from smoking, or make it more difficult for smokers to quit. Even those who haven't read the relevant statistical evidence have probably either heard about it or else understand intuitively that peer effects strongly influence smoking decisions. Regulators could take peer influences into account without having to broadcast conspicuous public commentary about them.

In any case, accepting that our choices are often influenced by external forces is clearly compatible with the belief that society has a legitimate interest in holding us accountable for those choices. But because people faced with the decision of whether to smoke do have greater agency than those who are damaged by secondhand smoke, it is also fair to require regulators to meet a stiffer burden of proof in the first case than in the second.

What no one questions, however, is that an increase in smoking rates makes each nonsmoker more likely to smoke. It is thus a statistical certainty that if additional people take up smoking, that fact alone will cause further increases in the overall number of smokers, even though each additional smoker was free to have abstained. People who say regulators should ignore peer effects are thus saying, in effect, that regulators should ignore any injuries that people suffer as a direct result of their own choices.

To call this a controversial position would be an understatement. Although libertarians often object to seat-belt laws and bicycle-helmet requirements for adults, for example, many acknowledge the attractiveness of such measures when applied to children. And in the smoking example, children are the ones most vulnerable to peer influences. Opposition to attempts to shield children from such influences would therefore seem difficult to defend, even for those most inclined to believe that regulators should ignore behavioral contagion.

Many respected scholars have also defended regulations whose apparent aim is to protect adults from the consequences of ill-advised choices. An important class of examples involves decisions that entail self-control. Psychologists have long known that people often succumb to temptation to engage in behavior they would prefer to avoid. When an inferior but earlier reward becomes imminently available, many exhibit a strong tendency to choose it over a much larger reward that occurs with significant delay.[7] Put another way, when the benefit of an option occurs right away but the costs come only with significant delay, the option often becomes misleadingly attractive. Tellingly, those who choose the early reward typically voice regret over having done so. Many awaken the next morning wishing they'd drunk a little less the night before, while many fewer wish they'd drunk a little more.

The extent to which the state should try to shield people from the consequences of insufficient self-control of course remains a matter of spirited debate. When the negative consequences are sufficiently small, the consensus is that people should resist temptation on their own. But when larger outcomes are at stake, that consensus quickly breaks down.

A case in point is the regulation of radiation exposure in the workplace. Workers' willingness to accept delayed risks to their health and safety for extra current pay is vividly illustrated by practices in the nuclear power industry, where it is occasionally necessary to clean up radiation spills. This task commands a significant and immediate pay premium, but also large and significantly delayed health risks from exposure to ionizing radiation. Even so, there is a ready supply of applicants eager to perform these tasks.

Federal regulations currently limit the amount of radiation to which these workers may be exposed, and workers get a bonus if they burn out, or exceed those limits. The cleanup workers, who are known in the industry as glow worms, invariably do burn out, often deliberately, and, were it not for the federal limits, would willingly expose themselves to even higher doses of radiation.

Do these rules constitute regulatory overreach? Reasonable people can disagree. On their face, they appear to violate John Stuart Mill's position that "the only purpose for which power can be rightfully exercised over any member of a civilized community, against his will, is to prevent harm to others." But some philosophers have defended seemingly paternalistic regulations by elaborating on what Mill may have meant by the phrase "against his will." Thus, as Gerald Dworkin writes,

> There is an emphasis on what could be called future-oriented consent—on what the child will come to welcome rather than on what it does welcome. Extensions of paternalism are argued for by claiming that in various respects, chronologically mature individuals share the same deficiencies in capacity to think rationally and the ability to carry out decisions that children possess. Hence, in interfering with such people we are in effect doing what they would do if they were fully rational.[8]

In this view of the problem, regulations that limit exposure to ionizing radiation are not really contrary to the will of those affected by them. Dworkin and others are arguing, in effect, that with the wisdom of hindsight, people would often resent not having been prevented from behaving in self-destructive ways when they were younger. Regulators who respect Mill's plea must still decide whose will deserves greater weight—that of the current self or that of the future self? To rule in favor of the future self is to limit the current self's freedom of action, yes. But failure to restrict the current self ignores the future self's well-considered wish to be protected against being harmed by his current self's myopic choices.

Work in behavioral economics has carried this line of thinking much further.[9] Scholars in this rapidly growing field work primarily at the intersection of psychology and economics, but also draw on insights from other disciplines. One of their most robust findings is that quite apart from issues involving self-control, people often violate the fundamental assumptions of rationality, behaving and choosing in ways that fail to serve their own interests. As these scholars have emphasized, collective action can often steer people toward choices they prefer without significantly restricting their freedom to choose as they see fit. Often this can be accomplished by simply rearranging the way choices are presented, without restricting behavior in any way.[10] (More on this point in chapter 11.)

But for the sake of discussion, suppose we adopt the extreme libertarian view that regulators should ignore injuries that people suffer as a direct result of their own choices. Even that view does not imply that regulators should ignore behavioral contagion, because smoking caused by behavioral contagion harms not only the new smokers themselves, but also many others who have no practical means to avoid injury.

Consider, for example, those parents who have already taken every reasonable step to discourage their children from smoking. Given what we now know about the health consequences of smoking, could anyone second-guess their pursuit of this goal? Perhaps they have attempted to achieve it by refraining from smoking themselves, by choosing friends who do not smoke, by steering their children away from public spaces where others smoke, and by repeatedly advising their children about the dangers of smoking. Perhaps they could have done even more. But evidence from adolescent psychology suggests the possibility that more extreme measures might well have proved counterproductive. Push teenagers too hard, and they become more likely to smoke, not less.

What is certain is that in any large group of such parents, many more will fail to achieve their goal in environments in which a higher proportion of their children's peers are smokers. These parents, like the victims of secondhand smoke, have no recourse. And although the harm they suffer may be hard to quantify, it is surely no less worthy of consideration on that account. And it is not just parents who are harmed. When a smoker dies prematurely, hundreds of other relatives and friends suffer too.

Free-market enthusiasts may underestimate this harm because of their tendency to emphasize self-interest as the most important human motivation. Opponents of regulation, who are overrepresented in this group, often cite Adam Smith's Invisible Hand approvingly. In their telling, market forces channel individual self-interest to serve the broader interests of society. It's a powerful narrative, to be sure, yet Smith himself understood that self-interest alone wouldn't create a just community. He believed that markets could function adequately only in the context of an elaborate foundation of laws and ethical norms of the sort he described in *The Theory of Moral Sentiments*, published almost two decades before *The Wealth of Nations*.

But even the most carefully crafted laws and regulations aren't sufficient. People must also be motivated not to violate them even when no one is looking. In Adam Smith's view, empathy was a primary source of such motivation. As the primatologist Frans de Waal has written, a "fundamental yet rarely asked question is why natural selection designed our brains so that we're in tune with our fellow human beings and feel distress at their distress, and pleasure at their pleasure. If the exploitation of others were all that mattered, evolution should never have got into the empathy business. But it did."[11]

As discussed in chapter 6, empathy motivates good behavior even when narrow self-interest weighs against it. Some people pour unwanted pesticides down their basement drains rather than take the time and trouble to dispose of them safely. But most people don't take this shortcut. Some people don't leave tips after dining in restaurants they don't expect to visit in the future. But most people tip at the expected rate even in these circumstances. Empathy is an important source of such restraint. People exercise restraint out of concern that failure to do so would cause pain to others.

Empathy's most powerful effects are seen in the behavior of parents toward their children. People who have never had children sometimes wonder how they could endure several hours trying to comfort an inconsolably colicky baby in the middle of the night. Once they become parents, however, the child's discomfort affects them more powerfully than their own, and failure to help is not even an option.

Some utilitarian moral philosophers insist that in a decision between saving the life of one's own child and saving the lives of two strangers, the right choice is to save the strangers. But if parents were equipped with a psychology compatible with that choice, few children would receive the care required to emerge as well-functioning adults. Far better to live among people raised by parents who would save a child's life over those of two strangers than to live among those raised by strict utilitarians.

Given the power and importance of parental empathy, it is hardly a mystery that parents hope their children don't grow up to be smokers. But again, if many of their children's peers are smokers, a large proportion of those parents are destined for disappointment. Do those who insist that peer effects are not a proper basis for regulating smoking believe that preventing the injury suffered by these parents is less important than protecting the right of people to smoke without restraint? If so, what arguments might support such a belief in the face of evidence that more than 90 percent of smokers wish they'd never started?

Any such arguments deserve careful scrutiny, because peer effects are strongly implicated in many other forms of harmful behavior besides smoking. Most parents want their children to grow up to be healthy adults, for example, but as we will see in chapter 13, many more of them will become obese if their childhood peers regularly drink thirty-two-ounce sugared soft drinks. Few parents want their children to become bullies, either, but here, too, the influence of peer behavior looms large.[12]

Even in the absence of persuasive arguments that regulators should ignore peer effects, lawmakers have largely confined their attention to behavior that causes significant direct harm to others.

They have ignored the fact that when people suffer harm because of their own choices, others who care about those people also suffer harm. That asymmetry may help explain why regulators have been quick to cite the dangers of direct exposure to secondhand smoke as their defense for taxing cigarettes. As noted, however, that particular harm falls well short of the threshold necessary to justify the relatively extreme measures we have taken to discourage smoking. But if we also consider smoking's indirect harm via behavioral contagion, even stronger antismoking measures could easily be justified.

Again, it's the situation, not the person. That brief sentence captures the long-standing consensus among social scientists that we can better predict what someone will do by examining the social environment than by looking at individual traits of character or personality. Because social environments influence us so strongly—sometimes for good, but often for ill—we have compelling reasons to use public policy to shape them to our advantage.

Yet the dangers of regulatory overreach are also evident. For example, on March 23, 2015, Chris Christie, then governor of New Jersey, signed a law prohibiting church organizations from selling memorial headstones. The law was championed by the Monuments Builders Association of New Jersey, whose members had seen their share of sales of headstones decline significantly after the Archdiocese of Newark, New Jersey, began selling them in 2013.[13]

As the journalist Tanya Marsh described this law's history, it "was adopted at the behest of a group of private market participants for a reason no more noble than to protect themselves from competition. This blatantly anti-competitive effort is even more stunning because the product at issue—headstones and memorial tablets—are not regulated. No license is required to manufacture or sell them. Literally anyone in New Jersey can manufacture and sell tombstones, vaults, and private mausoleums—everyone, that is, except religious organizations and non-profit corporations that own or manage cemeteries."[14]

Laws like these are said to result from *regulatory capture*, which has been defined as "the result or process by which regulation . . . is consistently or repeatedly directed away from the public interest and toward the interests of the regulated industry, by the intent and action of the industry itself."[15] Regulatory capture is widespread, but it is hardly the only source of bad regulation.

Consider again the question of safety regulation. The mere fact that a market failure may exist is no guarantee that regulations as implemented will reliably improve matters. Markets are imperfect, but so are government bureaucrats. During the many decades in which I have been writing about regulation, one of the most vivid examples of ineffective state intervention I have come across remains the following passage from the Occupational Health and Safety Administration's thirty double-columned pages of safety requirements for ladders in its 1976 manual of workplace safety standards:

> The general slope of grain in flat steps of minimum dimension shall not be steeper than 1 in 12, except that for ladders under 10 feet in length the slope of grain shall not be steeper than 1 in 10. The slope of grain in areas of local deviation shall not be steeper than 1 in 12 or 1 in 10 as specified above. For all ladders, cross grain not steeper than 1 in 10 are permitted in lieu of 1 in 12, provided the size is increased to afford at least 15 percent greater calculated strength than for ladders built to minimum dimensions. Local deviations of grain associated with otherwise permissible irregularities are permitted.[16]

It strains credulity to imagine that the cost of attempting to understand, much less comply with, these requirements would be exceeded by the value of any resulting gain in safety.

But we can oppose regulatory capture and ineptly executed regulation without endorsing the view that all regulation is counterproductive. Adam Smith was correct that market forces often channel self-interest for the common good. But he also was a firm advocate of regulation as a remedy for the market's shortcomings. Individual interest and society's interest coincide much of the time, but not always. As we saw in chapter 1, for example, the individual business owner's interest dictates erecting a sign that stands out relative to those of neighboring businesses. But when all owners pursue this interest without restriction, we get visual cacophony. And this has led most cities to enact zoning regulations that limit the placement, height, surface area, brightness, and other characteristics of signs, often with the enthusiastic support of business owners who are restricted by those regulations. In the same spirit, zoning ordinances in most cities do not permit my neighbor to operate a pig farm in a densely settled residential area like ours.

Not even the most extreme libertarians are willing to argue that restrictions on individual freedom are never justified. To embrace that position would be to rule out traffic lights and laws against homicide. As even a moment's reflection makes clear, the state's refusal to limit anyone's freedom of action would entail a wholesale reduction in other highly valued freedoms for everyone.

Scholars who work at the intersection of law and economics have argued that, over the millennia, the law has tended to evolve in the direction of efficiency.[17] Although the process is imperfect and exceptions abound, laws and regulations that address behavior that causes harm to others have been revised in a clearly identifiable way: they are more likely to restrict people from acting as they please when the costs to those restricted are smaller than the harm to others thus prevented. There are cogent reasons to have expected this tendency, for as Ronald Coase and others have emphasized, when the activities of two parties interfere with one another, it is in the shared interest of both to resolve the problem in the least costly way.[18]

This perspective about the law does not imply that all cases involving behavior with negative side effects will be easily resolved. Costs and benefits are often difficult to measure, not least because of strategic posturing. But the same perspective also identifies many cases that are not close calls. Consider an activity that causes considerable harm to others yet is not highly valued by those who engage in it. Smoking is exactly such an activity. It causes great harm to others—most of it indirect—and the overwhelming majority of smokers acknowledge that their habit is personally harmful. Restricting smoking easily meets the efficiency test.

But we have taken far more stringent steps to discourage smoking than would be warranted if our only aim were to protect people from the hazards of secondhand smoke. Once we acknowledge behavioral contagion as a legitimate basis for regulation, however, it becomes clear that the regulatory steps we have taken have not been nearly strong enough. And as we saw in chapter 7, smoking is not the only activity that fits this description.

Few would deny the value of encouraging people to accept responsibility for the consequences of their own behavior. That belief has, as noted, encouraged many to oppose restrictions whose aim is to foster more supportive peer environments. It is each individual's responsibility, these critics insist, to identify which peer examples are worthy of emulation and which are best to avoid.

Yet many who hold this view are also sympathetic toward analogous restrictions on corporate behavior. One reason for this asymmetry could be a general belief that whereas our peers are seldom actively trying to harm us, the same cannot be said of corporations. Firms generally try to persuade us to serve their ends, even when those ends conflict with our own. More troubling, corporations also have enormous power to bend us to their will. When it suits them, they deploy every weapon in the modern marketing arsenal to induce us to engage in deeply self-destructive behavior.[19] Such observations are plausibly cited as justifications for government regulation of firm behavior that harms others.

But the same observations also support regulating consumer behavior because of its effects on peer environments. Corporate marketers now understand, after all, that the surest way to boost demand for their products is to invest in making it more likely that potential buyers' peers will recommend them. Billions of dollars once spent on ads touting a product's features to consumers directly are now spent on sophisticated social media campaigns aimed at launching viral conversations about those products.[20] Businesses have fully grasped the power of peer influences and are heavily investing in new ways to harness them in the service of corporate goals.

As a purely descriptive matter, it follows that to regulate business behavior is often to regulate for the explicit purpose of discouraging negative peer influences. How, then, can those who accept the legitimacy of such regulation consistently oppose the regulation of individual behavior for similar ends? Consistency, of course, isn't everything. As Ralph Waldo Emerson wrote, "A foolish consistency is the hobgoblin of little minds, adored by little statesmen and philosophers and divines." But not every desire for consistency is foolish. Shouldn't the burden of proof here rest with those who argue against the legitimacy of regulating individual behavior to discourage harmful peer influences?

I should also note that ham-fisted prohibitions are not the only way to discourage people from engaging in activities that cause undue harm to others. As we will see in the next chapter, for example, such activities are generally much more efficiently discouraged by our taxing them. The tax approach, as I will explain, embodies multiple advantages in comparison with prohibition and other prescriptive measures. Not least is that it affords those who especially value the activity to continue engaging in it. Another is that it also helps to pay for public services we value. No one enjoys paying taxes, of course, but every dollar we raise from a tax on harmful activities is a dollar less we need to raise from existing taxes on useful activities.

Regulators are well-advised to be humble, to be cautious about using the power of the state to limit people's freedom of action. But caution, like other virtues, is best exercised in moderation. Social influences are extremely powerful. By declaring them off limits as a basis for regulatory intervention, we have been too cautious by far. We have foreclosed valuable opportunities to foster social environments that would help bring out the best in us. We could seize many such opportunities without demanding painful sacrifices from anyone.

11

Creating More Supportive Environments

We differ from one another along many important dimensions. Yet when trying to understand why we behave as we do, psychologists argue, it's generally far more fruitful to examine the social circumstances that surround us than to ask what kind of people we are.

As we have seen, for example, whether someone becomes a smoker is much better predicted by the proportion of her friends who smoke than by examining her traits of personality and character. But the causal arrows run not just from the group to the individual, but also in the opposite direction: if someone smokes, that predicts a slightly greater likelihood that her friends will smoke as well. But because the group's total influence on her is so much greater than her influence on the group, she has little reason to worry that doing so might affect others' likelihood of smoking.

Some social environments influence us for the better. But as in the case of smoking, others have at least the potential to lead us astray. By analogy to the economist's language for describing the harm caused by environmental pollution, I refer to the effects of the latter environments as negative behavioral externalities.

Although society has sometimes been slow to implement economists' recommendations for curbing environmental externalities, the legitimacy of policies like effluent taxation and regulation is generally no longer debated. But that has not been true for policies to curb behavioral externalities. In the smoking example, regulators defend cigarette taxes and smoking prohibitions as necessary for protecting innocent bystanders from harms caused by secondhand smoke. Such measures are almost never portrayed as ways of curbing negative peer influences.

My central thesis in this book has been that we have a legitimate public interest in policies whose explicit purpose is to foster more supportive social environments. By far the greatest benefit of cigarette taxes and smoking prohibitions has been their contribution to the creation of social environments that make our children less likely to become smokers. Such measures could be aptly described as encouraging people to behave as if they worried that becoming a smoker would make others more likely to smoke. These measures don't affect people's attitudes directly, of course, but their effect is the same as what we would predict from policies that encouraged them to care that their own behavior could affect the social environment adversely.

Like policies that discourage behavior that causes direct physical harm, policies that discourage harmful social environments also prevent harm to innocent bystanders. By that criterion, then, the latter policies are neither more nor less legitimate than the former ones. In all cases, the practical question is whether the harm prevented by a policy outweighs the cost of implementing it.

Once we acknowledge that policies to curb behavioral externalities are legitimate in principle, the next step is to investigate how such policies might be most effectively implemented in practice. Because behavioral externalities are completely analogous to physical externalities like air and water pollution, our attempts to mitigate those traditional forms of pollution offer useful lessons.

Economic analysis of environmental pollution begins with the observation that people and firms pollute not because of any desire to harm others, but simply because clean methods of production

FIG. 11.1. Arthur Cecil Pigou, 1877–1959. Chronicle / Alamy Stock Photo.

and consumption are more costly than dirty ones. If clean methods had been cheaper, pollution would not have been a problem in the first place. From the perspective of society as a whole, polluting processes are misleadingly attractive because the harm from emissions falls largely on others.

The British economist Arthur C. Pigou was the pioneer of the tax approach to curbing environmental externalities. In his most influential work, *The Economics of Welfare*, he argued that the best way to discourage the use of dirty processes is to make them more expensive by taxing the pollution they emit.[1] Such levies are commonly described as *Pigouvian taxes* (or, as some economists call them, Pigovian taxes).

The tax approach, Pigou explained, creates incentives to achieve any given emissions target at the lowest possible cost. Suppose, for example, that regulators want to reduce total emissions of a pollutant by some fraction relative to current levels. The traditional regulatory approach would be to require each firm to reduce its emissions by that same fraction. The problem with that approach, Pigou argued, is that some firms can reduce emissions much more cheaply than others can. Requiring all firms to reduce emissions by the same proportion would thus be significantly more costly than if cleanup efforts could somehow be concentrated in the hands of firms that could reduce emissions most efficiently.

And that's precisely what Pigouvian taxes accomplish. Suppose a tax of $1,000 was levied on each emitted ton of a specific industrial pollutant. Firms would then ask the following question: Can emissions be reduced by one ton at a cost of less than $1,000? If so, it will be in the firm's interest to remove that ton rather than pay the $1,000 tax on it. Firms naturally turn first to their cheapest methods of reducing emissions before implementing more expensive ones. They will continue to remove emissions until the cost of removing the next ton rises to $1,000. Beyond that point, the cost of further reductions will exceed the corresponding reductions in tax liability.

Firms with access to technologies that permit them to reduce emissions cheaply will be driven by tax incentives to achieve much larger emissions reductions than other firms. Compared to the alternative of requiring all firms to reduce emissions by the same proportion, the tax approach thus meets the same aggregate emissions target at significantly lower cost.

It might seem unjust to saddle firms that can reduce pollution most cheaply with the lion's share of the cleanup effort. But on closer inspection, Pigouvian taxes are not only efficient, but also fair. Because firms that can reduce emissions most cheaply also reduce emissions by much larger amounts, they also end up paying significantly less in pollution taxes.

Pigou's approach reminds us that society has an interest in reducing pollution only up to a point. Further reductions make sense whenever their cost is less than the value we assign to cleaner surroundings. But once the cost of removing additional pollution exceeds that value, we should stop. In short, the socially optimal level of pollution is not zero. By analogy, most of us value living in a clean house, yet we do not spend all day every day vacuuming and dusting. When the cost of removing additional dirt rises past a certain point, we say, "Good enough."

Pigou's approach also emphasizes that the cost to society of environmental pollution depends primarily on the total amount of it, not on the identities of the specific actors who put it there. That insight makes clear that Pigou's approach not only is efficient and fair, but also shows greater respect for the liberty of individuals and firms. Some firms can curtail their emissions cheaply, but others have far more limited options. Prescriptive regulation that requires every firm to achieve a uniform pollution target might force firms in the latter category to go out of business. Pigou's approach preserves their option of continuing to operate while paying a tax reflecting the damage caused by their emissions. By the same token, some people find it much more difficult to curtail behaviors that cause harm to others, and here too Pigouvian taxes afford greater liberty of action.

Functionally equivalent to the Pigouvian tax approach is what economists call the *cap-and-trade* approach. Cap-and-trade requires firms to have a permit for each ton of pollutant emitted and establishes a market in which these permits can be bought and sold. One attraction of cap-and-trade is that the desired pollution target can be set in advance by policy makers. Under the tax approach, by contrast, policy makers may have to experiment with different tax rates to discover the level that achieves a chosen target.

Despite the seemingly compelling advantages of the Pigouvian tax and cap-and-trade approaches to curbing negative environmental externalities, the political system was slow to embrace them. In the 1970s and 1980s, for example, regulators continued to attack the problem of acid rain with prescriptive regulation rather than with taxes or tradable effluent permits. The source of the problem was sulfur dioxide emissions from coal-burning power plants in the Midwest. Blown eastward by prevailing winds, those emissions precipitated out as acid rain (H_2SO_4) over states in the Northeast, causing extensive damage to forests and fisheries.

As early as the mid-1960s, economists had proposed the creation of a market for tradable sulfur dioxide permits, a limited supply of which would have substantially reduced the level of permissible emissions by utilities in the Midwest. Environmental groups mocked this proposal, likening it to a scheme that would allow utilities to pollute to their heart's content. This criticism was comically wrong-headed. First, since the number of permits granted was to have been significantly smaller than then-current emissions levels, the proposal would hardly have allowed utilities to engage in a pollution spree. More important, consider the bizarre model of firm motivation implied by the criticism, which suggests that firms pollute because their owners derive pleasure from doing so. Utter nonsense! As Pigou and other economists had long emphasized, firms pollute simply because it costs money to reduce emissions.

In the end, the proposed market for tradable sulfur dioxide permits was not established until the amendments to the Clean Air Act were adopted by Congress in 1990. In the wake of that move, damage from acid rain plummeted much more quickly and at far lower expense than under the prior approach of prescriptive regulation, just as economists had predicted. Relative to specific elements of the prior approach, estimates of the cost savings from adopting cap-and-trade ranged from 15 to 90 percent.[2] As a 2011 Harvard University panel assigned to review the program concluded,

> More than twenty years later, the introduction of the national SO_2 allowance-trading program as part of the Clean Air Act Amendments of 1990 remains widely regarded as a landmark step in the worldwide history of environmental regulation. The program, while not without flaws, is viewed as a success by almost all measures. Certainly it demonstrated that broad-based cap-and-trade systems can be used to achieve significant emissions reductions, that firms can navigate and regulators can enforce the compliance requirements of such systems, and that giving the private sector the flexibility to pursue a range of abatement op-

tions can simultaneously protect the environment, stimulate innovation and diffusion, and reduce aggregate costs.[3]

General hostility to taxation has been one source of resistance to the implementation of pollution taxes. But at least some of this hostility is grounded in magical thinking. Those who denounce taxation as theft, for example, seem to embrace the view that society would fare better if governments lacked the authority to levy mandatory taxes. If taxes were suddenly made voluntary, some might continue to pay them in the short run, but resentment would quickly build as their diminished relative purchasing power continued to limit their ability to achieve basic goals. As more and more people ceased paying taxes, government would soon be unable to offer basic services. And no matter what your attitudes about the proper scope of government might be, a moment's reflection reveals that having no government at all would be deeply problematic.

A society without a government, for example, would not be able to field an army. Lacking the means to defend itself, it would soon be invaded and conquered by some other country's army, a force maintained by that country's mandatory tax payments. The end result, then, would be an obligation to pay taxes to the conquering country's government.

When realists discuss tax policy, there are only two interesting questions: What should we tax, and at what rates? The second question is much harder than the first, for its answer depends on difficult-to-reconcile philosophical differences about the proper scope and scale of government. But Pigou's analysis suggests a relatively simple answer to the first question: *we should tax activities that cause harm to others*.

Pigouvian taxes kill two birds with one stone. They not only generate revenue to pay for essential government services, but they also discourage behaviors whose costs outweigh their benefits. In a rational world, Pigouvian taxes would be completely uncontroversial. We would continue to implement them unless there were no remaining untaxed activities that caused undue harm to others. Even if citizens agreed that no additional public expenditures were necessary, it would be in our interest to impose revenue-neutral Pigouvian taxes on any additional activities that caused undue harm to others. (A revenue-neutral tax on an activity is one whose revenues are returned to taxpayers in amounts that do not depend on taxpayer pursuit of the activity.)

Perversely, however, virtually every government currently raises a substantial share of its revenue by taxing activities that are socially beneficial. The payroll tax in the United States, for example, discourages companies from hiring additional workers. The income tax is also a tax on saving, so it discourages much-needed saving and investment. Every dollar of additional revenue generated by a Pigouvian tax would mean one dollar less we would need to collect from taxes on useful activities.

Although substituting Pigouvian taxes for taxes on beneficial activities would produce net benefits, it would not automatically make every individual better off. And those who would be hurt typically wield political influence far out of proportion to their numbers. That's in part because of loss aversion, discussed in chapter 2, which holds that the reduction in satisfaction that results from a loss of a given magnitude is much larger than the increase in satisfaction caused by a gain of the same size. The political scientists' version of loss aversion is embodied in their *iron law of politics*: the losers always cry louder than the winners sing.

The challenge posed by loss aversion is compounded by distributional concerns, since any new Pigouvian tax is bound to affect at least some low-income persons. For example, in 2007, when then New York City mayor Michael Bloomberg proposed the imposition of congestion fees on vehicles entering central Manhattan during business hours, city councilman Lewis A. Fidler objected that the move would place an unacceptable burden on the poor. "It creates a city of haves and have-nots," he said, adding that "those who can afford it may come and those who cannot afford it may not."[4] The city council went on to approve the mayor's proposal, but its implementation was blocked by state government officials who raised similar distributional objections.

The power of such concerns to derail otherwise compelling public policy proposals first became clear to me in a case involving regulated telephone rates in New York State. Shortly after I began my teaching career at Cornell in 1972, the economist Alfred Kahn left his post as dean of the university's College of Arts and Sciences to chair the New York State Public Service Commission, the agency that regulated the state's utilities. One of the first measures he championed upon his arrival in Albany was the imposition of a ten-cent charge for each directory assistance call. At the time, subscribers could simply dial 411 and tell the operator who answered the name and city of the party whose number they wanted. They would then hear her (it was always a woman) searching for the number as she turned pages in a phone book just like the one sitting on the table in front of them. Because subscribers were not charged for 411 calls, they had no incentive to look up numbers on their own. Yet telephone companies had to employ scores of operators and substantial amounts of capital equipment to provide this service. Those costs were then recovered through the imposition of higher rates on everyone, even those who never called 411. Kahn recognized this arrangement as not only inefficient, but also unfair.

He was therefore taken completely by surprise by the violent protests triggered by his proposal. Preposterously, experts testified before the commission that the new charge threatened to disrupt vital networks of communication in New York's communities.

Rather than see the proposal fail, Kahn amended it slightly. There would still be a ten-cent charge for each call to directory assistance, he announced, but each subscriber's bill would also include a thirty-cent monthly credit, paid for by the savings from the anticipated reduction in directory assistance calls. Under the new proposal, only those subscribers who averaged four or more directory assistance calls a month would experience an increase in their phone bills. Those who averaged fewer than three calls would actually see their bills go down. Once the new proposal was unveiled, opposition evaporated almost instantly. Today, any proposal to make directory assistance calls free again would seem bizarre.

The lesson I took from my conversations with Kahn about this experience was that distributional concerns can derail the adoption of efficient policies even when the monetary sums involved are utterly trivial. The standard of living of even the poorest families would have experienced no real change if Kahn's original proposal had been adopted. Yet failure to address the distributional objections to his proposal would have almost surely resulted in its defeat.

In many other domains, the Pigouvian taxes required to curb externalities would of course be far larger than Kahn's directory assistance charge. Yet moves similar to Kahn's thirty-cent credit offer could also parry distributional objections in those cases. Some of the revenues from congestion fees, for example, could be used to reduce vehicle registration fees, or even provide low-income motorists with a limited number of tradable vouchers for travel during congested periods. Those who needed to travel during peak periods could use the vouchers themselves, while others with more flexible schedules could earn extra cash by selling them. Revenue from cigarette taxes could be used to finance reductions in the payroll tax, or to support a more generous social safety net. Similar palliatives could be implemented for virtually any other Pigouvian tax.

As virtually all climate scientists and economists agree, a Pigouvian carbon dioxide tax must be a central pillar of any serious effort to curb greenhouse gas emissions. Such a tax would attack the problem in multiple ways. The most direct effect, and the only one emphasized by advocates, is that by making the discharge of carbon dioxide more expensive, it would provide a strong incentive for producers and consumers to emit less of it.

But because behavioral contagion amplifies people's tendency to make energy-intensive choices, the adoption of a carbon dioxide tax not only would reduce energy-intensive activities by making them more expensive, but would also generate powerful social feedback effects. On the negative side, for instance, by making SUVs more expensive to operate, it would lead fewer people to buy them, which, in turn, would make them still less attractive to others. An example on the positive side is that by raising the economic return from installing solar panels, it would lead more people to install them, which would induce still others to follow suit.

But the biggest gains from adopting a stiff carbon dioxide tax would come not from incentives to apply existing conservation methods more intensively, but instead from the wave of technological innovations it would stimulate. Our planet's continued viability may well depend on the emergence of these innovations.

Many scientists believe, for example, that even reducing carbon dioxide emissions to zero on the timetable prescribed by the IPCC would not be sufficient to avoid calamitous damage from global warming.[5] In their view, it will also be necessary to remove significant quantities of carbon dioxide already dispersed in the atmosphere.

Techniques for doing this already exist, but they are difficult to scale and are far more costly to implement than existing methods of reducing new emissions. Our best hope is that innovation will bring down the cost of these techniques and make them scalable. And that may well be the most important reason for adopting a stiff tax on carbon dioxide as soon as possible.

Even under the most optimistic assumptions, the carbon dioxide tax required to keep global warming under control would be large. The UN IPCC has estimated, for example, that a carbon tax of at least $135 per ton would be needed to meet its 2030 emissions targets.[6] That would translate to an increase of more than $1.20 in the price of each gallon of gasoline.[7] No one can doubt that a levy that large would provoke powerful distributional objections.

But every dollar raised by a tax on carbon dioxide is a dollar by which other taxes can be reduced. The actual cost of reducing carbon dioxide emissions would be only those costs associated with the cleaner processes we would be led to adopt. And those costs promise to be low.

Experience in other countries suggests, for example, that even a carbon tax that doubled the price of gasoline would result in cars that are more than twice as fuel-efficient as current US models. In the United Kingdom, high gasoline taxes produce fuel prices at the pump that are roughly twice those in the United States, with the result that new cars sold in the United Kingdom in 2017 averaged nearly fifty-six miles per gallon.[8]

The implication is that even in the absence of a rebate of carbon dioxide tax revenue, American drivers could adapt to a levy even twice as large as that proposed by the IPCC without having to strain their budgets. A carbon dioxide tax of $270 per ton, for example, would raise the price of gasoline by less than $2.50 per gallon, causing less than a doubling of the price of gasoline at the pump. A family could swap its aging Jeep Grand Cherokee (15 mpg) for a newer VW wagon (29 mpg), which not only handles better but also has virtually the same cargo capacity. Even at the sharply higher gasoline prices, the family's cost per mile driven would be roughly the same as before. And as higher gasoline prices led manufacturers to develop more fuel-efficient models, costs per mile driven would hold steady over the years, even in the face of the steadily rising carbon dioxide taxes called for by the IPCC. Although the price of gasoline at the pump is already more than twice as high in many European countries as in the United States, Europeans typically spend less on gasoline than Americans do, and there is no evidence that they are any less happy with the cars they drive.

The objection that we cannot afford a stiff carbon dioxide tax is further undermined by evidence that we're poised to bear dramatically higher costs from extreme weather associated with the warming trend.[9] The net cost of a carbon dioxide tax would properly include a deduction for the resulting decline in weather damage.

Other critics have argued that a carbon dioxide tax would destroy jobs. But if it were announced today that such a tax would be phased in during the coming years, the immediate effect would be to create a large number of new jobs. Because an impending carbon tax would render many existing energy-using processes obsolete, it would create strong incentives for corporations to put their mountains of idle cash to work right away. Investment spending on development of more efficient processes, with attendant hiring, would begin immediately. Even in the absence of a carbon dioxide tax, new jobs in the renewables sector have been greatly outpacing job reductions in the fossil fuels sector in recent years.[10]

Still other critics have conceded that carbon taxation might be a good idea in the abstract, but go on to argue that it would be pointless because no single country's tax would solve global warming. An effective assault on the problem will indeed require a coordinated effort by all major nations. But at this point, American intransigence is one of the biggest obstacles to collective action. If both the United States and Europe adopted a steep carbon dioxide tax, broader co-operation could be summoned by the threat of border adjustment levies on goods imported from countries that do not tax carbon dioxide. Other nations desperately need access to American and European markets, which gives us real leverage. World trade groups have indicated their receptivity to taxation of imported goods in proportion to their carbon dioxide emissions if exporting countries failed to enact carbon taxes at home.[11]

To repeat, if a proposed policy change is efficient, it will always be possible in principle to ensure that everyone affected by it will come out ahead. An efficient policy is, by definition, one whose total benefit is greater than its total cost. The gains from adopting such a policy are therefore necessarily sufficient to support transfers to those who would otherwise be net losers. Kahn's thirty-cent credit on the monthly phone bill is the form taken by those transfers in the directory assistance example.

Yet politicians have consistently failed to address the distributional objections inevitably provoked by Pigouvian taxation. France's president Emmanuel Macron, for example, could have easily avoided the violent Gilets Jaunes protests provoked by the country's recently imposed fuel tax. Low- and middle-income voters live in smaller houses and drive smaller, more efficient cars than their wealthy fellow citizens. They also take many fewer plane trips to distant destinations. As the results summarized in figure 11.2 indicate, the wealthiest 10 percent of the world's population accounts for almost half of all carbon emissions each year.[12] The lion's share of any carbon-based tax would thus be paid by a country's most prosperous citizens. More important, Macron missed an opportunity by failing to emphasize that the purpose of the fuel tax was not to raise additional revenue, but rather to reduce emissions. A simple version of a revenue-neutral

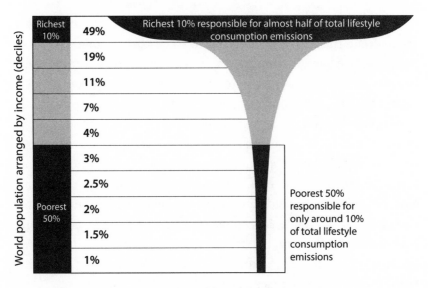

FIG. 11.2. Percentage of CO$_2$ emissions by world population. Oxfam.

carbon tax would redistribute the total revenue collected in equal lump-sum amounts to all taxpayers. Those with below-average carbon footprints would thus get more money back than they had paid in carbon taxes.

If Macron had made it clear at the outset that every euro of revenue generated by the tax would be returned in equal per capita cash payments to all households, both low- and middle-income families would have understood immediately that the amount they would pay in fuel taxes would be substantially smaller than the resulting rebates they would receive, making them net beneficiaries under the policy. That low- and middle-income families have experienced income stagnation in recent decades is simply no reason to avoid a carbon tax. On the contrary, a revenue-neutral tax would be more accurately described as a partial remedy for the income stagnation these families have experienced.

People with the highest incomes would of course pay more, on balance, even under a revenue neutral tax. But they could still easily afford everything they might reasonably be said to need, and as we will see in chapter 12, because the tax would not affect their relative purchasing power, it would also leave their ability to purchase life's little extras largely unaffected. And because carbon-intensive activities would be more expensive even under a revenue-neutral tax, the incentive to reduce emissions would be just as strong as if government spent the tax revenue in other ways.

But Macron did not describe his proposal in these terms, and the violent demonstrations against the initiative portend a significant setback to climate mitigation efforts around the globe. The title of a prominent piece published on the *New York Times* opinion page in the wake of France's cancellation of the fuel tax: "Forget the Carbon Tax for Now."[13]

To forget the carbon tax, however, would be to abandon all hope of meeting the emissions targets necessary to hold climate change in check. It's true that when most voters hear the words "carbon tax," they think the policy would make them poorer. But isn't that a solvable communication problem, rather than a reason to abandon carbon taxes? What leaders need to do is to explain in plain language why everyone's life would be much better with a stiff carbon dioxide tax than without one.

The explanation isn't complicated. Billionaire Tom Steyer's Next-Gen foundation has spent lavishly in support of measures to reduce greenhouse gases. Why not support an ad campaign explaining why a revenue-neutral carbon tax would have benign distributional effects?

No one doubts that achieving widespread adoption of carbon taxes will be a tall order. In the face of heavily financed opposition from the oil industry, for example, even the environmentally conscious voters of Washington State rejected a 2018 referendum calling for a carbon fee.[14] But there are also glimmers of hope. In the spring of 2019, four additional Canadian provinces adopted carbon taxes that are scheduled to rise from an initial level of $15.00 a ton to $37.50 a ton by 2022.[15] More than forty governments worldwide and nine US states have already imposed some form of price on carbon.[16]

Pigouvian taxes are in fact one of the few issues for which the traditional partisan divide is essentially nonexistent among serious students of public policy. For example, N. Gregory Mankiw, a conservative Harvard economist who served as chairman of the Council of Economic Advisers under President George W. Bush, was inspired by his enthusiasm for Pigouvian taxes to found the Pigou Club in 2006. Membership in this group now includes a long list of economists, politicians, pundits, and others from virtually every point along the political spectrum.[17]

In our politically fractious era, it would be a challenge to find any group that represented a broader span of viewpoints than those of Pigou Club members. (Can anyone find another organization that includes both Paul Krugman and Grover Norquist?) Club members attest that their presence on the group's roster constitutes a public endorsement of Pigou's argument that effluent taxes are the most efficient and fairest way of curbing environmental pollution.

Club members were not asked whether they also saw taxation as the remedy of choice for curbing behavioral externalities. But the case for taxing behavioral externalities is identical in every respect to the case so persuasively made by Pigou for effluent taxation.

As noted in chapter 8, regulations are data. By observing patterns in the rules, regulations, and social norms adopted in societies around the world, we can learn something about what people value. If behavioral externalities lead to inefficiencies like the ones caused by environmental externalities, we would expect to see widespread examples of measures whose effect is to curb behavioral externalities, even if those measures are not described explicitly in those terms. And indeed, patterns of taxation and regulation in countries around the world provide strong support for this conjecture. Most countries, for example, impose significant taxes on alcohol and tobacco, consumption of both of which is heavily shaped by behavioral contagion. Most countries also enforce zoning laws that limit the size and other features of signs that businesses erect.

But by far the largest source of waste caused by behavioral externalities results from distortions in our basic spending patterns. And here, too, there have been widespread attempts to curtail expenditures seen as wasteful.

Centuries before Christ, for example, Roman laws attempted to constrain outlays for funerals and mausoleums, even specifying that funeral pyres be constructed from unfinished wood rather than polished wood.[18] Under Chinese sumptuary laws during the seventeenth century, commoners were prohibited from wearing fine silks or using precious metal ornamentation for household articles and saddles.[19] Many jurisdictions in medieval Europe proscribed linen and lace garments.

Like prescriptive regulation of sulfur dioxide emissions, most of these measures were notoriously ineffective. If people's preferred forms of consumption were prohibited, they quickly found effective substitutes. Thus, as I described the history of responses to sumptuary laws in an earlier work,

The prohibition against wearing linen and lace led to attempts to signal status by wearing costly buttons, which by the fourteenth century "were worn as ornaments and fastenings from the elbow to the wrist and from the neckline to the waist." The appearance of gold, silver, and ivory buttons quickly became an indication of wealth and rank, leading some jurisdictions to pass further sumptuary laws restricting the use of buttons. . . . During the Tokugawa period of Japan (1603–1867), members of the increasingly prosperous merchant class "were barred by sumptuary laws from wearing jewelry as well as certain kinds of clothes and from owning certain kinds of traditional fine art works, all of which were reserved for those who held the rank of samurai and above." In response, the merchant class simply developed its own art forms, among them the exquisitely detailed miniature sculptures called netsuke. And there was essentially no limit on what one could spend on ever more elaborately carved netsuke. Medieval Florence had a sumptuary law that limited the number of courses that could be served during the evening meal. This law quickly inspired the pastry-wrapped meat-and-pasta torte and many other elaborate one-dish meals, which were no less time-consuming and expensive to prepare than the multi-course meals they replaced.[20]

By comparison to sumptuary laws, which try to discourage waste by banning the purchase of specific luxury items, the imposition of taxes on those same items offers several potential advantages. For one, it generates revenue that can be used to reduce taxes on beneficial activities. Taxing a luxury is also less coercive than an outright ban, since it preserves the right of those who derive greatest value from the product to continue buying it.

As a practical matter, however, taxes on specific luxuries have been almost as big a failure as sumptuary laws. In the most recent example from the American context, Congress passed a law in 1991 that levied a 10 percent tax on all expenditures above specific threshold amounts thought to define luxury for autos ($30,000), boats ($100,000), aircraft ($250,000), and furs and jewelry ($10,000). Here, too, because only some categories were taxed, buyers could easily find attractive substitutes. Boats purchased abroad, for example, were exempt from the tax, as were expenditures for refurbished used luxury yachts. Many luxury car buyers switched to luxury SUVs, which did not face the surtax.

In the first eighteen months following the enactment of these taxes, government revenues from them totaled less than $13 million, at the time too small a sum to run the Department of Agriculture for even three hours.[21] One of the main effects of the new levies was to cause widespread bankruptcies and financial losses among domestic boat builders, furriers, jewelers, and private-plane manufacturers. The taxes were unceremoniously repealed in 1993.

The theoretically ideal way to moderate mutually offsetting forms of consumption would be to tax every good in proportion to its positionality. Recall that a good is more positional the more heavily its value to consumers depends on how much they spend on it relative to what others spend. As a practical matter, however, we lack fine-grained measures of the positionality of the millions of goods and services traded each year in the marketplace. We are simply in no position to levy this ideal positional consumption tax.

But a 1942 book by the economist Irving Fisher and his brother Herbert suggests how simple modifications to the current income tax system could create a close approximation of the ideal positional consumption tax.[22] Their proposal was to replace the current income tax with a more steeply progressive tax on each household's annual consumption expenditure. This description summons a dismaying image of households having to keep track of thousands of receipts to document their spending to the tax authorities. But as the Fishers pointed out, the need for that step vanishes once we recognize that a family's total income falls into only two bins: what it spends and what it saves. To compute the family's total spending, therefore, we need only two numbers: its annual income and its annual additions to its total savings.

Families already document their incomes to the tax authorities, and many also document their annual savings, as required by 401(k) accounts and similar tax-sheltered retirement savings plans. With those two numbers in hand, the family's total taxable consumption would then be calculated as its income minus its savings, less a large standard deduction—say, $10,000 per person—in recognition of the tendency of lower-income families to save at lower rates than others.

Marginal tax rates on taxable consumption would start low, so that low- and middle-income families would face the same or lower tax bills as under the current income tax. Rates would then rise steadily as taxable consumption rose. Under the current income tax, economists caution against letting top rates rise too steeply, lest incentives to save and invest be diminished. Under a progressive consumption tax, by contrast, that concern vanishes: higher top marginal rates on consumption actually strengthen incentives to save and invest.

Suppose, for example, that the top marginal tax rate on taxable consumption rose to 100 percent for families with taxable consumption of at least $4 million annually—meaning that for each additional dollar spent above $4 million, the family would owe an additional dollar of tax. If a wealthy family were considering an addition to its mansion that would cost $1 million under the current income tax system, that same addition would then cost $2 million—$1 million for the addition itself, and another $1 million in extra taxes.

Even the wealthiest consumers build smaller when prices are higher. In Manhattan, for example, where prices per square foot are higher than in any other American city, many billionaires are content to live in apartments of five thousand square feet, whereas in cheaper real-estate markets many would choose houses more than twice that size.

Therein lies a hint at how a progressive consumption tax would create vast sums of free money out of thin air. Once houses reach a certain size, there is no evidence that further across-the-board increases cause any measurable increase in their owners' well-being. On the contrary, the hassles of managing a larger property suggest that wealthy people might actually become less happy when all build bigger. By slowing the growth in high-end consumption, then, the progressive consumption tax would require no real sacrifice from wealthy consumers. But it would free up resources that could improve everyone's lives in a variety of palpable ways.

For instance, some of the additional revenue could be used to refurbish infrastructure that would benefit families up and down the income scale. And because the tax would slow the rate of growth of top earners' spending, it would also slow the expenditure cascades that have made it more difficult for families further down the income ladder to make ends meet.

The economist Laurence Seidman has proposed that the progressive consumption tax be phased in gradually, starting with a progressive consumption surtax levied only on the taxable consumption of families who report annual incomes greater than $1 million.[23] A family with income below that amount would pay only those taxes required under the current income tax. Families with income greater than $1 million would report their annual savings and then pay a surtax on the difference between their income and their savings. As policy makers gained experience with the response to this progressive consumption surcharge, rates could be adjusted and the threshold gradually lowered. Over time, the new levies would gradually replace the income tax.

An initial effect of this gradual phase-in would be a small reduction in the rate of growth of high-end consumption and a corresponding increase in savings. Greater savings, in turn, would spawn greater investment, as capital markets steered additional funds to the most promising new projects. Additional investment would then boost productivity growth. Total spending would remain essentially the same at first, as would total employment.

As the progressive consumption tax continued to displace the income tax, the share of national income devoted to private consumption would fall gradually, while the share devoted to private and public investment would rise. But because higher investment would boost the growth rate of national income, absolute consumption levels under a progressive consumption tax would eventually overtake those of an economy that had remained on the income tax. The switch to a progressive consumption tax would thus be a policy change that would yield both private and public gains for virtually everyone.

Many people don't realize that most Americans are already living under a tax system that is nearly equivalent to a progressive consumption tax. This majority consists of the taxpayers who currently take less than full advantage of the deductions permitted for funds added to retirement savings instruments like IRAs and 401(k) accounts. (The 2019 maximum annual exemption for 401(k) plans, for example, is $19,000.)[24] For most Americans, therefore, the incentive to consume less and save more under the current income tax is much the same as it would be under a progressive consumption tax.

But there is an important qualification. Most high-income taxpayers already save far more than the maximum exemptions permitted under current retirement savings plans. And it is the spending of this group that has launched the expenditure cascades that have made things more difficult for low- and middle-income households. Adopting higher top marginal rates and eliminating caps on savings deductibility are thus the two key steps required to unleash the fiscal alchemy inherent in the progressive consumption tax. Without painful sacrifices on anyone's part, resources that would otherwise be squandered on fruitless positional arms races could instead support genuinely useful private and public investment.

High-income households are generally better able than others to take advantage of tax-exempt savings opportunities, and high top marginal rates would also give them a more powerful incentive to do so. Although replacing the income tax with a progressive consumption tax would have the desirable effect of reducing consumption inequality over time, it would also tend to increase wealth inequality. Because the wealthy would die with larger estates under a progressive consumption tax system, it would therefore be important to retain a robust inheritance tax.

This requirement is a feature, not a bug, of proposals to adopt a progressive consumption tax. Recent attempts to eliminate the estate tax have in fact been seriously misguided, for it is one of the fairest and most efficient ways to pay for valued public services. In essence, it works like a lawyer's contingency fee contract.

Such contracts enable people to access the legal system who otherwise could not afford to do so. A lawyer who believes an injury claim has merit, for example, may agree to argue a client's case on a contingency basis: if they lose, the client pays nothing, and if they win, the lawyer is paid a share of the judgment, normally 30 or 40 percent. The estate tax is functionally identical to this arrangement.

Young people typically don't know whether they will become wealthy by the end of their lives, although the strong likelihood is that most will not. By voting in favor of an estate tax at the start of their careers, they will enjoy a lifetime of enhanced public services made possible by its revenues. Almost none of them or their heirs will ever pay a penny in estate taxes. The tiny minority who end up lucky enough to trigger the tax have no more reason to complain than a winning plaintiff faced with a bill for his lawyer's contingency fee.

The most thoughtful members of that small group are also mindful of the danger that extremely large bequests pose for their children. Launching successful careers typically requires a series of difficult steps. Young people who expect to inherit big trust funds by age twenty-five often lack the motivation and self-discipline to take those steps.

Current law, which exempts estates of up to $11.4 million per person, attempts to chart a middle course. Under a threshold that high, the estate tax does nothing to harm parents who work hard and save prudently in the hope of being able to provide opportunities for their children to succeed. Maintaining an estate tax at least as strong as the current version would be an important political priority if we adopted a progressive consumption tax.

————

Because many behavioral economists had the wisdom to recognize that hell might freeze over before voters embraced Pigouvian tax remedies, practitioners in that field have instead focused on nontax policy manipulations that can improve the quality of people's choices. The economist Richard Thaler and legal scholar Cass Sunstein coined the term *choice architecture* to describe the practice of influencing choice by changing how options are presented.[25]

The strategic use of default options, for example, has proven remarkably effective in many settings. Because people tend to undersave, they often enter retirement with insufficient assets to support even half their preretirement standard of living. Low participation rates in payroll savings plans are one reason for this shortfall. Under the once-common practice whereby employers required workers to sign up for payroll savings plans, for instance, participation rates were often 50 percent or lower. But in an influential experiment by the economists Brigitte Madrian and Dennis Shea, a large employer made participation in its payroll savings plan the default option. Employees were automatically enrolled unless they took an active step to opt out. Under this arrangement, the participation rate of new employees shot up to 86 percent.[26]

Default options also encourage better decisions in many other domains. Most people feel it would be a good thing to be an organ donor, but when an active step is required to volunteer, few take that step. Yet most people are happy to remain organ donors when that status is the default option, even though they could opt out by simply filling out a form.[27] Simple changes like these often have surprisingly large effects. Reductions in the default size for beer servings in pubs, for example, have been shown to reduce the incidence of problem drinking.[28]

In confirmation of an important premise of the arguments in this book, behavioral scientists have also shown that direct references to peer behavior are among the most powerful ways to influence people's choices.[29] The psychologist Robert Cialdini and his collaborators made this point by examining the failed messaging strategies of hotels hoping to encourage their guests to save energy by reusing bathroom towels. A typical example was a card placed in the bathroom with the message "HELP SAVE THE ENVIRONMENT: *You can show your respect for nature and help save the environment by reusing your towels during your stay.*" Guests who saw this message reused their towels only 38 percent of the time.

A second message card widely used by hotels tried to evoke a cooperation theme by offering to share the energy savings from towel reuse with environmental groups: "PARTNER WITH US TO HELP SAVE THE ENVIRONMENT: *In exchange for your participation in this program, we at the hotel will donate a percentage of the energy savings to a nonprofit environmental protection organization. The environment deserves our combined efforts. You can join us by reusing your towels during your stay.*" This message was even less effective. Only 36 percent of guests who saw it reused their towels.

The researchers then tried a message card of their own design, one that made guests aware of how peers had responded. It read, "JOIN YOUR FELLOW GUESTS IN HELPING TO SAVE THE ENVIRONMENT: *Almost 75% of guests who are asked to participate in our new resource savings program do help by using their towels more than once. You can join your fellow guests to help save the environment by reusing your towels during your stay.*" This message was by far the most effective of the three: 48 percent of guests who saw it used their towels more than once.[30]

Choice architecture can also improve people's choices by physically manipulating the positions in which specific options are presented. Thaler and Sunstein, for example, argue that more healthful food choices can be encouraged by the context in which foods are presented in cafeteria lines. Healthful foods are more often chosen if placed closer to the beginning of the line and at eye level. Using spotlights to highlight healthful items also makes them more likely to be chosen, as does placing them near the cashier's station, where bottlenecks often occur. And fruits are more likely to be chosen if displayed in wire baskets rather than in opaque buckets.[31]

The nudge movement spawned by Thaler and Sunstein has been spectacularly successful around the globe. A 2017 review in the *Economist* described how policy makers were beginning to embrace insights from behavioral science:

> In 2009 Barack Obama appointed Mr Sunstein as head of the White House's Office of Information and Regulatory Affairs. The following year Mr Thaler advised Britain's government when it established BIT, which quickly became known as the "nudge unit". If BIT did not save the government at least ten times its running cost (£500,000 a year), it was to be shut down after two years.
>
> Not only did BIT stay open, saving about 20 times its running cost, but it marked the start of a global trend. Now many governments are turning to nudges to save money and do better. In 2014 the White House opened the Social and Behavioural Sciences Team. A report that year by Mark Whitehead of Aberystwyth University counted 51 countries in which "centrally directed policy initiatives" were influenced by behavioural sciences. Nonprofit organisations such as Ideas42, set up in 2008 at Harvard University, help run dozens of nudge-style trials and programmes around the world. In 2015 the World Bank set up a group that is now applying behavioural sciences in 52 poor countries. The UN is turning to nudging to help hit the "sustainable development goals", a list of targets it has set for 2030.[32]

Given the astronomical rates of return being delivered by nudge units, governments have every reason to keep expanding them. But many of the biggest policy opportunities will continue to elude us unless we can discover ways of making Pigouvian tax remedies more palatable to voters. Invoking a social norm, for example, is effective in getting people to reuse their hotel towels, and putting healthful foods within easy reach is effective in getting more people to choose them. But when the stakes are considerably higher, more powerful incentives are often necessary.

As noted, for example, scientists agree that the existential threat posed by catastrophic climate change cannot be parried without the adoption of a stiff Pigouvian tax on carbon dioxide. Similarly, it is difficult to imagine a simple nudge that would dissuade parents from bidding as vigorously as they could for houses in the best possible school districts. Past success in summoning restraint in high-stakes situations like these has required making restraint the only feasible option. Firms stopped belching sulfur dioxide into the air, for example, only when we required costly tradable permits for doing so. And workers had to moderate their bidding for houses in better school districts when they no longer had preretirement access to the money that financed Social Security checks.

An encouraging sign is that when policy makers have succeeded in implementing Pigouvian taxes, the community has generally been quick to recognize their efficacy. Such was the case, for example, with the cap-and-trade system for sulfur dioxide emissions and, on a smaller scale, with the imposition of charges for directory assistance calls.

Before the city of Stockholm adopted congestion fees in 2006, public support for such fees was hovering near 30 percent, and officials were understandably apprehensive about going forward. But convinced that the policy was sound, they enacted the fees on an experimental basis.[33] Defying the predictions of naysayers, the move was an overnight success.

Car traffic across the congestion zone quickly dropped by 20 percent, leading to sharply reduced travel times and significant improvements in air quality. At the end of a six-month trial period, more than 52 percent of Stockholm residents voted to make the fees permanent. Five years later, public support for the program stood at almost 70 percent and was above 50 percent even among those motorists most directly affected by the fees.[34]

On the basis of this experience, Stockholm transportation director Jonas Eliasson has urged leaders in other cities to be more bold. "The closer you get to implementation, the more the drawbacks stand out," he said, adding that "if you survive this valley of political death . . . then support starts going up again."[35]

Behavioral contagion affects not just the opinions and choices of private citizens but also those of public officials and policy makers. It took some thirty years to persuade members of Congress to embrace economists' recommendations to adopt the Pigouvian taxation solution to acid rain. But each time the approach has been tried and has succeeded, the hurdles facing additional attempts get a little lower.

There are other encouraging signs. After decades of resistance, for example, New York City will at last begin implementing congestion fees for cars and trucks that enter Manhattan south of Sixtieth Street during business hours.[36] And there is evidence that peer influences like the ones discussed for individuals in chapter 3 may also be important at the city level. Officials in several other traffic-plagued cities that are also weighing the adoption of congestion fees are closely monitoring the policy's effects in New York. "New York's use of congestion pricing could be a game-changer," said Travis Brouwer, an Oregon transportation official, in reference to Portland's pending decision about congestion pricing. Los Angeles, San Francisco, Philadelphia, and Seattle have also been considering the adoption of congestion fees, and officials in those cities are described as encouraged by New York City's move.[37]

Recent signs of movement notwithstanding, let no one doubt that political polarization remains a formidable obstacle to the adoption of Pigouvian taxation. In the next chapter, I'll suggest that antitax sentiment stems largely from a simple but powerful cognitive illusion.

12

The Mother of All Cognitive Illusions

If Pigouvian taxation is typically a less intrusive, more efficient, and more equitable remedy for behavioral externalities than the alternatives of prescriptive regulation and outright prohibition, why have legislators been so reluctant to embrace Pigou's approach?

A plausible answer is that politicians' first order of business is to win reelection. They resist tax solutions to externalities for fear of incurring the wrath of voters.

But that raises the obvious question: If tax remedies are so advantageous, why would they provoke the ire of voters? Here I will suggest that voters generally, and prosperous voters in particular, suffer from what I call *the mother of all cognitive illusions*: they believe that having to pay higher taxes would make it more difficult to buy what they want. Like many illusory beliefs, this one may strike most people as self-evidently true. And yet, as I will explain, it is completely baseless.

Many prosperous voters are of course willing to be taxed more heavily to support the common good. But that doesn't mean they regard taxes as painless. For most of these voters, the perceived value of additional public investment trumps their reluctance to endure what they imagine will be unpleasant reductions in disposable income.

Far more numerous, however, have been prosperous voters who reached the opposite conclusion: their perceived benefits from additional public investment were insufficient to compensate for the personal sacrifices they believed higher taxes would entail. And so they have resisted tax increases with all the formidable levers at their disposal.

Regardless of where they stand on tax policy, then, most prosperous voters believe that higher taxes would necessitate unpleasant reductions in personal consumption spending.

I call this belief the mother of all cognitive illusions because it has caused more damage than any other illusion yet identified by behavioral scientists. And the harm it has caused to date pales in comparison with the future damage it threatens.

The good news is that the cognitive processes that underlie the illusion are relatively simple. An average middle-schooler could easily grasp the logic that drives them. And once someone grasps that logic, the illusion is robbed of its destructive power.

Before I attempt to describe the specific mental heuristics, or rules of thumb, that give rise to the mother of all cognitive illusions, it will be helpful to begin with a few observations about the nature of cognitive illusions generally.

Life is complicated. We are bombarded by terabytes of information each day, far more than we are able to process consciously. To cope, our nervous systems employ various heuristics. As we saw in chapter 2, these rules of thumb often operate completely out of conscious awareness. They work reasonably well much of the time. But because of important design constraints, they are imperfect.

In figure 12.1, which square is darker, A or B? If you think A looks darker, your eyes and brain are functioning normally. But in this instance, your judgment is incorrect. In what's called the checker-shadow illusion, square A is exactly the same shade of gray as square B. Look at the figure carefully. If your brain is like mine, it should be telling you, "That can't be true!" And yet it is.

The psychologist Richard Wiseman offers this explanation:

FIG. 12.1. Edward H. Adelson, MIT, http:persci.mit.edu
/gallery/checkershadow.

Your eyes and brain see that the two squares are the same shade
of gray, but then think, 'Hold on—if a square in a shadow reflects
the same amount of light as a square outside of the shadow, then
in reality [square B] must be a much lighter shade of gray.' As a
result, your brain alters your perception of the image so that you
see what it thinks is out there in the real world.[1]

That explanation, plausible though it sounds, is insufficient to
convince most people. But now study the amended image in figure
12.2, and note the complete lack of contrast between squares A and
B and the added strip that joins them. Only upon seeing this second
image was I able even to consider the possibility that A and B might
actually be the same shade of gray.

As the checker-shadow illusion dramatically illustrates, a statement that seems incontrovertibly true ("Square A is darker than
square B.") may in fact be false. This example should affirm at least
the possibility that self-evidently true beliefs about the effect of
higher taxes may be false as well.

With that thought in mind, I'll describe a brief time line of the
experiences that called my attention to the mother of all cognitive
illusions, which I failed to recognize as an illusion at first.

I began teaching economics at Cornell University in the fall of
1972, shortly after receiving my PhD at UC Berkeley earlier that year.

FIG. 12.2. Edward H. Adelson, MIT, http:persci.mit.edu
/gallery/checkershadow.

Having earned a bachelor's degree in mathematics and a master's degree in statistics along the way, I was well-equipped to pursue the formal analytical approach to research that dominated economics during that era.

But the extreme manifestation of that approach that I encountered in Cornell's economics department led me to reject that path. At Berkeley, my classmates and I had been encouraged to prefer the simpler of any pair of behavioral models that were equally consistent with observed data. But among Cornell's economists of that era, the ordering seemed to be the reverse: when they considered someone's attempt to model a specific behavior, their immediate reaction was to reach for ways to make the model more mathematically formal and complex.

It was thus a breath of fresh air to leave Ithaca for Washington, DC, in the fall of 1978 for my first sabbatical. There, I served as director of the Civil Aeronautics Board's Office of Economic Analysis, where the economists on my staff were little concerned with mathematical formalism. For the first time in my professional career, I felt free to indulge my natural affinity for nontechnical speculation about puzzling human behavior.

Because I was at the time unsure whether I would return to Cornell, I applied for and was granted permission by the university to extend my sabbatical in Washington for a second year. And it was during that second year that I first noticed the behavioral consequences of the mother of all cognitive illusions.

The specific behavior that most puzzled me was how self-employed members of the building trades navigated the inevitable trade-offs between earnings and workplace safety. In the course of renovating a row house I had bought near my office, I hired a crew of four to do finishing work and painting on walls and ceilings. Rather than set up sturdy scaffolding to work on areas that were too high to reach, their practice was to stack five-gallon buckets of joint compound three high and then bridge them with a stout 2 × 12 plank. This worked well enough most of the time, but at least several times a week the structure would collapse in a heap. Although no serious injuries resulted during the project, several of the men suffered painful cuts and bruises.

Each time I witnessed one of these episodes, I asked why they didn't set up scaffolding platforms for hard-to-reach areas. Invariably they responded that the necessary equipment was not only costly, but also time-consuming to set up and move frequently.

They were saying, in effect, that the cost of proper scaffolding exceeded the value they assigned to the extra safety. Because rational safety decisions always require weighing the relevant costs and benefits, there was of course nothing intrinsically illogical in this response. Extra safety is costly, and no matter how much one spends, it is impossible to eliminate all risk. The sensible decision rule is to keep investing in safety until further risk reduction would be less valued than alternative uses of the same money. Where that point occurs clearly depends on the decision maker's income and preferences. People of great means and cautious temperaments typically invest more heavily in safety than others. And as people who have lived or traveled extensively in poor countries are well aware, people with low incomes often accept substantial safety risks in return for even marginal increments in income.

What struck me as strange, however, was that the crews working on my project embraced risks that would have been cheap to avoid even though they were anything but poor. Each of them, for example, arrived at my project each day behind the wheel of a nearly new van equipped with lushly carpeted walls and an expensive, state-of-the-art audio system. "Wouldn't it be better," I asked crew members, "to drive a slightly used van and use the savings to get some scaffolding?" Their inevitable response: an older van was simply out of the question!

But why wouldn't a slightly used van have been acceptable? What seemed clear to me at the time was that each worker would have found a two-year-old vehicle perfectly adequate, *but only if that was what coworkers also drove.* The same used van would seem shabby by comparison if most of one's coworkers continued to drive new ones. These observations formed the outlines of the positional-arms-race narrative I sketched in chapter 8, according to which individual decisions result in underinvestment in nonpositional goods like safety. Another implication of this narrative, recall, is that mutually offsetting spending on positional goods spawns annual waste of more than $2 trillion in the US economy alone.

At the time, I saw this phenomenon as a simple collective-action problem. Since the satisfaction from additional consumption beyond some point is almost entirely context-dependent, no individual could curb waste by unilaterally reducing her own spending on positional goods. To be effective, all would need to act in tandem.

Although I continue to consider this an accurate description of the problem, I should have been more troubled than I was by my failure to ask the obvious follow-up question: If prosperous voters would be happier if they spent less on positional goods and lived in environments with more generously funded public sectors, why didn't they just elect politicians who would deliver what they wanted? As I see now but didn't see then, the answer is that prosperous voters suffer from what I am calling the mother of all cognitive illusions.

In the fall of 1980, after two years in Washington, I resumed my teaching duties at Cornell. Shortly after my return, I met Richard Thaler, who had started teaching economics in the university's business school in 1979. Over the next several years, he and I spent long hours in conversation about how our own observations of people's behavior were often strikingly at odds with the predictions of standard economic theory.

Thaler had spent his own recent first sabbatical working with the Israeli psychologists Daniel Kahneman and Amos Tversky, whose pioneering work on cognitive errors I described in chapter 2. Thaler's 1980 article "Toward a Positive Theory of Consumer Choice,"[2] which drew on that work, is now widely viewed as the paper that launched the behavioral economics revolution. In October of 2017, he was awarded the Nobel Prize in economics in recognition of his role as the founder of this vibrant new field. Even critics who had once bitterly resisted his ideas were quick to celebrate his receipt of the award.

Cornell's Behavioral Economics and Decision Research Seminar, started by Thaler in the mid-1980s, is by far the longest-running and most visible faculty research forum in the field he founded. In collaboration with Yale and Berkeley, Cornell is also one of three universities that serve as hosts of the annual gathering of the world's behavioral economists. Cornell, in short, can be fairly described as the birthplace of behavioral economics.

In 1983, I offered the first-ever undergraduate behavioral economics course. Its title was Departures from Rational Choice, which seemed fitting since most of the material I planned to discuss entailed departures from the predictions of the traditional rational choice models favored by economists. (Because that title led to many largely unproductive debates about the meaning of rationality, however, I eventually came to regret it.)

There was of course no standard syllabus for a behavioral economics course in 1983. After considerable reflection and consultation, the one I came up with had two main headings:

A. DEPARTURES FROM RATIONAL CHOICE WITH REGRET

Material under this heading focused on examples of behavior motivated by cognitive errors. For example, rational choice theory counsels that when deciding whether to take an action, we should consider only those current and future costs and benefits that would result from taking the action. An implication is that we should ignore sunk costs (which are costs that have already been incurred and cannot be recovered no matter what we do).

When deciding how many slices to eat at an all-you-can-eat pizza buffet, for instance, the fixed fee for the meal should be irrelevant, since it will be the same no matter how many slices you eat. Yet people who have paid the fee tend to eat substantially more slices than others who are given the opportunity to attend the lunch for free. People who pay are clearly influenced by a sunk cost.

When people learn why sunk costs are irrelevant for rational decision making, most seem to regret such behavior and feel motivated to change it.

B. DEPARTURES FROM RATIONAL CHOICE WITHOUT REGRET

Material under this heading focused on examples of collective-action problems, of behavior that is individually rational but collectively irrational. For example, when all stand to get a better view, no one sees any better than if all had remained comfortably seated. Standing is irrational from a collective vantage point, but makes perfect sense from each individual's perspective.

In such situations, people typically don't regret standing, since the alternative would be not to see at all.

Behavioral economics as it developed over the next decades did not follow the road map outlined in my syllabus. Instead, it has focused almost exclusively on behavior under my first heading, departures with regret.

This work on cognitive errors has had enormous impact among policy makers. As noted in the preceding chapter, for example, governments around the globe have been inspired by it to set up behavioral science advisory groups, popularly known as nudge units, to help citizens make better decisions.

In striking contrast, work that falls under my departures-without-regret heading has been far less extensive—so much so that an instructor putting together a syllabus for a behavioral economics course today might find that heading from my early-1980s syllabus somewhat puzzling.

I continue to believe, however, that economic losses under the without-regret heading are larger by several orders of magnitude than those under the with-regret heading. The former losses stem largely from the wasteful spending patterns discussed in chapter 8, but also include those associated with many other examples of behavioral contagion.

The economic losses from departures without regret are not only substantially larger; they are also more stubborn. That's because losses resulting from cognitive errors can be remedied by unilateral individual action. Once someone learns that it is a mistake to take sunk costs into account, for example, it becomes possible to ignore them unilaterally. Collaboration with others isn't required.

Collective-action problems are a different matter. Parents may learn, for example, that bidding against one another for houses in better school districts serves only to drive up the prices of those houses; but that doesn't alter the fact that it is rational for individual families to continue bidding, since the alternative would be to consign one's children to lower-quality schools. Problems of this sort can be solved only if parents can find some way to act collectively. Effective remedies typically entail policies that alter people's incentives, which are often by their very nature impossible for individuals to implement unilaterally.

If behavioral economics had evolved along the two-branch path I had initially envisioned, I would not have thought to question my continuing membership in the field. But as behavioral economists became ever more heavily focused on cognitive errors, the overlap between my own work and theirs continued to shrink. Eventually, it felt misleading to describe myself as a member of the field.

I should have known better. Having now realized that the biggest barrier to solving the most important collective-action problems we face is itself a cognitive error, I no longer hesitate to identify myself as a behavioral economist. As the Turkish proverb has it, if the mountain won't come to Muhammad, then Muhammad must go to the mountain.

My claim is not that prosperous voters are stupid. Most of them believe, quite naturally, that higher taxes would make it harder to buy what they want. Meeting someone who didn't believe that would be like meeting someone who thought squares A and B were the same shade of gray in the checker-shadow illusion. Yet prevailing beliefs about the effect of higher taxes are false.

What I'm calling the mother of all cognitive illusions provides the answer to the question I failed to ask earlier: If prosperous voters would be happier with less positional consumption and more public investment, why don't they vote accordingly? The reason is that the illusion prevents them from seeing why such a reallocation would be advantageous. It has thus prevented us from raising the revenue required to deal with the many pressing challenges we face, most notably the climate crisis. But if enough people understood why higher taxes wouldn't require painful sacrifices, progress against these challenges would suddenly become possible.

In the checker-shadow illusion, there were cogent reasons for the normal brain to reach a confident but erroneous conclusion. A similarly plausible sequence of cognitive steps give rise to the mother of all cognitive illusions.

When someone asks, "How will an event affect me?" the natural first step is to try to recall the effects of similar events in the past. When parents are trying to decide whether to take their children to Disney World, for example, they might try to summon memories of how well they had enjoyed past visits to similar theme parks. In like fashion, when high-income people try to imagine the impact of higher taxes, Plan A is to summon memories of how they felt in the wake of past tax increases.

But that strategy doesn't work in the current era, since most high-income people alive today have experienced steadily declining tax rates. In 1966, when I graduated from Georgia Tech, the top marginal tax rate in the United States was 70 percent. In 1982 it was 50 percent, and it is now just 37 percent. Apart from brief and isolated increases almost too small to notice, top marginal tax rates have fallen steadily since their 92 percent peak during World War II. Similar declines have occurred in other countries.

When Plan A fails, we go to Plan B. Because paying higher taxes means having less money to spend on other things, a plausible alternative cognitive strategy is to estimate the effect of tax hikes by recalling earlier events that resulted in lower disposable income—an occasional business reverse, for example, or a losing lawsuit, or a divorce, or a house fire, maybe even a health crisis. Rare is the life history that is completely devoid of events like these, which share a common attribute: they make people feel miserable.

More important, such events share a second feature, one that is absent from an increase in taxes: they reduce our own incomes while leaving others' incomes unaffected. Higher taxes, in contrast, reduce all incomes in tandem. This difference holds the key to understanding the mother of all cognitive illusions.

As most prosperous people would themselves be quick to concede, they have everything anybody might reasonably be said to need. If higher taxes pose any threat, it would be to make it more difficult for them to buy life's special extras. But "special" is an inescapably relative concept. To be special means to stand out in some way from what is expected. And almost without exception, special things are in limited supply. There are only so many penthouse apartments with sweeping views of Central Park, for instance. To get one, a wealthy person must outbid peers who also want it. The outcomes of such bidding contests depend almost exclusively on relative purchasing power. And since relative purchasing power is completely unaffected when the wealthy all pay higher taxes, the same penthouses end up in the same hands as before.

A plausible objection is that higher tax rates on prosperous Americans would put them at a disadvantage relative to oligarchs from other countries in the bidding wars for trophy properties in the United States. But that disadvantage could be eliminated easily by the imposition of a purchase levy on nonresident buyers.

To repeat, when we try to imagine how higher taxes would affect us, our history of steadily falling tax rates prevents us thinking back to times when our taxes rose. Plan B is to recall times when our incomes fell. But most of those declines were ones in which our own incomes fell while the incomes of others stayed the same. When our relative income declines, we feel pain. But tax increases don't reduce anyone's relative income.

Emotions and memory are tightly coupled. The more closely an experience is paired with a powerful emotion, the more likely we are to remember it.[3] Strong emotions are provoked by divorces, home fires, business reverses, health crises, and other events that cause individual incomes to fall sharply. These emotions imbue the associated memories with three properties: they are vivid, painful, and easy to retrieve. Those properties greatly strengthen the illusion that tax increases will hurt.

The illusion is compounded by the phenomenon of loss aversion, according to which people experience the pain of a loss much more intensely than they experience the pleasure of a gain of the same magnitude. Psychologically, the imagined loss of private goods one already possesses outweighs the prospective gains from public investments that haven't yet been made. But given the speed with which people generally adapt to losses, this asymmetry merits little weight in policy decisions.

In sum, it's little wonder that people would believe that higher taxes would make them feel bad. Yet this is a cognitive illusion, pure and simple. And because of the magnitude of the resulting losses, I do not exaggerate in the slightest by calling it the mother of all cognitive illusions.

As I've discovered while teaching introductory economics for many decades, repetition is an important key to effective learning. So I'll close this chapter with a simple thought experiment that encapsulates my central point.

Imagine two independent worlds, in one of which the wealthy are taxed more heavily than in the other. In the high-tax world, the wealthiest drivers buy Porsche 911 Turbos for $150,000 rather than $333,000 Ferrari F12 Berlinettas, the vehicle of choice of wealthy drivers in the low-tax world. But because the lowly Porsche includes every design feature that materially affects handling and

performance, the absolute differences between these cars are minuscule. In both cases, drivers would take the same pride in owning
the best car on the road. Available evidence suggests that even if
all other features of the two worlds were exactly the same, it would
be difficult to detect any measurable happiness differences between
wealthy drivers in these environments.

But of course other features would not be the same. Even if governments in both worlds were highly wasteful, at least some of the
extra revenue in the high-tax world would go for public investment,
including better road maintenance. So the real question is this: "Who
is happier, someone who drives a $333,000 Ferrari on roads riddled
with foot-deep potholes, or someone driving a $150,000 Porsche
on well-maintained roads?"

It's an uninteresting question. No serious driver would prefer to
drive a Ferrari on bad roads rather than a Porsche on good ones.

The mother of all cognitive illusions implies that societies can
enjoy the fruits of additional public investment without having to
demand painful sacrifices from anyone. If that strikes you as a radical
claim, that's because it is.

Yet the claim follows logically from only one simple premise—that
beyond a point (one that has long since been passed in the West),
across-the-board increases in most forms of private consumption
do little more than raise the bar that defines what people consider
adequate.

This premise is perhaps the least controversial finding from many
decades of careful research on the determinants of human well-being.
Those who insist that higher taxes on the wealthy require painful
sacrifices face a formidable hurdle: to sustain their position they must
refute the validity of a large body of carefully gathered evidence.

———

Although no one who appreciates the gravity of our current challenges denies that we must act with dispatch, we have consistently
failed to do so. Total carbon dioxide emissions in the United States,

for example, were actually 3.4 percent higher in 2018 than they had been just a year earlier.[4]

But the growing body of research on behavioral contagion offers grounds for hope. As that research amply demonstrates, sweeping change is sometimes a less remote possibility than most of us dare to imagine. The key will be to launch contagious conversations broadly and quickly.

How we might spur progress on that front is our topic in the next and final chapter.

13

Ask, Don't Tell

Harmful forms of behavioral contagion create losses on an epic scale. But because the logic of contagion is often poorly understood, we have made little progress in mitigating those losses, or indeed even in recognizing them. Although this is a lamentable state of affairs in one sense, in another sense it is an opportunity.

The bad news is that our failure to deal effectively with problems caused by behavioral contagion has been costing us literally trillions of dollars annually. The good news is that it would be relatively simple to alter the individual incentives that give rise to these losses. We could greatly increase the amount of resources at our disposal—resources that could be used to solve pressing problems, including the threat posed by the climate crisis—without having to demand painful sacrifices from anyone. My deepest hope in writing this book has been to encourage conversations about how to get started on this project.

The challenges facing this enterprise are formidable indeed. Many decades elapsed, after all, before Congress adopted economists' recommendations about mitigating air and water pollution. Such a delay in the face of truly compelling arguments for effluent taxes and massive investments in renewable energy sources suggests that our failure to act more quickly often stems not from flaws in the policy remedies themselves but from our shortcomings as advocates for them. Persuading legislators to embrace innovative solutions to policy problems is just inherently difficult.

But not impossible. Scholars who study communication have identified strategies that have enabled progress in similar circumstances. Many of these strategies involve eschewing attempts to persuade listeners to do something in favor of launching conversations that enable them to conclude for themselves that action is warranted.

Psychotherapists report, for instance, that telling a woman she is in an abusive relationship often sparks a defensive reaction that may actually increase her likelihood of remaining with her partner. Much more effective, apparently, is simply asking her to describe her relationship. In response, she'll often portray it in ways that make it difficult not to see clearly that things aren't right.[1]

Consider also the history of attempts to persuade voters to support greater investment in infrastructure. During the election campaign of 2012, President Obama and then Massachusetts Senate candidate Elizabeth Warren attempted to remind successful business owners of the importance of such investment. As transcripts of their speeches reveal, both told entrepreneurs that because they had shipped their goods to market on tax-financed roadways, hired workers trained in public schools, were protected by community-sponsored police and firefighters, and enjoyed various other advantages under our free-enterprise system, they should embrace their obligation to invest in the next generation's opportunities to succeed.

Yet many heard a profoundly different message. To them, the speeches seemed to be saying that business owners couldn't claim credit for the successes they'd achieved, that they weren't really entitled to the lofty positions they held. Both quickly became known as the "you-didn't-build-that" speeches. Video excerpts went viral, spawning millions of outraged comments.

Business owners react differently, however, if we don't remind them that their success stemmed in part from external factors. If we instead simply ask whether they can recall examples of external factors that may have facilitated their paths to the top, they seem to enjoy thinking about the question and often take evident pleasure in describing examples of their good fortune. In the wake of such conversations, they often volunteer suggestions about additional public investments we ought to be making.

If conversations about policies for mitigating environmental pollution were far more difficult than suggested by a dispassionate assessment of the merits of those policies, conversations about policies for mitigating behavioral externalities promise to be still more difficult. But because the potential gains involved are so large, it behooves us to think more carefully about how to approach these conversations.

My own interest in how styles of conversation affect the adoption of new ideas stems in part from the striking difference between policy discussions I had over a span of several years with two senior university administrators. One was my university's president, the other a dean of one of its colleges. In separate conversations with these men about specific academic policy initiatives I advocated, each ruled in my favor in about the same proportion of cases. More often than not, they ruled against me. What came as a surprise, therefore, was that my reaction to their decisions depended much less on whether they were in my favor than on the quality of the discussions preceding them.

When the first administrator would rule against me, my admiration of him remained undiminished. Yet each ruling from the second administrator, positive or negative, caused my opinion of him to dip another notch. The first administrator paid careful attention to my arguments and provided clear evidence that he not only understood them but could also restate them in ways that would enable others to recognize their force. When I said something unclear or incomplete, he was quick to notice and pose insightful follow-up questions. And when he did rule against me, he was usually able to explain why he felt that doing so was necessary to protect the university's ability to advance some other goal I valued.

My experience with the second administrator was not like that at all. He was an inattentive listener, and I cannot recall even a single question he ever asked about any of my proposals. Nor did he ever give any indication that he understood why I thought they had merit. When he ruled against me, he made little attempt to explain why. And when he ruled in my favor, it seemed likely that it was for his own reasons.

At the time, I recall feeling skeptical about the asymmetry of my reactions to these men. Had I merely been charmed by the first administrator? Was my low opinion of the second too harsh a judgment for behavior that might reflect little more than a deficit of social skill? Brief reflection erased these worries. Genuine charm springs from emotional intelligence—not only an impulse to care about others, but also an ability to see the world through their eyes. Since those are traits I'd want my children to have, why not admire them in the first administrator? And why not lament their absence in the second?

Scholars who study the content of human conversations would have no difficulty explaining why I reacted so differently to these two administrators. A consistent finding in this field is that questioning is a uniquely powerful tool for promoting progress toward the shared goals of conversation partners. Questions of several different types are abundant in most conversations, but follow-up questions appear to have special power. As Alison Wood Brooks and Leslie John, two leaders in this field, wrote, "They signal to your conversation partner that you are listening, care, and want to know more. People interacting with a partner who asks lots of follow-up questions tend to feel respected and heard."[2]

One method employed by conversation researchers is to interview subjects just after they have engaged in discussions such as job interviews, first dates, or work meetings. Unbidden, subjects leaving these discussions often voice complaints like "I wish [s/he] had asked me more questions" and "I can't believe [s/he] didn't ask me any questions."[3]

One study analyzed thousands of conversations in which people were attempting to learn more about one another in fifteen-minute online chats or in-person speed dates. Some participants were instructed to ask at least nine questions during their exchanges, while others were told to ask no more than four. In the online chats, those who asked more questions were significantly better liked by their partners. Speed-daters, for their part, were more likely to express interest in a second meeting with partners who asked more questions.[4]

Active questioning has been a core element in Western philosophic traditions since at least the time of Socrates and had even earlier origins in Eastern philosophies. In the Upanishad texts of Hinduism, for example, pupils pose six questions to a wise teacher. The Buddha encouraged questioning by his disciples, a tradition that survives in modern Buddhism. The emphasis on questioning is thought to have evolved independently in the Eastern and Western traditions, and, as one researcher put it, "both developed this skill through a high degree of discipline and practice."[5]

Socratic questioning, which has long been a core teaching method in law schools, has also seen growing emphasis in other disciplines. A careful study by the high school biology teachers Ginat Brill and Arnat Yarden, for example, demonstrated that assigning research papers stimulated students to adopt a more question-oriented approach to learning. As these teachers wrote,

> Question-asking is a basic skill, required for the development of scientific thinking. However, the way in which science lessons are conducted does not usually stimulate question-asking by students. To make students more familiar with the scientific inquiry process, we developed a curriculum in developmental biology based on research papers suitable for high-school students. Since a scientific paper poses a research question, demonstrates the events that led to the answer, and poses new questions, we attempted to examine the effect of studying through research papers on students' ability to pose questions. Students were asked before, during, and after instruction what they found interesting to know about embryonic development. In addition, we monitored students' questions, which were asked orally during the

lessons. Questions were scored according to three categories: properties, comparisons, and causal relationships. We found that before learning through research papers, students tend to ask only questions of the properties category. In contrast, students tend to pose questions that reveal a higher level of thinking and uniqueness during or following instruction with research papers. This change was not observed during or following instruction with a textbook.[6]

As marketers have long known, people's opinions are more readily influenced by personal experience and by the experiences of friends than by ostensibly more informative statistical evidence. And so my own opinions about the importance of asking questions have undoubtedly been shaped by long personal experience with this approach in the classroom.

I have been teaching introductory economics courses for more than four decades, during the first two of which my offerings were much like the traditional version of this course taught in universities around the country. These courses, like the traditional biology courses described by Brill and Yarden, do little to encourage questions. Millions of person-hours are devoted to them annually in the United States alone. Yet, according to a nationwide study, when students are given tests that probe their knowledge of basic economic principles six months after they've completed one of these courses, they do not perform significantly better than others who had never even taken the course![7] I have no evidence that students from my own early courses would have done any better.

In the late 1980s, however, I altered my approach. That's when Cornell's Knight Writing Program included my course in an initiative whose purpose was to encourage instructors in a range of disciplines to require students to write papers about their subject matter. Thus was born what became my "economic naturalist" writing assignment, in which I ask students to pose an interesting question about some pattern of events or behavior they have personally experienced or observed, and then use economic principles discussed in the course to craft a plausible answer to it.

As I wrote in my syllabus, "Your space limit is 500 words. Many excellent papers are significantly shorter than that. Please do not lard your essay with complex terminology. Imagine yourself talking to a relative who has never had a course in economics. The best papers are ones that would be clearly intelligible to such a person, and typically these papers do not use any algebra or graphs."

An interesting question is one that makes the listener instantly curious to learn the answer. At first, students find it challenging to come up with such questions, but with practice, they get better quickly. A good test for whether a question is interesting, I tell them, is to pose it to friends and observe their reactions.

One of my all-time favorite submissions was from my former student Greg Balet: Why do regulators require that toddlers be strapped into government-approved safety seats for even a two-block drive to the grocery store, yet permit them to sit unrestrained on parents' laps on five-hour flights from New York City to Los Angeles?

Greg told me that when he posed this question to classmates, it appeared to spark interest. And when he then asked them to try to answer it, the most common response he got was that if a plane crashes, everyone is likely to die anyway, so being strapped in wouldn't matter. He quickly realized, however, that this couldn't be the explanation, since the main reason for being restrained in flight is to reduce the risk of injury caused by severe air turbulence. In the early history of commercial aviation, that risk, apparently, was much greater than the risk of injury from auto accidents, which may explain why regulators mandated seat belts in planes long before they were required in cars.

One of the most important economic concepts I try to teach is the cost-benefit principle, which holds that an action should be taken only if its benefit is at least as great as its cost. This simple principle led Greg to conclude that because the benefit of being restrained in flight was greater than that of being restrained while driving, any economically rational basis for not requiring toddler restraint in flight would have to lie on the cost side of the cost-benefit test. And sure enough, that proved the key insight.

Once you've set up a safety seat in your car, the cost of strapping your toddler in is negligible, just the few moments of effort required to do so. In contrast, if you're traveling across the country on a full flight, strapping your toddler in would require an additional ticket, which might boost the cost of your trip by several hundred dollars or more. Although regulators might not feel comfortable describing their thinking in these terms explicitly, the reason they don't require toddler restraints in flight is that it would be too costly do so.

I don't have any systematic evidence that encouraging my students to ask questions produced a dramatic increase in their long-run mastery of basic economic principles. But since traditional introductory economics courses appear to add no lasting value, I'm confident that my switch to that approach cannot have done significant harm, either. And there are at least some indications that it may have helped. Many students report, for example, that when they go home for Thanksgiving break, their holiday dinner-table conversations often involve the best economic naturalist questions submitted by their classmates. And every year during alumni reunion weekend, former students who graduated years earlier stop by my office to share questions they've posed and answered in the interim.

Some of the best questions entail an element of paradox or contradiction. A personal favorite was posed by my former student Jennifer Dulski: Why do brides spend thousands of dollars on a wedding dress they will never wear again, while grooms, who may attend scores of future events requiring formal attire, generally rent a cheap tuxedo? Posing a question like this creates an instant conversational asset. So it's perhaps little wonder that many students are motivated to keep thinking about this assignment long after their last paper was due. My 2007 collection of my favorite student submissions has sold many more copies than any of my other books.[8]

There is also evidence that asking good questions helps create value in organizations. Author Paul Sloane, for example, reports that one of Greg Dyke's first moves on becoming director general of the BBC in 2000 was to greet his assembled staff by asking, "What is the one thing I should do to make things better for you?"[9] The staff, which had been expecting the usual long, boring presentation, reacted warmly to Dyke's recognition that, as a newcomer, he could learn more from them than they could from him. Sloane reports that the assembled BBC workers indeed had "many wonderful ideas that they were keen to share," and that Dyke went on to implement many of them.

Further evidence of the importance of asking questions comes from studies showing that mere exposure to opposing opinions does little to change people's minds about partisan issues. In one recent experiment, for example, a large sample of Democratic and Republican Twitter users were asked to follow the Twitter accounts of prominent members of the opposing party. At intervals, subjects were asked about their views on ten issues of the sort that reliably separate Democrats from Republicans, including environmental regulation, immigration, affirmative action, LGBTQ rights, corporate profits, and government waste.

This experiment was designed to test the hypothesis that political polarization results from segregation into like-minded groups that seldom hear opposing views. This hypothesis received no support at all. On the contrary, rather than reducing political polarization, exposure to opposing views had the opposite effect: it made Republicans substantially more conservative and Democrats slightly more liberal.[10]

Well-posed questions, in contrast, have been shown to shift opinions on even the most polarizing issues. A careful field experiment demonstrated, for example, that structured conversations lasting no longer than ten minutes can reduce opposition even to highly polarizing initiatives like transgender rights laws.[11] In the hope of discovering methods to mitigate backlash to the Miami-Dade County Commission's 2014 ordinance protecting transgender people from various forms of housing and employment discrimination, experimenters asked local voters to talk with them about these issues. The central feature in these conversations was that canvassers were instructed to listen rather than try to persuade. As David Broockman and Joshua Kalla, the study authors, wrote,

> Canvassers first asked each voter to talk about a time when they themselves were judged negatively for being different. The can-

vassers then encouraged voters to see how their own experience offered a window into transgender people's experiences, hoping to facilitate voters' ability to take transgender people's perspectives. The intervention ended with another attempt to encourage active processing by asking voters to describe if and how the exercise changed their mind. The conversations lasted around 10 minutes on average.[12]

Canvassers also created a control group by conducting ten-minute conversations about recycling with a second large group of voters. Participants in both the treatment and control groups were sent four follow-up surveys at three days, three weeks, six weeks, and three months following the initial conversations.

This simple intervention proved astonishingly effective. Recall from chapter 4 the unusual rapidity with which opposition to same-sex marriage eroded during the first fifteen years of this century. Broockman and Kalla report that their Miami-Dade intervention produced an even larger change in attitudes much more quickly. Those ten-minute conversations, they wrote, "substantially reduced transphobia, with decreases greater than Americans' average decrease in homophobia from 1998 to 2012."[13]

For some participants, the authors experimented with an attempt to undo the effect of the original conversations by including an antitrans attack ad in the six-week survey. This ad highlighted the baseless claim that trans-rights laws encourage predation against young girls in women's restrooms. As expected, members of the treatment group who received this version of the survey registered reduced support for the trans-rights ordinance relative to their two earlier responses. But they were still significantly more supportive of it than control-group members. More telling, the ad's effect on treatment-group members proved transitory. By the three-month survey, it had vanished completely.[14]

The conversational technique employed by Broockman and Kalla was developed by political organizer Dave Fleischer and his colleagues at the Leadership LAB, a gay rights organization in Los Angeles. Their aim was to discover why California voters had rejected legalization of same-sex marriage in 2009's Prop 8 referendum.

Fleischer calls their technique *deep canvassing*, and its essence is having the voter do most of the talking. "We ask open-ended questions and then we listen. And then we continue to ask open-ended questions based on what they just told us."[15]

Learning theorists explain that we absorb information more effectively when we reason our way to a conclusion actively rather than when someone else states it for us.[16] A 2018 meta-analysis of sixty-four earlier studies involving more than five thousand subjects confirms that students learn more effectively if they are asked to explain a concept to themselves than if it is presented to them in other ways. The included studies compared learning outcomes from prompted self-explanation to those produced by a variety of other instructional approaches, including lectures by instructors, solving problems, studying worked problems, and studying text.[17]

In my own experience outside the classroom, one of the most vivid illustrations of the power of self-explanation has come in conversations with opponents of the Affordable Care Act. First, some brief background: The act as drafted had three central features—the requirement that insurers make policies available at the same rates for all participants, even those with serious preexisting medical conditions; a mandate, under which those who elected not to buy insurance were required to pay a fine; and the provision of subsidies for low-income persons. Among those who had an opinion about the Affordable Care Act, the first and third of these provisions enjoyed broad support. The mandate, however, was widely attacked by Obamacare opponents and was deeply unpopular in many circles. Drafters of the Affordable Care Act tried repeatedly to explain to voters why the act couldn't function unless each of its three central features was in place. Those attempts, however, were spectacularly unsuccessful.

Yet the underlying concepts were not complex at all. And if legislators had only thought to pose the right questions, their constituents would have been able to grasp them without difficulty. As my own experience in conversations with Obamacare opponents demonstrated convincingly, the single most important question to have posed was this: What would happen to home insurers if the government forced them to offer fire insurance at affordable rates to people whose homes had already burned down?

The question almost answers itself. Fire insurance policies are available on the market at a price of only several hundred dollars a year, and if companies were forced to offer them at that price to people whose homes had already burned down, no rational consumer would buy insurance unless his home had, in fact, already burned down. Because each policy sold would then obligate the insurer to replace a home costing several hundred thousand dollars, insurers would quickly go out of business. The fire insurance market works only because insurers know that most homes they insure won't burn down. That's why they know the revenue from selling thousands of policies at reasonable prices will be sufficient to cover the cost of replacing the occasional home that is lost.

But an unregulated market for health insurance can't work the same way. A patient with serious preexisting medical conditions is exactly analogous to a homeowner whose home has already burned down. Both the insurer and the patient know that the company will lose an enormous amount of money if the insurer is forced to cover this patient at an affordable price. The only way private insurers can insure such patients is if they're part of a pool that consists mostly of healthy people. And that's precisely why the mandate was an essential feature of Obamacare.

Someone can discover that reason all by herself if she's prompted to consider what would happen to home insurers if they were forced sell cheap fire insurance to people whose homes had already burned down. But because no one thought to ask that question, the mandate's rationale proved elusive to voters despite countless attempts to explain it.

Asking questions is of course not the only strategy for promoting more effective communication on important policy issues. The psychologists Matthew Baldwin and Joris Lammers have shown, for example, that temporal framing can dramatically affect how liberals and conservatives evaluate different environmental policy options.[18] Their work starts with the observation that conservatives tend to focus on the past, while liberals are more likely to focus on the future.

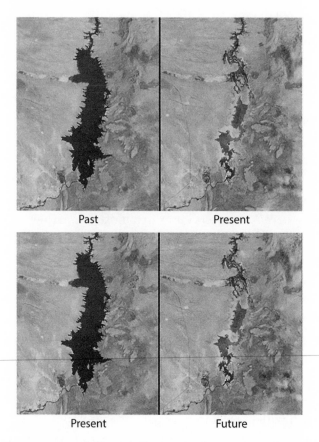

Past   Present

Present   Future

FIG. 13.1. Temporal framing affects support for environmental protection measures. NASA.

As an exaggerated, but informative, characterization of this difference might put it, conservatives think that because the present is worse than the past, we need to restore earlier policies, whereas liberals think that because the future will be worse than the present, we need to change existing policies.

Baldwin and Lammers go on to show that self-identified conservatives are far more likely to embrace environmental protection measures when confronted with contrasts between past and present conditions, and far less likely to support those same measures when the contrasts are described in current-versus-future terms.

One vivid example of this finding occurred when two groups of conservatives were shown identical pairs of photos purporting to depict changes in the health of a specific river basin. One group was told that the two photos at the top of figure 13.1 compared the river's condition in the past with its present condition. A second group was shown the two photos in the bottom pair and told that they described current and future states of the same river basin. Conservatives' support for measures to protect the river was substantially stronger among the past-present group than among the present-future group.

The implication is that someone who wants to boost conservatives' support for environmental protection measures would do well to call attention to aspects of environmental quality that are lower today than in the past. Baldwin and Lammers report that liberals' views were not significantly altered by the same temporal-framing manipulation.

In related research, other psychologists have shown that people are generally ineffective in deploying moral arguments in discussions with opponents of policies they favor. According to Moral Foundations Theory, moral reasoning is typically anchored in discrete emotional modules.[19] The five most commonly listed ones are these:

1. *Care*: cherishing and protecting others
2. *Fairness* or *proportionality*: rendering justice according to shared rules
3. *Loyalty* or *ingroup*: standing with your group, family, nation
4. *Authority* or *respect*: submitting to tradition and legitimate authority
5. *Sanctity* or *purity*: abhorrence for disgusting things, foods, actions

According to the psychologist Jon Haidt and other proponents of Moral Foundation Theory, liberals tend to emphasize the first two of these modules, while conservatives tend to emphasize the last three. In an influential paper, the psychologists Matthew Feinberg and Robb Willer demonstrated that when people from both sides of the political aisle employ moral arguments in support of policies they favor, they tend to invoke the specific modules favored by their own side, a strategy that renders their arguments much less effective with opponents.[20]

For present purposes, their more interesting finding was that in attempts to engage with political adversaries, arguments are far more effective if couched in terms of the moral concerns emphasized by their opponents. Although conservatives were in general strongly opposed to Obamacare, for example, their opposition was significantly more likely to soften when they read a defense of the program framed in purity concerns (e.g., as a way of reducing exposure to sick people) than when they read a defense framed in justice or fairness concerns.

———

With the findings of communications theorists in mind, I'll now try to imagine a conversation with a small-government conservative that might make him more likely to consider the possibility that behavioral contagion is a proper target for policy intervention. Since my hope is to expand the range of issues on which we can agree, I'll refer to him as my partner rather than my opponent. But lest my task seem hopeless at the outset, I'll handicap my partner by assuming him to be a member of the Pigou Club—that is, someone who has already endorsed the proposition that taxation is by far the most efficient and fair way of curbing environmental pollution (see chapter 11).

To avoid claiming too big an advantage for myself, I'll try to defend a policy that has consistently drawn heavy fire from small-government conservatives: specifically, I'll recommend taxing sugared soft drinks as a reasonable response to evidence that high levels of sugar consumption have contributed to a range of serious health problems associated with the obesity epidemic.[21] Mexico, which has experienced an even larger increase in obesity rates than the United States, recently began taxing sugared soft drinks in the hope of curbing the epidemic. Consumption there declined 5.5 percent in the first year after adoption of the tax, and 9.7 percent in the second year.[22]

Of course, many small-government conservatives would object to the imposition of any new taxes. But that objection would not be available to my partner. As fellow members of the Pigou Club, he and I are both on record as favoring taxation as the best way to curb environmental pollution. But if I did happen to find myself in conversation with someone who insists that all taxation is theft, a useful question to ask would be the following: What would happen in a society in which paying taxes was purely voluntary? As we saw in chapter 11, that question highlights the deep contradictions inherent in the taxation-is-theft position. So I'll assume here that my partner agrees that we must tax *something*. I'll note, too, that we both like the idea of taxing pollution, because doing so would reduce the harm that pollution causes to others.

At first opportunity, I would ask my partner, "Do you agree that soda consumption is a social activity?" If he's not sure, I'd point out that in virtually every domain, evidence suggests that our consumption patterns tend to mirror those of others in our social circle. And since this tendency is stronger for children than for adults, it seems reasonable to believe that greater consumption of sugared soft drinks by some children will lead to greater consumption by others as well. If my partner agrees, then he and I also agree that consumption of sugared soft drinks and the emission of toxic pollution have an important feature in common: both are behaviors that cause harm to others. And since the quantity demanded of any good declines when its price rises, it follows that taxation would reduce harm in both cases.

Another common objection to soda taxation has been that people should have the freedom to decide for themselves what beverages to consume. But taxing sugared soft drinks would of course not deprive anyone of that freedom. It would merely make the consumption of sugared soft drinks more costly and, by so doing, result in reduced levels of consumption. We've already agreed that we must tax something, and we both agree that it's desirable in the abstract to tax activities that cause harm to others. So the obvious next question is "Are there *better* things to tax than sugared soft drinks?"

I'll venture that my partner would readily agree that there are many *worse* things to tax than sugared soft drinks. As noted, for example, a large proportion of federal tax revenue in the United States currently comes from the payroll tax. Because this tax makes it 12.4 percent more expensive to hire a worker, it prevents a host of mutually beneficial transactions. If hiring someone would add $20 an hour to a firm's net revenue, for instance, and if that person would be willing to work for as little as $18 an hour, both the firm and the worker would want this hire to occur. But because of the payroll tax, which would boost hiring costs by more than $2 in this instance, it would not. I can therefore assume without even asking that my partner would consider that an undesirable side effect of the payroll tax.

Since money is fungible, every dollar we raised by taxing soft drinks would mean one dollar less we would need to raise from the payroll tax. Wouldn't that switch be a good thing on balance? My partner might support my proposal if soft drinks were the only thing we could tax that would enable reduced taxes on socially beneficial activities. But perhaps he would object that there are even better things to tax than soft drinks. In that case, I'd ask, "What specific things do you have in mind?" He might well come up with examples that I'd find persuasive, activities that cause even more harm than sugar consumption. But in addition to the payroll tax, I could also come up with other examples of beneficial activities that we currently tax. In this fashion, we might compile lists of the best and worst things to tax and then discuss which specific changes we might agree on.

My partner might well object to taxing soft drinks for reasons akin to those offered against cigarette taxes as devices for mitigating peer influences on potential teenage smokers. People always retain the option of abstaining from sugared soft drinks, he might say, just as they also have the option of not smoking. It's a fair point, as I would be quick to concede.

But as we saw earlier, high teen smoking rates are statistically certain to injure many parents and others in ways they cannot escape. For parallel reasons, current beverage consumption patterns are destined to cause unavoidable injury to many others. My partner would surely agree that most parents and friends don't want people they care deeply about to become obese, or to suffer amputations, or kidney failure, or other grave consequences of diet-induced diabetes. Are those not legitimate aspirations?

The science is clear that our current social environment encourages heavy consumption of sugared soft drinks, which greatly increases the incidence of serious health problems. If current consumption patterns persist, it is thus a statistical certainty that millions of parents will fail to achieve the laudable goal of seeing their children grow up to be healthy adults. Would these parents have any recourse? There is only so much they can do to encourage their children to chart a course different from that of their peers. Beyond a certain point, further effort to influence them could easily prove counterproductive.

My partner might also object that to let bureaucrats tax sugared soft drinks would be to step onto a slippery slope that leads inexorably to the dreaded nanny state. In light of recent attempts to curtail speech on college campuses to protect others from injury, it is this objection that gives me greatest pause.[23] If I believe, for example, that the best response to people who are afraid that a campus speaker might injure their feelings is to urge them to grow a thicker skin, why don't I also believe that the best response to concerns about sugared soft drinks is just to urge people not to drink them? Why do I have faith that the bureaucrats will get the science right and tax only those activities that cause genuine harm to others for whom it would be prohibitively costly to escape that harm on their own?

Although I share the concerns that prompt these questions, they don't outweigh my concerns about the losses we suffer by *not* taxing sugared soft drinks. In addition to continuing increases in the serious health consequences of sugar consumption, those losses include the missed opportunity to reduce current taxes on genuinely useful activities. The taxation remedy is also more respectful of individual autonomy than the stereotypical regulatory excesses associated with the nanny state. And finally, taking the slippery slope argument seriously would require abandonment of all attempts to regulate behavior: no stop signs, no red lights, no laws against theft and murder. No reasonable person would advocate that position. Since we go partway down slippery slopes all the time, there can surely be no presumption that taxing soda would usher in a race to the bottom.

Finally, my partner might object (and one of my friends did, in fact, object) that a tax on soft drinks might simply induce people to switch to readily available untaxed substitutes. Just as the tax on luxury cars led drivers to switch to untaxed luxury SUVs, he might ask, wouldn't soda taxes simply lead people to consume more candy and cookies? A good question! As discussed in chapter 11, if much of high-end consumption is mutually offsetting and hence highly wasteful, a progressive tax on total consumption is far more effective than a tax on specific luxuries. Analogously, if excess sugar consumption is the problem, taxing food and drink on the basis of total sugar content is a far better solution than taxing sugared soft drinks alone. Here my partner's objection is not to soda taxes per se, but rather to the failure to tax other forms of dietary sugar as well.

In short, my own view is that seeing Pigouvian taxation as the remedy of choice for environmental externalities would appear to commit Pigou Club members to a parallel conclusion regarding behavioral externalities, even in the most bitterly contested example of soda taxes. The logic of the supporting arguments, after all, is in every detail the same in both cases. Would my small-government conservative conversation partner see things that way? On the basis of many actual conversations about this very issue, I can report that the answer is sometimes, but not always.

But if you care about public policy, even occasional successes make conversations like these well worth having.

———

One of my themes in an earlier book was that because successful people often fail to appreciate the importance of seemingly minor random events in life, they tend to develop an exaggerated sense of entitlement to the enormous material rewards they command in the marketplace.[24] To be sure, most successful people have worked hard and are also highly talented. But at critical junctures, they must also have been lucky. There are plenty of others, after all, who were equally talented and hardworking, yet didn't earn nearly as much.

The problem is that when people think their success was entirely their own doing, they often become more reluctant to support taxes necessary for the investments that would create similar opportunities for the next generation. Any attempt to remind them of the importance of luck in their lives, however, seems to kindle hostile reactions.

Quite by accident, I discovered that the quickest way over this hurdle was to eschew any attempt to remind my successful friends that they'd also been lucky. If I instead simply asked whether they could recall examples of lucky breaks they'd enjoyed along their paths to the top, they didn't react angrily or defensively at all. Instead, their eyes lit up as they scanned their memories for relevant examples. And when they dredged one up, they were eager to tell me about it. The process of recounting it would often kindle the memory of another example, which they also eagerly described. In many cases, they then wanted to discuss possible investments government might undertake to spur progress going forward.

On other occasions, asking people to recall examples of times they'd been lucky just led to interesting stories. Here's one from a friend from graduate school days:

In 1970 while working the midnight shift in Southern Pacific's Oakland railroad yard, I realized that I had left my baseball-style hat at home. Not a big deal—until it started to rain. Another employee lent me a spare hard hat from his truck. Later that night, a 200-pound plate of iron fell from one of the tri-level auto carriers and hit me. I was knocked several feet and rendered unconscious. I spent three days in the hospital and six weeks recuperating. On my first day back at work, a member of the crew from the night of the accident handed me the hard hat, suggesting that I might want it as a memento. I was stunned to see that the metal plate had sheared most of the way through it. Without a doubt, had I not forgotten my baseball hat, that metal plate would have bisected my skull. I kept my "lucky" hard hat until it disappeared during our move to Virginia.

On another occasion, I asked a former college classmate with whom I had recently shared a draft copy of my luck book about his own experiences with chance events. After graduation, he had become a highly successful entrepreneur whose dealings with regulators had made him deeply skeptical about government. In response to my question, he began with a similarly memorable account:

> You may not know that I was struck by lightning back in '85 and was really dead. (It fades to black, with no lights, music, or angels.) If there hadn't been a man there with CPR and leadership skills, I wouldn't be here either. Also, as a small child I ran in front of a 1940 car on Main Street in Jemison, Alabama. The driver never did see me, so I was hit right in the chest by the bumper. Fortunately, the blow caused my arms to reflexively wrap around the upright member that cars of that era always had. That allowed me to be dragged along without being thrown under the wheels. People on the street saw what happened and chased the driver to get him stopped.

But our conversations didn't end there. Although he's still deeply conservative, he told me that being prompted to think about the various ways in which he'd been lucky had made him feel much more supportive of investments to strengthen the social safety net.

You're more likely to learn something new if you spend at least some of your time in conversation with people who don't share your every view. *Confirmation bias* is the psychologists' term for one of the most important cognitive biases to which we are prone. A good scientist looks for evidence that her hypothesis might be wrong, but the natural impulse of most of us is to be more receptive to information that confirms our initial beliefs. Blindness to contradictory information is especially powerful when you feel strongly motivated to believe an idea. Someone who wants to believe asks, "*Can* I believe it?" In contrast, someone who wants an idea to be false asks, "*Must* I believe it?" We're much more likely to avoid confirmation bias if we spend at least some of our time in conversation with people who disagree with us.

But some conversation partners are of course better to avoid. In recent years, it has become increasingly clear that many people publicly support positions that they almost certainly know to be false.[25] Unless you are invited to expose the positions of such people in a public debate forum, there's little reason to waste energy talking with them.

But despite growth in the number of people willing to embrace alternative facts, most people continue to hold their beliefs in good faith. As noted, however, mere exposure to opposing views not only does not alter those beliefs; it actually tends to reinforce them.[26] Yet experimental evidence also shows clearly that conversations structured in a certain way have the power to produce large and durable changes in both beliefs and attitudes.[27]

Someone determined to be strategic in her efforts to persuade others might elect whenever possible to focus on conversation partners who enjoy high esteem among their peers. As the psychologist Betsy Levy Paluck and her coauthors have shown, for example, interventions to curb bullying in schools are far more likely to succeed if focused on the students identified as most popular by social network data.[28] In a similar vein, the economist Juan David Robalino and the sociologist Michael Macy have demonstrated that these are also the students whose own smoking behavior has the largest and most persistent impact on the smoking choices of classmates.[29]

There is also reason to believe, however, that an overly strategic or goal-oriented approach to conversations may be counterproductive. Thus, as the essayist Andrew Merle wrote, "A question is really only a question if you actually care about the answer. Questions are meaningless if you aren't engaged or interested in the response. You can't just absentmindedly check a box with this exercise."[30]

Merle's view was implicit in my response to critics of an earlier book in which I attempted to show that because genuine trustworthiness is a valuable asset in potential trading partners, honest people can prosper in material terms in even the most bitterly competitive environments (see chapter 6).[31] If such people can be identified with sufficient accuracy, they can earn the premium rewards from successful ventures that require trust. Several critics wrote to complain that I had erred in offering material gain as a motive for behaving honestly. But that objection missed my point. The mechanism I described works only if people can detect genuine trustworthiness in others. Given the emotional signaling mechanisms involved, someone who was attempting to appear trustworthy merely to reap material rewards would be unlikely to be perceived as a genuinely trustworthy person. Any such attempt would be as futile as hoping to become more popular by dint of conscious effort to be more spontaneous.

More important, no hint of insincere intent is implied by a passionate concern to tell others about ideas of value. In my second book, published in 1985, I tried to explain why a long list of social ills had been misattributed by social critics on the left to exploitation by powerful employers, or a shortage of competition, or a variety of other market failures.[32] Those same ills, I argued, were instead a result of self-defeating excesses of competition. When the book was published in January of that year, I imagined that Congress would be enacting a progressive consumption tax and several of my other policy recommendations before the year was out. With virtually none of those recommendations having been adopted in the decades since, I am of course painfully aware of how naive those expectations were.

On finishing each of my previous books, I had no idea whether I would write another. That's true this time as well, but since life spans are finite, it's more likely than before that this book will be my last. I also know that even if everyone who reads it were completely persuaded of the wisdom of my recommendations, their number would be far too small to have any discernable impact on the policy debates I care most about. If my ideas are to affect those debates, it will therefore have to be because others became motivated to continue talking about them.

The same was true of ideas that many economists cared passionately about in the 1960s, in particular their proposal to attack acid rain by implementing a system of tradable sulfur dioxide permits.

That recommendation, which was ignored by legislators for decades, sparked a fruitful conversation. Economists talked about the proposal with their students, some of whom became interns or staff members on Capitol Hill, eager to discuss it with senators and representatives, who in turn discussed it with their colleagues. Progress didn't happen quickly, but these conversations eventually led to the adoption of a market for sulfur dioxide permits with Congress's 1990 amendments to the Clean Air Act.

Progress doesn't always take so long. As we saw in the evolution of the law's posture toward same-sex marriage, for instance, the awesome power of behavioral contagion can spur conversations that produce rapid change about even far more controversial policy proposals.

My appreciation of that power kindled my desire to learn more about what promotes fruitful conversations. In short order, I encountered the research described earlier about the effectiveness of posing the right questions. Early on, I watched a video of a TEDx Talk in which Dan Moulthrop, the CEO of the City Club of Cleveland, offered advice based on his long experience as an interviewer.[33] Many of his specific recommendations were supported by the findings of experimental studies cited earlier. But one of the points he made in his talk I have not seen mentioned elsewhere. He said that the most powerful and informative single question to ask someone is "What is your passion?"

No one had ever asked me that question before, and at first I had no idea how I might answer it. I'm an economist, a breed not known for its passions. (As a wag once said, an economist is someone who wanted to be an accountant but didn't have enough soul.) Maybe, I thought, economists aren't supposed to have passions. But brief reflection led me down a different path. In fact, most economists share a deep commitment to efficiency, and I'm no exception. Like most people, I care about many things, but efficiency is in fact my deepest passion, one that animates virtually everything I think and write about professionally.

It influences even my most inconsequential choices. When I spent a year on sabbatical at New York University, for example, it dictated where I sat on subway trains. The station closest to our apartment on Eighth Street that year had two separate entrances, one on Third Street, another on Eighth Street. When boarding northbound trains toward that station, I always sat in the lead car, and always in the last car on southbound trains, since in each case those choices minimized the number of steps to the Eighth Street exit.

But efficiency also lies at the heart of far more profound human concerns. Whenever we adopt a policy that leads to a more efficient outcome, it necessarily becomes possible for every person to achieve more of what he or she wants to accomplish. If inefficiency, especially inefficiency on a grand scale, were the result of deliberate choices, it would be properly denounced as a moral abomination.

There can be little question that the losses I have described here are genuinely titanic in scale and scope. In the case of wasteful spending patterns, these losses have been occurring for many decades. In the case of climate change, the most significant losses are yet to come. But both forms of loss are, for the most part, unintended side effects rather than a result of deliberate choices, and therefore not proper targets of moral outrage. Even so, losses of this magnitude are an entirely proper focus for our deepest passions. I have argued that simple policy changes could eliminate many of them without demanding painful sacrifices from anybody. I may not succeed in persuading a critical mass of people that I am right about this. But I don't think I could exit this world peacefully if I hadn't tried to do so.

Of course, many people need no instruction from me about how to conduct conversations effectively. Intrinsically curious and high in emotional intelligence, they are just naturally good at this. But as the conversation researcher Alison Wood Brooks wrote, "most of us don't ask enough questions, nor do we pose our inquiries in an optimal way. The good news is that by asking questions, we naturally improve our emotional intelligence, which in turn makes us better questioners—a virtuous cycle."[34]

My hope, then, is that you'll go forth and ask lots of questions. You won't always persuade skeptics to embrace your point of view. But you'll be sure to develop more satisfying relationships and hear many fascinating stories along the way.

Epilogue

Having written periodically about climate issues for more than a decade, I have followed the scientific literature on the subject more closely than most of my fellow economists have. In the process, I became deeply concerned about the seriousness of the threat posed by warming. Those concerns animated much of what I wrote in my first draft of chapter 9, which I completed in late December of 2018.

Shortly after the publication of *The Uninhabitable Earth* less than two months later, I was therefore startled by the strength of my reaction to David Wallace-Wells's comprehensive account of what researchers have thus far discovered about our planet's climate trajectory. Although I had already seen many of the most important papers he cited, I had completely failed to grasp the magnitude of the threat he portrayed. His comprehensive summary of the most authoritative climate studies to date amply supported his conclusion that things are indeed much worse than most of us had imagined.

Wallace-Wells also reported that many researchers were themselves reluctant to describe the full extent of the threat, fearing accusations of alarmism. Some worried, apparently, that more candid reporting might lead many to view the challenge as hopeless. But

The Uninhabitable Earth can also be read as supporting a strikingly different reaction.

More than half of all carbon dioxide currently circulating in our atmosphere was put there as a result of human activity since 1988, the year climatologist James Hansen testified before Congress that a dangerous warming trend was already well under way. Wallace-Wells notes that despite this awareness, we continue to spew greenhouse gases into the atmosphere at alarming rates. As he writes, "If this strikes you as tragic, which it should, consider that we have all the tools we need, today, to stop it all: a carbon tax and the political apparatus to aggressively phase out dirty energy; a new approach to agricultural practices and a shift away from beef and dairy in the global diet; and immense public investment in green energy and carbon capture."[1] In the end, he concludes, "the question of how bad things will get is not actually a test of the science; it is a bet on human activity. How much will we do to stall disaster, and how quickly?"[2]

We may safely assume that with the exception of a relatively small number of remaining denialists, a high proportion of the world's population would welcome opportunities to help slow the pace of climate change—especially if painful sacrifices weren't demanded of them. But pessimists are of course quick to cite the necessity of such sacrifices in support of their predictions that we will fail to act in time.

Their skepticism is hardly surprising. As Samuel Johnson said, "To do nothing is within the power of all men." Paralysis becomes the expected result when the power to do nothing is coupled with an intense and well-documented desire to do nothing.[3] A serious assault on global warming will require substantial lifestyle changes across multiple domains, but insofar as we are creatures of habit, our impulse is to resist such changes. Resistance to carbon taxes is especially intense, and in more than one jurisdiction their imposition has precipitated the defeat of political leaders who supported them. Perhaps it's little wonder, then, that we've made so little progress.

Yet despite the stubborn intransigence of the status quo, dramatic change sometimes happens more rapidly than anyone had thought possible. Recall that in the United States the proportion of smokers in the adult population fell by more than 60 percent in the space of just a few decades, and that sweeping changes in attitudes about same-sex marriage happened even more rapidly. Recall, too, that after decades with little visible evidence of political ferment, the governments of member states in the former Soviet Union fell like dominoes in less than a year.

In each of these instances, the most important driver of change was behavioral contagion. With smoking, new taxes and regulations were the initial disruptors, but the far more important force, as we saw in chapter 7, was that for every smoker who chose to quit, an additional member of that former smoker's peer group would also either quit or refrain from smoking. Andrew Sullivan's persuasive arguments that same-sex marriage would not harm others helped launch a national conversation on that subject, but as we saw in chapter 4, the most important reason for public opinion's rapid shift was that as some people announced their change of heart publicly, others felt safer to do likewise. And as also discussed in chapter 4, the fall of the former Soviet Union was another textbook illustration of the explosive power of behavioral contagion: with each additional citizen who spoke out against an oppressive regime, it became less risky for others to speak out as well.

Wallace-Wells asks not only whether we can summon the necessary motivation to challenge warming's trend, but also whether we can garner sufficient resources to succeed. Economists and climatologists view warming as a standard environmental externality, one that calls for rapid imposition of stiff carbon taxes around the globe and substantial investments in green technology. For anyone armed only with that view, it might seem prudent to predict failure.

That we have been permitted to emit greenhouse gases without penalty during the entire industrial era is indeed the root cause of the warming problem, just as the traditional account stresses. But the environmental externalities narrative overlooks behavioral contagion's critical role in the process. As we saw in chapters 8 and 9, behavioral externalities are by far the most important explanation for why we have been building bigger houses, driving heavier cars, and engaging in a host of other energy-intensive activities. We choose these options less because they are priced incorrectly than because that's simply what people like us tend to do.

The other side of that coin, of course, is that our strongest motive for altering our choices will also be that others like us are doing so. When neighbors put photovoltaic panels on their roofs, we too become much more likely to install them. When they buy plug-in electric vehicles, we too become far more likely to consider them. And when peers modify what they eat in response to environmental concerns, we too become much more likely to follow suit.

Understanding how behavioral contagion shapes our choices thus reveals how dramatically we underestimate the effectiveness of policies that encourage individuals to limit greenhouse emissions. Because behavioral externalities are so powerful, any policy that alters individual energy usage directly will also generate ripple effects that exceed the direct effects, often by substantial multiples.

Skeptics are of course correct to note widespread resistance to calls for significant financial sacrifice. But here, too, we have seen, many of the most important actions required to parry warming entail no such sacrifices. Because the wealthy consume far more energy than others, for example, the imposition of a steep but revenue-neutral carbon tax would actually increase the disposable income available to a substantial majority of taxpayers. Under a suitably designed rebate plan, as many as 90 percent of the population might be net financial beneficiaries.

The wealthy, of course, would be left with less money to spend under a revenue-neutral carbon levy. But don't cry for those taxpayers, who not only already have everything anyone might be reasonably said to need, but also would retain their ability to buy the extras they want, even under the steepest carbon tax ever proposed. The special extras in life, after all, are in short supply, requiring those who want them to bid against one another. And when the rich all pay higher taxes, their relative bidding power is completely unaffected. The same penthouse apartments overlooking Central Park would therefore end up in the same hands as before. The tax resistance that stems from failure to grasp that simple fact, I have argued, is the mother of all cognitive illusions (see chapter 12).

The same illusion has also prevented us from raising the general tax revenue required for large-scale public investment in green technology. If the voluminous literature on the determinants of human well-being can be said to demonstrate any single finding conclusively, it is that across-the-board increases in private consumption beyond some point produce no durable increases in life satisfaction.[4] The spending of the top 1 percent of US earners is well beyond that point. That group's share of national income, which now exceeds 21 percent, has grown sharply in recent decades and is higher than at any point since the 1920s. Higher taxes on this group alone could underwrite the massive investments we need in green technology without requiring painful sacrifices from anyone.

The mother of all cognitive illusions of course continues to fuel opposition by the wealthy to higher taxes. But cognitive illusions aren't set in stone. The underlying issues that give rise to this particular one are sufficiently straightforward that any middle school student could easily grasp them. (If there is a middle-schooler in your circle, test this claim!) A deeper understanding of the power of behavioral contagion holds genuine promise of dispelling the mother of all cognitive illusions.

Many climate advocates have cautioned that "conscious consumption" (voluntary individual restraint in energy usage) is no substitute for decisive action on the public policy front. As Wallace-Wells describes this concern,

> conscious consumption and wellness are both cop-outs, arising from that basic premise extended by neoliberalism that consumer choices can be a substitute for political action, advertising not just political identity but political virtue; that the mutual end-goal of market and political forces should be the effective refinement of contentious politics at the hand of market consensus, which would displace ideological dispute; and that, in the meantime, in the supermarket aisle or department store, one can do good for the world simply by buying well.[5]

I have long shared Wallace-Wells's view that there is little hope of parrying warming's threat on the strength of individual spending decisions alone. We will also need bold changes in public policy. But studying the power of behavioral contagion has persuaded me that conscious consumption may promote progress on the policy front in ways I had not previously appreciated. Installing solar panels, buying an electric vehicle, or adopting a more climate-friendly diet doesn't just increase the likelihood of others taking similar steps; it also deepens one's sense of identity as a climate advocate. In the process, it increases one's likelihood of supporting candidates who favor strong climate legislation and of knocking on doors to help them get elected.

Keeping warming at bay is indeed unlikely in the absence of a massive social movement, one that culminates in climate obstructionists being defeated resoundingly at the polls. But mounting such a movement becomes much easier when people's personal consumption choices become more heavily shaped by climate concerns. (Again, as Will Durant distilled Aristotle's wisdom about the power of habit, "we are what we repeatedly do.")

Another reason that behavioral contagion counsels hope is that we have already seen it spawn rapid and sweeping change in the domestic political arena, as it recently did in the state of California. In the not very distant past, California's political leaders were heavily focused on cutting taxes, slashing school funding, reducing infrastructure investment, and bashing immigrants. In these ways, they eerily anticipated the positions taken by many national political leaders today.

But no longer. California voters pushed back. And once voters drove leaders who stood in the way of fruitful collective action out of office, reform efforts surged dramatically. The state now enjoys a budget surplus, even in the face of its increased support for education, infrastructure, and environmental protection. Despite continued population growth, its total emissions of greenhouse gases have declined substantially. And despite dire predictions that the higher top tax rates necessary to pay for these efforts would drive the wealthy to leave the state in droves, outmigration by the top 1 percent has been lower than for any other income group.

As political scientists have long noted, what happens in California often happens in the rest of the country a decade or so later.

A deeper appreciation of the power of behavioral contagion also informs our thinking about political strategies for tackling the two most pressing problems we face, economic inequality and the climate crisis. Proponents of the Green New Deal have argued that unless we tackle both issues simultaneously, there's no prospect of assembling a sufficiently broad political coalition to break through our current gridlock. Their critics, many of them on the left, counter that tackling both issues at once would be so daunting and expensive as to all but guarantee failure in both domains. But this critique, which presumes that the progressive taxes required to reduce inequality would demand painful sacrifices from politically influential wealthy voters, ignores the mother of all cognitive illusions: if leaders explained to voters that higher top tax rates wouldn't alter their relative bidding power, most would be capable of grasping that no real sacrifices would be necessary.

In short, a two-front battle is the right path because the very same policies that would reduce economic inequality most efficiently would simultaneously reduce the economic cost of achieving carbon neutrality. By a rare stroke of good fortune, the best policies for attacking each problem separately turn out to be powerfully synergistic.

As I hope these observations make clear, pessimism about our ability to parry warming's threat is premature. There can also be no doubt that most people are strongly motivated to take action they know will make a difference. As the late Apple cofounder Steve Jobs once said, "We're here to put a dent in the universe. Otherwise, why else even be here?" Few of us, of course, are in a position to put much of a dent in the universe. Even so, the evidence is clear that most of us not only can but also strongly desire to make useful things happen.

I first became consciously aware of the strength of that basic motive when my oldest son was very young, perhaps five or six months old. With him perched on my arm, I walked up to a light switch on the wall and flicked it on and off. Immediately grasping the connection between the switch and the light, he lunged to flip the switch himself. The delight in his eyes as he experienced his ability to make the light to go on and off was palpable. At about the same age, his three younger brothers reacted in exactly the same way—as did my grandson, two granddaughters, and countless children of friends.

In its primitive form, this desire is relatively indiscriminate. Turning a light on and off is neither more nor less satisfying than ringing a doorbell repeatedly. As we mature, however, the desire becomes more focused. We care less about the mere fact of having made something happen and more about the actual effects of our actions. And as we quickly discover, the greatest satisfaction stems from causing something useful or praiseworthy to happen.

Clear evidence of this assertion is seen in the difficulty confronting employers seeking to fill jobs that summon social disapproval. Attracting ad copy writers to a tobacco company, for example, requires a substantial salary premium relative to those who write ad copy for the American Cancer Society. There is, in short, a deep reservoir of intrinsic human desire available to be tapped in service of the common good. A deeper understanding of the forces of behavioral contagion highlights the enormous potential power lurking in appeals to that desire.

Researchers were prudent to worry that knowing the full extent of the threat posed by climate change might cause many to abandon hope. But as Wallace-Wells asks, "Why should we be suspicious of our exceptionality, or choose to understand it only by assuming an imminent demise? Why not choose to feel empowered by it?"[6]

Alarm is a cogent reaction to the threat posed by the climate crisis. But since there is still time to act, and since our choice is between hope and despair, why choose despair? Instead, why not reach for the deep satisfaction that would stem from being part of a collaboration to preserve our planet's viability? For many of those who have managed to avoid being paralyzed by fear, confronting the challenge has been galvanizing. As the climate advocate Katharine Wilkinson put it, "It's a magnificent thing to be alive in a moment that matters so much."[7]

ACKNOWLEDGMENTS

Many have offered useful advice and encouragement during my work on this project. As always, I am especially grateful to my wife, Ellen McCollister, whose keen sense of language is one of the traits that attracted me so strongly to her when we first met. Her perceptive observations on my first draft were exceptionally valuable.

I'd also like to thank my sons, David, Jason, Chris, and Hayden, not only for their helpful observations and encouragement, but also for being the source of much of what I have learned about human nature. With apologies to those I neglect to mention explicitly, I'm also grateful to many others. Phil Cook, Dan Gilbert, Tom Gilovich, Mark Kleiman, and Larry Seidman are deeply knowledgeable about the issues discussed in this book and were extraordinarily generous in providing helpful and timely feedback. I also thank Karen Gilovich, who offered helpful comments on earlier drafts of chapters 5 and 13; Duncan Watts and Steven Strogatz, who helped me with the history of the small-worlds concept; Debra Dwyer and Mir Ali, who confirmed that I'd understood and reported their empirical work on smoking and drinking correctly. Kate Antonovics, Nick Barr, Tom Barson, Jag Bhalla, Alison Wood Brooks, Micky Falkson, Paul Greenberg, Ori Heffetz, Szu-Chi Huang, Leslie John, Duk Gyoo Kim, Michael Macy, Greg Mankiw, Dennis Reagan, David Rose, Kate Rubenstein, Sunita Sah, Leah Stokes, and Cass Sunstein offered helpful comments and suggestions. Paul Roberts and Li Mei Lin provided invaluable research assistance.

I'm also grateful to my agents, Andrew Wylie and James Pullen, whose early enthusiasm for my proposal was an important factor in my decision to undertake this project. And finally, I thank Joe

Jackson at Princeton University Press for his enthusiastic support and helpful guidance throughout, and Lauren Lepow for her superb work as the manuscript's copy editor.

Any remaining errors or other deficiencies in the work are of course entirely on me.

NOTES

Prologue

1. Jeffrey E. Stake, "Are We Buyers or Hosts? A *Memetic* Approach to the First Amendment" (2001), https://www.repository.law.indiana.edu/facpub/220.

2. David Wallace-Wells, *The Uninhabitable Earth: Life after Warming* (New York: Tim Duggan Books, 2019), p. 3.

3. William Strunk, Jr., and E. B. White, *The Elements of Style* (New York: Macmillan, 1959), p. xv.

4. Ibid.

Chapter 1

1. Simon Chapman, *Smoke Signals: Selected Writings* (Sydney, Australia: Sydney University Press, 2016), p. 314.

2. Geoffrey T. Fong, David Hammond, Fritz L. Laux, Mark P. Zanna, K. Michael Cummings, Ron Borland, and Hana Ross, "The Near-Universal Experience of Regret among Smokers in Four Countries: Findings from the International Tobacco Control Policy Evaluation Survey," *Nicotine & Tobacco Research* 6, suppl. 3 (December 2004): S341–S351.

3. Mir M. Ali and Debra S. Dwyer, "Estimating Peer Effects in Adolescent Smoking Behavior: A Longitudinal Analysis," *Journal of Adolescent Health* 45, no. 4 (October 2009): 402–408.

4. Henry J. Kaiser Family Foundation, "Percent of Adults Who Smoke by Gender" (2017), https://www.kff.org/other/state-indicator/smoking-adults-by-gender/?currentTimeframe=0&sortModel=%7B%22colId%22:%22Location%22,%22sort%22:%22asc%22%7D.

5. John Stuart Mill, *On Liberty*, The Library of Economics and Liberty, https://www.econlib.org/library/Mill/mlLbty.html.

6. Jonathan M. Samet, Erika Avila-Tang, Paolo Boffetta, Lindsay M. Hannan, Susal Olivo-Marston, Michael J. Thun, and Charles M. Rudin, "Lung Cancer in Never Smokers: Clinical Epidemiology and Environmental Risk Factors," *Clinical Cancer Research* 15, no. 18 (September 15, 2009): 5626–5645.

7. National Association of Attorneys General, Master Settlement Agreement Related Information, naag.org, 2019.

8. W. Kip Viscusi, "Cigarette Taxes and the Social Consequences of Smoking,"

National Bureau of Economic Research Working Paper No. 4891, October 1994, https://www.nber.org/papers/w4891.pdf.

9. Jonathan H. Gruber and Sendhil Mullainathan, "Do Cigarette Taxes Make Smokers Happier?" *B.E. Journal of Economic Analysis & Policy* 5 no. 1 (July 13, 2005): 1–45.

10. Ashlesha Datar and N. Nicosia, "Association of Exposure to Communities with Higher Ratios of Obesity with Increased Body Mass Index and Risk of Overweight and Obesity among Parents and Children," *JAMA Pediatrics* (January 22, 2018), https://www.rand.org/pubs/external_publications/EP67466.html.

11. Solomon E. Asch, "Effects of Group Pressure on the Modification and Distortion of Judgments," in *Groups, Leadership and Men*, ed. H. Guetzkow (Pittsburgh, PA: Carnegie Press, 1951), 177–190.

12. Stanley Milgram, "Behavioral Study of Obedience," *Journal of Abnormal and Social Psychology* 67, no. 4 (1963): 371–378.

13. Abraham Lincoln, "Temperance Address," Springfield, Illinois, February 22, 1842, http://www.abrahamlincolnonline.org/lincoln/speeches/temperance.htm.

14. Marshall Burke et al., "Global Non-linear Effect of Temperature on Economic Production," *Nature* 527 (October 2015): 235–239.

Chapter 2

1. Richard Layard, "Human Satisfactions and Public Policy," *Economic Journal* 90, no. 363 (1980): 727–750, p. 741.

2. For an extended discussion, see chap. 9 of Tom Gilovich, Dacher Keltner, Serena Chen, and Richard Nisbett, *Social Psychology*, 5th ed. (New York: W. W. Norton, 2018).

3. T. D. Wilson and N. Brekke, "Mental Contamination and Mental Correction: Unwanted Influences on Judgments and Evaluations," *Psychological Bulletin* 116, no. 1 (July 1994): 117–142.

4. The psychologist Daniel Kahneman refers to these mechanisms as "System 1." See Daniel Kahneman, *Thinking Fast and Slow* (New York: Farrar, Straus and Giroux, 2011).

5. Andrew M. Colman, "Titchener Circles," *A Dictionary of Psychology* (New York: Oxford University Press, 2009).

6. T. Pappas, "The Impossible Tribar," *The Joy of Mathematics* (San Carlos, CA: Wide World Publishers/Tetra, 1993).

7. "Escher's 'Waterfall' Explained," Optical Illusions, August 11, 2008, https://www.opticalillusion.net/optical-illusions/eschers-waterfall-explained/.

8. Richard Russell, "A Sex Difference in Facial Contrast and Its Exaggeration by Cosmetics," *Perception* 38 (2009): 1211–1219.

9. Nina Jablonsky and George Chaplin, "The Evolution of Skin Coloration," *Journal of Human Evolution* 39, no. 1 (July 2000): 57–106.

10. Gustav Theodor Fechner, D. H. Howes, and E. G. Boring, eds., *Elements of Psychophysics* (1860), vol. 1, trans. H. E. Adler (New York: Holt, Rinehart and Winston, 1966). Fechner was the student of Ernst Weber, whose experiments led

to his eponymous law. Fechner's law, articulated by Fechner himself, states that subjective sensation is proportional to the logarithm of the stimulus intensity. The term *Weber-Fechner law* is sometimes used to describe both relationships.

11. Stanislas Dehaene, *The Number Sense: How the Mind Creates Mathematics* (Oxford: Oxford University Press, 2011).

12. Lav R. Varshney and John Z. Sun, "Why Do We Perceive Logarithmically?" *Significance*, February 2013, 28–31.

13. Ibid., p. 28.

14. Lav R. Varshney, P. J. Sjostrom, and D. B. Chklovskii, "Optimal Information Storage in Noisy Synapses under Resource Constraints," *Neuron* 52, no. 3 (2006): 409–423.

15. Leslie Lamport, "Buridan's Principle," *Foundations of Physics* 42, no. 8 (August 2012): 1056–1066.

16. Amos Tversky and Itamar Simonson, "Context-Dependent Preferences," *Management Science* 39, no. 10 (October 1993): 1179–1189.

17. Daniel Kahneman and Amos Tversky, "Prospect Theory: An Analysis of Decision under Risk," *Econometrica* 47 (1979): 263–291.

18. Daniel Kahneman, Jack L. Knetsch, and Richard H. Thaler, "The Endowment Effect: Evidence of Losses Valued More than Gains," in *Handbook of Experimental Economics Results*, vol. 1 (Amsterdam: North-Holland, 2008), chap. 100.

19. Michael Lewis, "The Economist Who Realized How Crazy We Are," Bloomberg Opinion, May 29, 2015, https://www.bloomberg.com/opinion /articles/2015-05-29/richard-thaler-the-economist-who-realized-how-crazy -we-are.

Chapter 3

1. Paul Marsden, "Memetics and Social Contagion: Two Sides of the Same Coin?" *Journal of Memetics—Evolutionary Models of Information Transmission* 2 (1998), http://cfpm.org/jom-emit/1998/vol2/marsden_p.html.

2. Ibid.

3. For a general account, see Marco Iacobani, *Mirroring People: The New Science of How We Connect with Others* (New York: Farrar, Straus and Giroux, 2008).

4. Tanya L. Chartrand and John A. Bargh, "The Chameleon Effect: The Perception-Behavior Link and Social Interaction," *Journal of Personality and Social Psychology* 76, no. 6 (June 1999): 893–910.

5. Elaine Hatfield, J. T. Cacioppo, and R. L. Rapson, *Emotional Contagion* (New York: Cambridge University Press, 1994).

6. Sushil Bikhchandani, David Hirshleifer, and Ivo Welch, "A Theory of Fads, Fashion, Custom, and Cultural Change as Informational Cascades," *Journal of Political Economy* 100 (1992): 992–1026.

7. Timur Kuran and Cass Sunstein, "Availability Cascades and Risk Regulation," University of Chicago Public Law & Legal Theory Working Paper No. 181, 2007, https://chicagounbound.uchicago.edu/cgi/viewcontent.cgi?article=1036 &context=public_law_and_legal_theory.

8. Cass R. Sunstein, *How Change Happens* (Cambridge, MA: MIT Press, 2019).

9. Abhijit V. Banerjee, "A Simple Model of Herd Behavior," *Quarterly Journal of Economics* 107, no. 3 (August 1992): 797–817.

10. Stephani K. A. Robson, "Turning the Tables: The Psychology of Design for High-Volume Restaurants," *Cornell Hospitality Quarterly* 40, no. 3 (June 1999): 56–63.

11. Susan Cotts Watkins, *From Provinces into Nations: Demographic Integration in Western Europe, 1870–1960* (Princeton, NJ: Princeton University Press, 2016).

12. David F. Scharfstein and Jeremy Stein, "Herd Behavior and Investment," *American Economic Review* 80, no. 3 (June 1990): 465–479; Elihu Katz, Martin L. Levin, and Herbert Hamilton, "Traditions of Research on the Diffusion of Innovation," *American Sociological Review* 28, no. 2 (April 1963): 237–252.

13. Tatsuya Kameda, Keigo Inukai, Thomas Wisdom, and Wataru Toyokawa, "The Concept of Herd Behaviour: Its Psychological and Neural Underpinnings," in *Contract Governance*, ed. Stefan Grundmann, Florian Möslein, and Karl Riesenhuber (Oxford: Oxford University Press, 2015), chap. 2; Terry Connolly and Lars Åberg, "Some Contagion Models of Speeding," *Accident Analysis and Prevention* 25, no. 1 (1993): 57–66; and Alicia Oullette, "Body Modification and Adolescent Decision Making: Proceed with Caution," *Journal of Health Care Law and Policy* 15, no. 1 (2012), https://core.ac.uk/download/pdf/56355486.pdf.

14. Gordon B. Dahl, Katrine Løken, and Magne Mogstad, "Peer Effects in Program Participation," *American Economic Review* 104, no. 7 (July 2014): 2049–2074.

15. Edward L. Glaeser, B. Sacerdote, and J. A. Scheinkman, "Crime and Social Interactions," *Quarterly Journal of Economics* 111 (1996): 507–548.

16. Colin Loftin, "Assaultive Violence as a Contagious Social Process," *Bulletin of the New York Academy of Medicine* 62, no. 5 (June 1986): 550–555.

17. John Maynard Keynes, *The General Theory of Employment, Interest, and Money* (London: Macmillan, 1936).

18. Glenn C. Loury, "Self-Censorship in Public Discourse: A Theory of 'Political Correctness' and Related Phenomena," *Rationality and Society* 6, no. 4 (October 1994): 428–461.

19. Erving Goffman, *The Presentation of Self in Everyday Life* (Garden City, NY: Doubleday, 1959).

20. Philip J. Cook and Kristen A. Goss, "A Selective Review of the Social Contagion Literature" (unpublished manuscript, Sanford School of Public Policy, Duke University, 1996).

Chapter 4

1. Andrew Sullivan, "Here Comes the Groom: A (Conservative) Case for Gay Marriage," *New Republic*, August 28, 1989, https://newrepublic.com/article/79054/here-comes-the-groom.

2. Supreme Court of the United States, *Obergefell et al. v. Hodges, Director, Ohio Department of Health, et al.*, Decided June 26, 2015, https://www.supremecourt.gov/opinions/14pdf/14-556_3204.pdf.

3. Lyle Denniston, "Opinion Analysis: Marriage Now Open to Same-Sex Couples," SCOTUSblog, June 26, 2015.

4. Nate Silver, "Change Doesn't Usually Come This Fast," FiveThirtyEight, June 28, 2015, https://fivethirtyeight.com/features/change-doesnt-usually-come-this-fast/.

5. Ibid.

6. Justin McCarthy, "Two in Three Americans Support Same-Sex Marriage," Gallup, May 23, 2018, https://news.gallup.com/poll/234866/two-three-americans-support-sex-marriage.aspx.

7. Anna Brown, "Five Key Findings about LGBT Americans," Pew Research Center, June 13, 2017, https://www.pewresearch.org/fact-tank/2017/06/13/5-key-findings-about-lgbt-americans/.

8. McCarthy, "Two in Three Americans Support Same-Sex Marriage."

9. Sabrina Eaton, "Sen. Rob Portman Comes Out in Favor of Gay Marriage after Son Comes Out as Gay," *Cleveland Plain Dealer*, March 14, 2013, https://www.cleveland.com/open/2013/03/sen_rob_portman_comes_out_in_f.html.

10. "Cheney Backs Gay Marriage, Calls It a State Issue," NBC News, June 2, 2009, http://www.nbcnews.com/id/31066626/#.XTHa6HspC7l.

11. Paul Graham, "What You Can't Say," January 2004, http://paulgraham.com/say.html.

12. Pamela Duncan, "Gay Relationships Are Still Criminalized in 72 Countries, Report Finds," *Guardian*, July 27, 2017.

13. BBC Newsbeat, "The Countries Where People Still Eat Dogs for Dinner," BBC.com, April 12, 2017.

14. Again, see Duncan J. Watts and Steven H. Strogatz, "Collective Dynamics of 'Small World' Networks," *Nature* 393 (June 4, 1998): 440–442.

15. Timur Kuran, *Private Truths and Public Lies* (Cambridge, MA: Harvard University Press, 1997).

16. Everett Rogers, *The Diffusion of Innovations* (New York: The Free Press of Glencoe, 1962); Thomas C. Schelling, *Micromotives and Macrobehavior* (New York: W. W Norton, 1978); and Malcolm Gladwell, *The Tipping Point: How Little Things Can Make a Big Difference* (New York: Little Brown, 2000).

17. Edward N. Lorenz, "Deterministic Nonperiodic Flow," *Journal of the Atmospheric Sciences* 20, no. 2 (March 1963): 130–141.

18. Jules Henri Poincaré, "Sur le problème des trois corps et les équations de la dynamique: Divergence des séries de M. Lindstedt," *Acta Mathematica* 13, nos. 1–2 (1890): 1–270; Norbert Wiener, "Nonlinear Prediction and Dynamics," in *Proceedings of the Third Berkeley Symposium on Mathematical Statistics and Probability* (Berkeley: University of California Press, 1954–1955), 247–252; and James Gleick, *Chaos: Making a New Science* (London: Heinemann, 1987).

19. Sunstein, *How Change Happens*.

20. MeToo, 2006, https://metoomvmt.org/about/#history.

21. Jodi Kantor and Megan Twohey, "Harvey Weinstein Paid Off Sexual Harassment Accusers for Decades," *New York Times*, October 5, 2017, https://www.nytimes.com/2017/10/05/us/harvey-weinstein-harassment-allegations.html.

22. Ibid.

23. Ronan Farrow, "From Aggressive Overtures to Sexual Assault: Harvey Weinstein's Accusers Tell Their Stories," *New Yorker*, October 23, 2017 (print edition); online edition, posted on October 10, 2017, https://www.newyorker.com /news/news-desk/from-aggressive-overtures-to-sexual-assault-harvey-weinsteins -accusers-tell-their-stories.

24. Emily Shugerman, "Me Too: Why Are Women Sharing Stories of Sexual Assault, and How Did It Start?" *Independent*, October 17, 2017, https://www .independent.co.uk/news/world/americas/me-too-facebook-hashtag-why-when -meaning-sexual-harassment-rape-stories-explained-a8005936.html.

25. Andrea Park, "#MeToo Reaches 85 Countries with 1.7 Million Tweets," CBS News, October 24, 2017, https://www.cbsnews.com/news/metoo-reaches -85-countries-with-1-7-million-tweets/.

26. Ben Thompson, "Goodbye Gatekeepers," Stratechery, October 16, 2017, https://stratechery.com/2017/goodbye-gatekeepers/.

27. Hannah Hartig and Abigail Geiger, "About Six-in-Ten Americans Support Marijuana Legalization," Pew Research Center, October 8, 2018, https:// www.pewresearch.org/fact-tank/2018/10/08/americans-support-marijuana -legalization/.

28. William A. Galston and E. J. Dionne, Jr., "The New Politics of Marijuana Legalization: Why Opinion Is Changing," Governance Studies at Brookings, May, 2013, https://www.brookings.edu/wp-content/uploads/2016/06/Dionne -Galston_NewPoliticsofMJLeg_Final.pdf.

29. Jack S. Blocker, Jr., "Did Prohibition Really Work? Alcohol Prohibition as a Public Health Innovation," *American Journal of Public Health* 96, no. 2 (February 2006): 233–243.

30. Galston and Dionne, "The New Politics of Marijuana Legalization."

31. Graham, "What You Can't Say."

32. Ibid.

33. Silver, "Change Doesn't Usually Come This Fast."

34. Sullivan, "Here Comes the Groom."

35. Mychal Denzel Smith, "The Truth about 'The Arc of the Moral Universe,'" *Huffington Post*, January 18, 2018, https://www.huffpost.com/entry/opinion -smith-obama-king_n_5a5903e0e4b04f3c55a252a4.

36. Theodore Parker, "Of Justice and the Conscience," in *Ten Sermons of Religion* (Boston: Crosby, Nichols and Company, 1853), 84–85.

37. Cass R. Sunstein, Sebastian Bobadilla-Suarez, Stephanie Lazzaro, and Tali Sharot, "How People Update Beliefs about Climate Change: Good News and Bad News," Social Science Research Network, September 2, 2016, https://papers.ssrn .com/sol3/papers.cfm?abstract_id=2821919.

Chapter 5

1. Bill Petro, "History of the Summer of Love—1967: Sex, Drugs, and Rock & Roll," Medium, May 31, 2017, https://medium.com/history-of-the-holidays /history-of-the-summer-of-love-1967-sex-drugs-and-rock-roll-cf8f9d9db91f.

2. Gardiner Harris, "It Started More than One Revolution," *New York Times*, May 3, 2010.

3. Stuart Koehl, "Beyond the Pill: Looking for the Origins of the Sexual Revolution," First Things, May 11, 2010, https://www.firstthings.com/web-exclusives /2010/05/beyond-the-pill-looking-for-the-origins-of-the-sexual-revolution.

4. Claudia Goldin, "What 'the Pill' Did," CNN, May 7, 2010, http://www.cnn .com/2010/OPINION/05/06/pogrebin.pill.roundup/index.html.

5. Emma Gray, "Penicillin Started the Sexual Revolution, Not the Pill, Says Economist," *Huffington Post*, January 29, 2013, https://www.huffpost.com/entry /penicillin-sexual-revolution_n_2567622?guccounter=1.

6. Andrew M. Francis, "The Wages of Sin: How the Discovery of Penicillin Reshaped Modern Sexuality," *Archives of Sexual Behavior* 42, no. 1 (January 2013): 5–13, https://link.springer.com/article/10.1007/s10508-012-0018-4.

7. Quoted by Kerry Grens, "Sex and Drugs: Did 20th-Century Pharmaceutical and Technological Advances Shape Modern Sexual Behaviors?" *Scientist*, July 2014, https://www.the-scientist.com/notebook/sex-and-drugs-37242.

8. Ibid.

9. Lynn Duenil, *The Modern Temper: American Culture and Society in the 1920s* (New York: Hill and Wang, 1995), p. 136.

10. Quoted by Grens, "Sex and Drugs."

11. David John Frank, Bayliss J. Camp, and Stephen A. Boutcher, "Worldwide Trends in the Criminal Regulation of Sex: 1945–2005," *American Sociological Review* 75, no. 6 (December 2010): 867–893, https://journals.sagepub.com/doi/pdf /10.1177/0003122410388493.

12. Quoted by Grens, "Sex and Drugs."

13. Marina Adshade, *Dollars and Sex: How Economics Influences Sex and Love* (New York: Chronicle Books, 2013).

14. Donald Cox, "The Evolutionary Biology and Economics of Sexual Behavior and Infidelity" (unpublished manuscript, 2009). (Quoted by Adshade, *Dollars and Sex*.)

15. Ronald A. Fisher, *The Genetical Theory of Natural Selection* (Oxford: Clarendon, 1930).

16. Richard Harris, "Why Are More Baby Boys Born than Girls?" National Public Radio, March 30, 2015, https://www.npr.org/sections/health-shots/2015/03 /30/396384911/why-are-more-baby-boys-born-than-girls.

17. "Mid-Twentieth Century Baby Boom," Wikipedia, https://en.wikipedia.org /wiki/Mid-twentieth_century_baby_boom.

18. US Census, "Median Age at First Marriage, 1890 to Present," *Decennial Censuses*, 1890–1940, and *Current Population Survey, Annual Social and Economic Supplements*, 1947 to 2018, US Census Bureau, 2018, https://www.census.gov /content/dam/Census/library/visualizations/time-series/demo/families-and -households/ms-2.pdf.

19. Jeremy E. Uecker and Mark D. Regnerus, "BARE MARKET: Campus Sex Ratios, Romantic Relationships, and Sexual Behavior," *Sociological Quarterly* 51, no. 3 (2010): 408–435, https://www.ncbi.nlm.nih.gov/pmc/articles/PMC3130599/.

20. National Center for Education Statistics, Digest of Education Statistics: 2007, NCES 2008-022. March 2008, https://nces.ed.gov/programs/digest/d07/tables/dt07_179.asp?referrer=report.

21. Uecker and Regnerus, "BARE MARKET."

22. The authors attribute this thesis to Marcia Guttentag and Paul F. Secord, *Too Many Women? The Sex Ratio Question* (Beverly Hills, CA: Sage, 1983); and Kathleen A. Bogle, *Hooking Up: Sex, Dating, and Relationships on Campus* (New York: New York University Press, 2008).

23. Uecker and Regnerus, "BARE MARKET," p. 1.

24. Ibid.

25. Ibid., p. 10.

26. Ibid., p. 7.

27. Mark Regnerus and Jeremy Uecker, *Premarital Sex in America* (New York: Oxford University Press, 2011).

28. On this point, see George A. Akerlof, Janet L. Yellen, and Michael L. Katz, "An Analysis of Out-of-Wedlock Childbearing in the United States," *Quarterly Journal of Economics* 111, no. 2 (May 1996): 277–317.

29. Kate Taylor, "Sex on Campus: She Can Play That Game, Too," *New York Times*, July 12, 2013, https://www.nytimes.com/2013/07/14/fashion/sex-on-campus-she-can-play-that-game-too.html?pagewanted=all&_r=0.

30. Ibid.

31. Hanna Rosin, "Boys on the Side," *Atlantic*, September 2012, https://www.theatlantic.com/magazine/archive/2012/09/boys-on-the-side/309062/.

32. Leah Fessler, "A Lot of Women Don't Enjoy Hookup Culture—So Why Do We Force Ourselves to Participate?" *Quartz*, May 17, 2016, https://qz.com/685852/hookup-culture/.

33. Kathrin F. Stanger-Hall and David W. Hall, "Abstinence-Only Education and Teen Pregnancy Rates: Why We Need Comprehensive Sex Education in the U.S.," *PLOS ONE*, October 14, 2011, https://journals.plos.org/plosone/article?id=10.1371/journal.pone.0024658.

34. Planned Parenthood, "History of Sex Education in the U.S.," November 2016, https://www.plannedparenthood.org/uploads/filer_public/da/67/da67fd5d-631d-438a-85e8-a446d90fd1e3/20170209_sexed_d04_1.pdf.

Chapter 6

1. Plato, *Republic* (360 BCE), trans. Benjamin Jowett, bk. 2, http://classics.mit.edu/Plato/republic.3.ii.html.

2. O. B. Bodvarsson and W. A. Gibson, "Gratuities and Customer Appraisal of Service: Evidence from Minnesota Restaurants," *Journal of Socioeconomics* 23 (1994): 287–302.

3. David Sally, "A General Theory of Sympathy, Mind-Reading, and Social Interaction, with an Application to the Prisoners' Dilemma," *Social Science Information* 39, no. 4 (2000): 567–634.

4. Charles Darwin, *The Expression of Emotions in Man and Animals* (1872; Chicago: University of Chicago Press, 1965).

5. Paul Ekman, *Telling Lies* (New York: W. W. Norton, 1984).

6. Darwin, *The Expression of Emotions.*

7. For an extended discussion, see Sally, "A General Theory of Sympathy."

8. Opportunistic individuals have an obvious incentive to mimic whatever signs we employ for identifying reliable trading partners. Selection pressure should therefore favor capacities for deception, and examples of such capacities clearly abound in human interaction. If signals of emotional commitment could be mimicked perfectly and without cost, these signals would eventually cease to be useful. Over time, natural selection would mold false signals into perfect replicas of real ones, driving the capacity for signaling commitment to extinction.

But the mere observation that costless, perfect mimicry would render a signal useless does not rule out the possibility of an equilibrium that entails strategic signaling. Natural selection might be good at building a copy of a useful signal, but it might also be good at modifying an existing signal to evade mimicry. And because the original signal often has a substantial head start in this process, it may be a difficult target. At the very least, it is a moving one. Whether attempts to mimic it could keep pace simply cannot be settled on a priori grounds.

9. See, for example, Paul Ekman, W. V. Friesen, and S. Ancoli, "Facial Signs of Emotional Experience," *Journal of Personality and Social Psychology* 39 (1980): 1125–1134; Paul Ekman and E. Rosenberg, eds., *What the Face Reveals: Basic and Applied Studies of Spontaneous Expression Using the Facial Action Coding System (FACS)* (New York: Oxford University Press, 1997); and J.-M. Fernández-Dols, F. Sánchez, P. Carrera, and M.-A. Ruiz-Belda, "Are Spontaneous Expressions and Emotions Linked? An Experimental Test of Coherence," *Journal of Nonverbal Behavior* 23 (1997): 163–177.

10. See Sally, "A General Theory of Sympathy"; and David DeSteno, Cynthia Brazeal, Robert Frank, David Pizarro, J. Baumann, L. Dickens, and J. Lee, "Detecting the Trustworthiness of Novel Partners in Economic Exchange," *Psychological Science* 23 (2012): 1549–1556.

11. Robert H. Frank, Thomas Gilovich, and Dennis T. Regan, "The Evolution of One-Shot Cooperation," *Ethology and Sociobiology* 14, no. 4 (July 1993): 247–256.

12. In an extensive meta-analysis of empirical studies of the one-shot dilemma, Sally ("A General Theory of Sympathy") finds that such high rates of cooperation are not uncommon.

13. Aristotle, *Nicomachean Ethics* (350 BCE), trans. W. D. Ross, bk. 2, http://classics.mit.edu/Aristotle/nicomachaen.2.ii.html.

14. Will Durant, *The Story of Philosophy: The Lives and Opinions of the World's Greatest Philosophers*, pt. 7 (New York: Simon and Schuster, 1967).

15. Assuming the server pays no tax on the $500 a week he receives in tips, a 20 percent tax rate on a weekly wage of $350 would yield total after-tax income of $800.

16. See, e. g., M. G. Allingham and A. Sandmo, "Income Tax Evasion: A Theoretical Analysis," *Journal of Public Economics* 1 (1972): 323–338; and S. Yitzhaki, "A Note on Income Tax Evasion: A Theoretical Analysis," *Journal of Public Economics* 3 (1974): 201–202.

17. Bernard Fortin, Guy Lacroix, and Marie-Claire Villeval, "Tax Evasion and Social Interactions," *Journal of Public Economics* 91 (2007): 2089–2112.

18. James Andreoni, B. Erard, and J. Feinstein, "Tax Compliance," *Journal of Economic Literature* 36, no. 2 (1998): 818–860; James Alm, Gary H. McClelland, and William D. Schulze, "Changing the Social Norm of Compliance by Voting," *Kyklos* 52 (1999): 141–171, and James Alm, Gary H. McClelland, and William D. Schulze, "Why Do People Pay Taxes?" *Journal of Public Economics* 48 (1992): 21–38.

19. Brian Erard and Jonathan S. Feinstein, "The Role of Moral Sentiments and Audits Perceptions in Tax Compliance," *Public Finance/Finances Publiques* 49 (1994): 70–89 (Supplement); and "Honesty and Evasion in the Tax Compliance Game," *RAND Journal of Economics* 25, no. 1 (February 1994): 1–19.

20. M. Spicer and L. A. Becker, "Fiscal Inequity and Tax Evasion: An Experimental Approach," *National Tax Journal* 33, no. 2 (1980): 171–175.

21. Jörg Paetzold and Hannes Winner, "Tax Evasion and the Social Environment," VOX CEPR Policy Portal, December 17, 2016, https://voxeu.org/article/tax-evasion-and-social-environment.

22. Ahmed Riahi-Belkaoui, "Relationship between Tax Compliance Internationally and Selected Determinants of Tax Morale," *Journal of International Accounting, Auditing and Taxation* 13 (2004): 135–143.

23. Jesse Eisinger and Paul Kiel, "I.R.S. Tax Fraud Cases Plummet after Budget Cuts," *New York Times*, October 1, 2018.

24. Emily Horton, "Underfunded I.R.S. Continues to Audit Less," Center on Budget and Policy Priorities, April 18, 2018, https://www.cbpp.org/blog/underfunded-irs-continues-to-audit-less.

25. Ibid.

26. Ibid.

27. Jesse Eisinger and Paul Kiel, "The IRS Tried to Take on the Ultrawealthy. It Didn't Go Well," ProPublica, April 5, 2019, https://www.propublica.org/article/ultrawealthy-taxes-irs-internal-revenue-service-global-high-wealth-audits?utm_content=bufferd7919&utm_medium=social&utm_source=twitter&utm_campaign=buffer.

28. John A. Koskinen, Prepared Remarks before the Urban-Brookings Tax Policy Center, Washington, DC, April 8, 2015, http://www.taxpolicycenter.org/sites/default/files/alfresco/publication-pdfs/2000180-prepared-remarks-of-irs-commissioner-before-tpc.pdf.

29. David Barstow, Suzanne Craig, and Russ Buettner, "Trump Engaged in Suspect Tax Schemes As He Reaped Riches from His Father," *New York Times*, October 2, 2018, https://www.nytimes.com/interactive/2018/10/02/us/politics/donald-trump-tax-schemes-fred-trump.html.

30. George A. Akerlof and Robert J. Shiller, *Phishing for Phools: The Economics of Manipulation and Deception* (Princeton, NJ: Princeton University Press, 2015).

Chapter 7

1. George Washington, "From George Washington to Major General Stirling, March 5, 1780," Founders Online, US National Archives, https://founders.archives.gov/documents/Washington/03-24-02-0525.

2. L. Chassin, C. C. Presson, S. J. Sherman, D. Montello, and J. McGrew, "Changes in Peer and Parent Influence during Adolescence: Longitudinal versus Cross-Sectional Perspectives on Smoking Initiation," *Developmental Psychology* 22, no. 3 (1986): 327–334.

3. Charles Manski, "Identification of Endogenous Social Effects: The Reflection Problem," *Review of Economic Studies* 60 (1993): 531–542.

4. Mir M. Ali and Debra S. Dwyer, "Estimating Peer Effects in Adolescent Smoking Behavior: A Longitudinal Analysis," *Journal of Adolescent Health* 45, no. 4 (October 2009): 402–408.

5. Centers for Disease Control and Prevention, "Overweight and Obesity," 2016, https://www.cdc.gov/obesity/adult/defining.html.

6. Adela Hruby and Frank B. Hu, "The Epidemiology of Obesity: A Big Picture," National Institutes of Health, NCBI, 2015, https://www.ncbi.nlm.nih.gov/pmc/articles/PMC4859313/.

7. Patrick Basham and John Luik, "Is the Obesity Epidemic Exaggerated? Yes," *BMJ* 336, no. 7638 (February 2, 2008): 244.

8. Hruby and Hu, "The Epidemiology of Obesity."

9. Craig M. Hales, Cheryl D. Fryar, Margaret D. Carroll, David S. Freedman, and Cynthia L. Ogden, "Trends in Obesity and Severe Obesity Prevalence in US Youth and Adults by Sex and Age, 2007–2008 to 2015–2016," *Journal of the American Medical Association* 319, no. 16 (2018): 1723–1725.

10. Cynthia L. Ogden, Margaret D. Carroll, Brian K. Kit, and Katherine M. Flegal, "Prevalence of Childhood and Adult Obesity in the United States, 2011–2012," *Journal of the American Medical Association* 311, no. 8 (February 26, 2014): 806.

11. Ibid.

12. Nicholas A. Christakis and James H. Fowler, "The Spread of Obesity in a Large Social Network over 32 Years," *New England Journal of Medicine* 357 (July 26, 2007): 370–379.

13. Ibid., p. 371.

14. Ibid., p. 377.

15. Ann Smith Barnes and Stephanie A. Coulter, "The Epidemic of Obesity and Diabetes," *Texas Heart Institute Journal* 38, no. 2 (2011): 142–144.

16. Rebecca M. Puhl and Chelsea A. Heuer, "Obesity Stigma: Important Considerations for Public Health," *American Journal of Public Health* 100, no. 6 (June 2010): 1019–1028.

17. Y. Claire Wang, Klim McPherson, Tim Marsh, Steven L. Gortmaker, and Martin Brown, "Health and Economic Burden of the Projected Obesity Trends in the USA and the UK," *Lancet* 378, no. 9793 (August 27–September 2, 2011): 815–825.

18. Alesha Datar and Nancy Nicosea, "Assessing Social Contagion in Body Mass Index, Overweight, and Obesity Using a Natural Experiment," *JAMA Pediatrics* 172, no. 3 (January 22, 2018): 239–246.

19. Puhl and Heuer, "Obesity Stigma."

20. Philip J. Cook, *Paying the Tab: The Costs and Benefits of Alcohol Control* (Princeton, NJ: Princeton University Press, 2007).

21. "Alcohol: Weighing Risks and Potential Benefits," Mayo Clinic, https://www.mayoclinic.org/healthy-lifestyle/nutrition-and-healthy-eating/in-depth/alcohol/art-20044551.

22. National Institute on Alcohol Abuse and Alcoholism, National Institutes of Health, "Alcohol Facts and Statistics," https://www.niaaa.nih.gov/alcohol-health/overview-alcohol-consumption/alcohol-facts-and-statistics.

23. National Center for Statistics and Analysis, "2014 Crash Data Key Findings (*Traffic Safety Facts Crash Statistics*, Report No. DOT HS 812 219)," Washington, DC: National Highway Traffic Safety Administration, 2015, https://crashstats.nhtsa.dot.gov/Api/Public/ViewPublication/812219.

24. World Health Organization, *Global Status Report on Alcohol and Health*, 2014 edition, https://www.who.int/substance_abuse/publications/global_alcohol_report/msb_gsr_2014_1.pdf?ua=1.

25. Jennie Connor and Sally Caswell, "Alcohol-Related Harm to Others in New Zealand," *New Zealand Journal of Medicine* 125, no. 1360 (August 24, 2012): 11–27.

26. Michael Kremer and Dan Levy, "Peer Effects and Alcohol Use among College Students," *Journal of Economic Perspectives* 22, no. 3 (Summer 2008): 189–206.

27. Ibid., p. 196.

28. Ibid., p. 198.

29. Ibid., p. 200.

30. Ibid., p. 198.

31. See, for example, A. Clark and Y. Loheac, "It Wasn't Me, It Was Them! Social Influence in Risky Behavior by Adolescents," *Journal of Health Economics* 26, no. 4 (2007): 763–784; N. Evans, E. Gilpin, A. J. Farkas, E. Shenassa, and J. P. Piere, "Adolescents' Perception of Their Peers' Health Norm," *American Journal of Public Health* 85, no. 8 (1995): 1064–1069; P. Lundborg, "Having the Wrong Friends? Peer Effects in Adolescent Substance Use," *Journal of Health Economics* 25 (2006): 214–233; and E. Norton, R. Lindrooth, and S. Ennett, "Controlling for the Endogeneity of Peer Substance Use on Adolescent Alcohol and Tobacco Use," *Health Economics* 7 (1998): 439–453.

32. Mir M. Ali and Debra S. Dwyer, "Social Network Effects in Alcohol Consumption among Adolescents," *Addictive Behaviors* 35, no. 4 (April 2010): 337–342.

33. Ibid., p. 340.

34. Christakis and Fowler, "The Spread of Obesity," p. 378.

Chapter 8

1. Fred Hirsch, *Social Limits to Growth* (Cambridge, MA: Harvard University Press, 1976).

2. Scott Coulter, "Advancing Safety around the World," Occupational Health and Safety, February 1, 2009, https://ohsonline.com/Articles/2009/02/01/Advancing-Safety-World.aspx.

3. Thomas C. Schelling, "Hockey Helmets, Concealed Weapons, and Daylight Saving: A Study of Binary Choices with Externalities," *Journal of Conflict Resolution* 17, no. 3 (1973): 381–428.

4. Robert H. Frank, "The Demand for Unobservable and Other Nonpositional Goods," *American Economic Review* 75 (March 1985): 101–116.

5. Thorstein Veblen, *The Theory of the Leisure Class* (1899; New York: Penguin, 1994); James Duesenberry, *Income, Saving, and the Theory of Consumer Behavior* (Cambridge, MA: Harvard University Press, 1949); Harvey Leibenstein, "Bandwagon, Snob, and Veblen Effects in the Theory of Consumers' Demand," *Quarterly Journal of Economics* 64, no. 2 (May 1, 1950): 183–207; Richard Easterlin, "Does Economic Growth Improve the Human Lot? Some Empirical Evidence," in *Nations and Households in Economic Growth: Essays in Honor of Moses Abramowitz*, ed. Paul A. David and Melvin W. Reder (New York: Academic Press, 1974), 89–125; and Richard Layard, "Human Satisfactions and Public Policy," *Economic Journal* 90, no. 363 (1980): 737–750.

6. Marianne Bertrand and Adair Morse, "Trickle-Down Consumption," *Review of Economics and Statistics* 98, no. 5 (December 2016): 863–879; Ed Diener, Ed Sandvik, Larry Seidlitz, and Marissa Diener, "The Relationship between Income and Subjective Well-Being: Relative or Absolute?" *Social Indicators Research* 28 (1993): 195–223; Bill Dupor and Wen-Fang Liu, "Jealousy and Equilibrium Overconsumption," *American Economic Review* 93, no. 1 (2003): 423–428; Ada Ferrer-i-Carbonell, "Income and Well-Being: An Empirical Analysis of the Comparison Income Effect," *Journal of Public Economics* 89, nos. 5–6 (2004): 997–1019; Jordi Galí, "Keeping Up with the Joneses: Consumption Externalities, Portfolio Choice and Asset Prices," *Journal of Money, Credit and Banking* 26, no. 1 (1994): 1–8; Mark Grinblatt, Matti Keloharju, and Seppo Ikaheimo, "Social Influence and Consumption: Evidence from the Automobile Purchases of Neighbors," *Review of Economics and Statistics* 90, no. 4 (2008): 735–753; Ori Heffetz, "A Test of Conspicuous Consumption: Visibility and Income Elasticities," *Review of Economics and Statistics* 93, no. 4 (2011): 1101–1117; Norman Ireland, "Status-Seeking, Income Taxation and Efficiency," *Journal of Public Economics* 70 (1998): 99–113; Olof Johansson-Stenman, Fredrik Carlsson, and Dinky Daruvala, "Measuring Future Grandparents' Preferences for Equality and Relative Standing," *Economic Journal* 112, no. 479 (2002): 362–383; Duk Gyoo Kim, "Positional Concern and Low Demand for Redistribution of the Poor," *European Journal of Political Economy* 56 (January 2019): 27–38; Lars Ljungqvist and Harald Uhlig, "Tax Policy and Aggregate Demand Management under Catching Up with the Joneses," *American Economic*

Review 90, no. 3 (2000): 356–366; Erzo Luttmer, "Neighbors as Negatives: Relative Earnings and Well-Being," *Quarterly Journal of Economics* 120, no. 3 (August 2005): 963–1002; Michael McBride, "Relative-Income Effects on Subjective Well-Being in the Cross-Section," *Journal of Economic Behavior and Organization* 45, no. 3 (2001): 251–278; David Neumark and Andrew Postlewaite, "Relative Income Concerns and the Rise in Married Women's Employment," *Journal of Public Economics* 70, no. 1 (1998): 157–183; Yew-Kwang Ng, "Relative-Income Effects and the Appropriate Level of Public Expenditure," *Oxford Economic Papers* 39, no. 2 (1987): 293–300; Andrew J. Oswald, "Altruism, Jealousy and the Theory of Optimal Non-linear Taxation," *Journal of Public Economics* 20, no. 1 (1983): 77–87; Robert A. Pollak, "Interdependent Preferences," *American Economic Review* 66, no. 3 (1976): 309–320; Luis Rayo and Gary S. Becker, "Evolutionary Efficiency and Mean Reversion in Happiness" (mimeographed, University of Chicago, 2004); Arthur J. Robson, "Status, the Distribution of Wealth: Private and Social Attitudes to Risk," *Econometrica* 60, no. 4 (1992): 837–857; Larry Samuelson, "Information-Based Relative Consumption Effects," *Econometrica* 72, no. 1 (2004): 93–118; Laurence S. Seidman, "Relativity and Efficient Taxation," *Southern Economic Journal* 54, no. 2 (1987): 463–474; Amartya Sen, "Poor, Relatively Speaking," *Oxford Economic Papers* 35, no. 2 (1983): 153–169; Sara J. Solnick and David Hemenway, "Is More Always Better? A Survey on Positional Concerns," *Journal of Economic Behavior and Organization* 37, no. 3 (1998): 373–383; Nigel Tomes, "Income Distribution, Happiness and Satisfaction: A Direct Test of the Interdependent Preferences Model," *Journal of Economic Psychology* 7 (1986): 425–446; Bernhard M. S. Van Praag, and Arie Kapteyn, "Further Evidence on the Individual Welfare Function of Income: An Empirical Investigation in the Netherlands," *European Economic Review* 4, no. 1 (1973): 33–62; Ruut Veenhoven, "Is Happiness Relative?" *Social Indicators Research* 24 (1991): 1–24.

7. Donald J. Boudreaux, "Monkeying Around with Redistribution," Café Hayek, https://cafehayek.com/2013/05/monkeying-around-with-redistribution.html.

8. John Maynard Keynes, "Economic Possibilities for Our Grandchildren," in *Essays in Persuasion* (New York: Harcourt Brace, 1932), 358–373.

9. Elizabeth Warren and Amelia Warren Tyagi, *The Two-Income Trap: Why Middle-Class Mothers and Fathers Are Going Broke* (New York: Basic Books, 2003).

10. John Sullivan, "McCain Warns against Hasty Mortgage Bailout," *New York Times*, May 25, 2008, https://www.nytimes.com/2008/03/25/us/politics/25cnd-mccain.html.

11. "1955 Thunderbird Road Test: Remembering Motor Trends," *Motor Trend*, June 2, 1999.

12. Honda 0-60 Times, https://www.zeroto60times.com/vehicle-make/honda-0-60-mph-times/; K. C. Colwell, "2015 Porsche Spyder Tested: 2.2 Seconds to 60!" *Car and Driver*, November 2016, https://www.caranddriver.com/features/a15111035/the-2015-porsche-918-spyder-is-the-quickest-road-car-in-the-world-feature/.

13. Inequality.org, "Income Inequality in the United States," https://inequality.org/facts/income-inequality/.

14. Colleen Egan and Melissa Minton, "Playboy Mansion Sold for $100 Million," *Architectural Digest*, August 16, 2016, https://www.architecturaldigest.com/gallery/playboy-mansion-for-sale-200-million-hugh-hefner-staying.

15. Candace Jackson, "Who Wants to Buy the Most Expensive House in America?" *New York Times*, December 23, 2017.

16. Nicholas Kulish and Michael Forsythe, "World's Most Expensive Home? Another Bauble for a Saudi Prince," *New York Times*, December 16, 2017.

17. Candace Jackson, "Would You Pay $1 Billion for This View?" *New York Times*, July 28, 2018.

18. Kulish and Forsyte, "World's Most Expensive Home?"

19. Joe Pinsker, "Are McMansions Making People Any Happier?" *Atlantic*, June 11, 2019.

20. "Cost of US Weddings Reaches New High As Couples Spend More per Guest to Create an Unforgettable Experience, according to The Knot 2016 Real Weddings Study," PRNewswire, February 2, 2017, https://www.prnewswire.com/news-releases/cost-of-us-weddings-reaches-new-high-as-couples-spend-more-per-guest-to-create-an-unforgettable-experience-according-to-the-knot-2016-real-weddings-study-300401064.html.

21. Andrew Francis-Tan and Hugo M. Mialon, "A Diamond Is Forever and Other Fairy Tales: The Relationship between Wedding Expenses and Marriage Duration," *Economic Inquiry* 53, no. 4 (October 2015): 1919–1930.

22. Robert H. Frank, Adam Seth Levine, and Oege Dijk, "Expenditure Cascades," *Review of Behavioral Economics* 1 (2014): 55–73.

23. Ibid.

24. Ibid.

25. Sarah A. Donovan and David H. Bradley, "Real Wage Trends: 2001–2017," Congressional Research Service, March 15, 2018, https://fas.org/sgp/crs/misc/R45090.pdf.

26. Robert H. Frank, "Supplementing Per-Capita GDP as Measure of Well-Being" (paper presented at the annual meetings of the American Economic Association, Denver, Colorado, January 2010).

27. George Loewenstein and Shane Frederick, "Hedonic Adaptation: From the Bright Side to the Dark Side," in *Understanding Well-Being: Scientific Perspectives on Enjoyment and Suffering*, ed. Daniel Kahneman, Ed Diener, and Norbert Schwartz (New York: Russell Sage, 1998).

28. Stephen J. Galli, Mindy Tsai, and Adrian M. Pilioponski, "The Development of Allergic Inflammation," *Nature* 454, no. 7203 (July 24, 2008): 445–454.

29. See chap. 6 of Robert H. Frank, *Luxury Fever* (New York: The Free Press, 1999).

30. Leaf Van Boven and Thomas Gilovich, "To Do or to Have? That Is the Question," *Journal of Personality and Social Psychology* 85, no. 6 (2003): 1193–1202.

31. Amit Kumar, Matthew Killingsworth, and Thomas Gilovich, "Waiting for

Merlot: Anticipatory Consumption of Experiential and Material Purchases," *Psychological Science* 25, no. 10 (2014): 1924–1931.

32. Sara J. Solnick and David Hemenway, "Is More Always Better? A Survey on Positional Concerns," *Journal of Economic Behavior and Organization* 37 (1998): 373–383.

33. Heffetz, "A Test of Conspicuous Consumption."

34. See chap. 8 of Robert H. Frank, *Choosing the Right Pond: Human Behavior and the Quest for Status* (New York: Oxford University Press, 1985).

35. I say "almost," because nations could in principle compete to offer more and better public goods for their citizens. But in most countries, only a small fraction of citizens travel abroad regularly, and fewer still would consider moving to a different country, so competition of this sort is likely to be of only minor importance.

36. InfrastructureReportCard.Org, 2017 Report Card on Infrastructure: Roads, https://www.infrastructurereportcard.org/wp-content/uploads/2017/01/Roads -Final.pdf.

37. InfrastructureReportCard.Org, 2017 Report Card on Infrastructure: Bridges, https://www.infrastructurereportcard.org/wp-content/uploads/2017/01 /Bridges-Final.pdf.

38. InfrastructureReportCard.Org, 2017 Report Card on Infrastructure: Dams, https://www.infrastructurereportcard.org/wp-content/uploads/2017/01/Dams -Final.pdf.

39. Bruce Bartlett, "Are the Bush Tax Cuts the Root of Our Fiscal Problem?" *New York Times*, July 26, 2011.

40. Jim Tankersley, "How the Trump Tax Cut Is Helping to Push the Federal Deficit to $1 Trillion," *New York Times*, July 25, 2018.

41. Sara Solnick and David Hemenway, "Are Positional Concerns Stronger in Some Domains Than in Others?" *American Economic Review, Papers and Proceedings* 95, no. 2 (May 2005): 147–151; and Solnick and Hemenway, "Is More Always Better?" For additional evidence on cross-category differences in positionality, see A. X. Yang, C. K. Hsee, and X. Zheng, "The ABIS: A Survey Method to Distinguish between Absolute versus Relative Determinants of Happiness," *Journal of Happiness Studies* 13, no. 4 (2011): 729–744.

42. Renée M. Landers, James B. Rebitzer, and Lowell J. Taylor, "Rat Race Redux: Adverse Selection in the Determination of Work Hours in Law Firms," *American Economic Review* 86 (1996): 329–348.

43. David Neumark and Andrew Postlewaite, "Relative Income Concerns and the Rise in Married Women' Employment," *Journal of Public Economics* 70 (1998): 157–183.

Chapter 9

1. D. R. Reidmiller, C. W. Avery, D. R. Easterling, K. E. Kunkel, K.L.M. Lewis, T. K. Maycock, and B. C. Stewart, eds., *Impacts, Risks, and Adaptation in the United*

States: Fourth National Climate Assessment, vol. 2, U.S. Global Change Research Program (Washington, DC: US Government Publishing Office, 2018), p. 1.

2. Ibid.

3. A. P. Sokolov, P. H. Stone, C. E. Forest. R. Prinn, M. C. Sarofim, M. Webster, S. Paltsev, and C. A. Schlosser, "Probabilistic Forecast for Twenty-First-Century Climate Based on Uncertainties in Emissions (without Policy) and Climate Parameters," *Journal of Climate* 22 (October 2009): 5175–5204.

4. Summary for Policymakers, in *Global Warming of 1.5°C*, IPCC, 2018, https://www.ipcc.ch/sr15/.

5. Coral Davenport, "Major Climate Report Describes a Strong Risk of Crisis as Early as 2040," *New York Times*, October 8, 2018.

6. James Inhofe, *The Greatest Hoax: How the Global Warming Conspiracy Threatens Your Future* (Washington, DC: WND Books, 2016).

7. National Oceanographic and Atmospheric Administration, "2017 Was the Third-Warmest Year on Record for the Globe," January 18, 2018, https://www.noaa.gov/news/noaa-2017-was-3rd-warmest-year-on-record-for-globe.

8. Ibid.; and Laura Geggel, "Data Confirm That 2018 Was 4th Hottest Year on Record, NASA Finds," LiveScience, February 6, 2019, https://www.livescience.com/64700-2018-heat-record.html.

9. Summary for Policymakers, in *Climate Change 2001: The Scientific Basis*, IPCC, 2001, "Figure 1: Variations of the Earth's surface temperature over the last 140 years and the last millennium," https://www.ipcc.ch/site/assets/uploads/2018/03/WGI_TAR_full_report.pdf; National Research Council, *Committee on Surface Temperature Reconstructions for the Last 2,000 Years* (Washington, DC: National Academies Press, 2006).

10. André Stephan and Robert H. Crawford, "The Relationship between House Size and Life-Cycle Energy Demand: Implications for Energy Efficiency Regulations for Buildings," *Energy* 116 (2016): 1158–1171.

11. US Department of Transportation Federal Highway Administration, 2017 National Household Travel Survey, table 27, https://nhts.ornl.gov/assets/2017_nhts_summary_travel_trends.pdf.

12. Dave Barry, *Dave Barry Is Not Taking This Sitting Down* (New York: Crown, 2000).

13. "Number of U.S. Aircraft, Vehicles, Vessels, and Other Conveyances," US Department of Transportation, https://www.bts.gov/content/number-us-aircraft-vehicles-vessels-and-other-conveyances.

14. "SUVs and Crossovers Overtake Sedans to Become Most Popular Vehicle Body Style in the U.S., IHS Automotive Finds," IHS Markit, July 16, 2014, https://news.ihsmarkit.com/press-release/automotive/suvs-and-crossovers-overtake-sedans-become-most-popular-vehicle-body-style-.

15. Nathan Bomey, "Honda, Toyota, Nissan Car Sales Plunge, but SUVs Rise: U.S. Auto Sales Likely Up in August," *USA Today*, September 4, 2018.

16. Keith Bradsher, *High and Mighty: The Dangerous Rise of the SUV* (New York: Public Affairs, 2002).

17. Mark J. McCourt, "Upwardly Mobile," *Hemmings Motor News*, December, 2012.

18. Summary for Policymakers, in *Global Warming of 1.5°C*, IPCC, 2018.

19. Rebecca Bellan, "The Grim State of Electric Vehicle Adoption in the U.S.," CityLab, October 15, 2018, https://www.citylab.com/transportation/2018/10/where-americas-charge-towards-electric-vehicles-stands-today/572857/.

20. "Energy Use in Food Production," Choose Energy, November 19, 2015, https://www.chooseenergy.com/blog/energy-101/energy-food-production/.

21. Ezra Klein and Susannah Locke, "Forty Maps That Explain Food in America," Vox, June 9, 2014, https://www.vox.com/a/explain-food-america.

22. Susan Bredlowe Sardone, "Wedding Statistics and Honeymoon Facts & Figures," TripSavvy, December 24, 2018, https://www.tripsavvy.com/wedding-statistics-and-honeymoon-facts-1860546.

23. Saqib Rahim, "Finding the 'Weapons' of Persuasion to Save Energy," *New York Times*, June 21, 2010.

24. Ibid.

25. Ibid.

26. Hunt Allcott, "Social Norms and Energy Conservation," *Journal of Public Economics* 95 (March 21, 2011): 1082–1095.

27. Ibid.

28. Bryan Bollinger and Kenneth Gillingham, "Peer Effects in the Diffusion of Solar Photovoltaic Panels," *Marketing Science*, November–December, 2011, 900–912.

29. Marcello Graziano and Kenneth Gillingham, "Spatial Patterns of Solar Photovoltaic System Adoption: The Influence of Neighbors and the Built Environment," *Journal of Economic Geography* 15 (2015): 815–839.

30. David F. Scharfstein and Jeremy Stein, "Herd Behavior and Investment," *American Economic Review* 80, no. 3 (June 1990): 465–479; Elihu Katz, Martin L. Levin, and Herbert Hamilton, "Traditions of Research on the Diffusion of Innovation," *American Sociological Review* 28, no. 2 (April 1963): 237–252.

31. Felix Richter, "The Global Rise of Bike Sharing," Statista, April 10, 2018, https://www.statista.com/chart/13483/bike-sharing-programs/.

32. Patrick Sisson, "Electric Scooters Growing at 'Unprecedented Pace,' Finds New Transit Survey," Curbed, July 24, 2018, https://www.curbed.com/2018/7/24/17607698/electric-scooter-bird-lime-spin-adoption-transit.

33. T. J. McCue, "Global Electric Bike Market Is Still Moving Fast," Forbes, April 12, 2018, https://www.forbes.com/sites/tjmccue/2018/04/12/the-global-electric-bike-market-is-still-moving-fast-sondors-e-bike-offers-glimpse/#7e5c5d2631ff.

34. Roland Irle, "USA Plug-in Sales for 2018 Full Year," EV-volumes.com, 2019, http://www.ev-volumes.com/country/usa/.

35. Jesper Berggreen, "Almost One Third of All New Car Sales in Norway in 2018 Were for Pure Electric Vehicles," CleanTechnica, January 3, 2019, https://cleantechnica.com/2019/01/03/almost-one-third-of-all-new-car-sales-in-norway-in-2018-were-for-pure-electric-vehicles/.

36. Franklin Schneider, "Is Walkability a Passing Fad, or Is It Here to Stay?" Urban Scrawl, May 12, 2016, https://urbanscrawldc.blog/2016/05/12/is-walkability-a-passing-fad-or-is-it-here-to-stay/.

37. "Walk Scores Are Now on Zillow," Zillow Group, February 24, 2009, https://www.zillowgroup.com/news/walk-scores-are-now-on-zillow/.

38. Gary Pivo and Jeffrey D. Fisher, "The Walkability Premium in Commercial Real Estate Investments," *Real Estate Economics* 10 (2011): 1–35.

39. Sheharyar Bokhari, "How Much Is a Point of Walk Score Worth?" RedFin, August 3, 2016, https://www.redfin.com/blog/how-much-is-a-point-of-walk-score-worth.

40. Ibid.

41. Maria Creatore et al., "Association of Neighborhood Walkability with Change in Overweight, Obesity, and Diabetes," *Journal of the American Medical Association* 315, no. 20 (2016): 2211–2220.

42. David Leonhardt, "The Story of 2018 Was Climate Change," *New York Times*, December 30, 2018.

43. Brian K. Sullivan, Alexandra Semenova, and Eric Roston, "Wall Street Embraces Weather Risk in New Era of Storms," *Bloomberg*, April 1, 2019.

44. Jeff Halverson, "The Second 1000-Year Rainstorm in Two Years Engulfed Ellicott City. Here's How It Happened," *Washington Post*, May 28, 2018.

45. Colin Campbell and Catherine Rentz, "How Ellicott City Flooded: A Timeline," *Baltimore Sun*, June 1, 2018.

46. Environmental Defense Fund, "How Climate Change Plunders the Planet," EDF, 2017, https://www.edf.org/climate/how-climate-change-plunders-planet.

47. Associated Press, "Global Warming Is Shrinking Glaciers Faster than Thought," *Los Angeles Times*, April 8, 2019.

48. Tapio Schneider, Colleen M. Kaul, and Kyle G. Pressel, "Possible Climate Transitions from Breakup of Stratocumulus Decks under Greenhouse Warming," *Nature Geoscience* 12 (2019): 163–167.

49. David L. Chandler, "Explaining the Plummeting Cost of Solar Power," *MIT News*, November 20, 2018, http://news.mit.edu/2018/explaining-dropping-solar-cost-1120.

50. David Keith, Geoffrey Holmes, David St. Angelo, and Kenton Heidel, "A Process for Capturing CO_2 from the Atmosphere," *Joule* 2, no. 8 (August 15, 2015): 1573–1594.

51. Wallace-Wells, *The Uninhabitable Earth*, p. 170.

52. David Roberts, "The Green New Deal and the Case against Incremental Climate Policy," Vox, March 28, 2019, https://www.vox.com/energy-and-environment/2019/3/28/18283514/green-new-deal-climate-policy.

53. Ibid.

Chapter 10

1. Derk Pereboom, *Free Will, Agency, and Meaning in Life* (New York: Oxford University Press, 2014).

2. Jasmine M. Carey and Delroy Paulhus, "Worldview Implications of Believing in Free Will and/or Determinism: Politics, Morality, and Punitiveness," *Journal of Personality* 81, no. 2 (April 2013): 130–141.

3. Kathleen D. Vohs and Jonathan W. Schooler, "The Value of Believing in Free Will," *Psychological Science* 19, no. 1 (2008): 49–54.

4. R. F. Baumeister, E. A. Sparks, T. F. Stillman, and K. D. Vohs, "Free Will in Consumer Behavior: Self-Control, Ego Depletion, and Choice," *Journal of Consumer Psychology* 18 (2008): 4–13.

5. Thomas Nadelhoffer, Jason Shepard, et al., "Does Encouraging a Belief in Determinism Increase Cheating? Reconsidering the Value of Believing in Free Will," OSF Preprints, May 5, 2019, https://osf.io/bhpe5/.

6. See Sam Harris, *Free Will* (New York: The Free Press, 2012).

7. George Ainslie, *Picoeconomics* (Cambridge: Cambridge University Press, 1992).

8. Gerald Dworkin, "Paternalism," in *Morality and the Law*, ed. Richard Wasserstrom (Belmont, CA: Wadsworth, 1971).

9. See, for example, Colin Camerer, Samuel Issacharoff, George Loewenstein, and Matthew Rabin, "Regulation for Conservatives: Behavioral Economics and the Case for 'Asymmetric Paternalism,'" *University of Pennsylvania Law Review* 151 (2003): 1211–1254.

10. See, especially, Richard H. Thaler and Cass R. Sunstein, *Nudge* (New Haven, CT: Yale University Press, 2008).

11. Frans de Waal, "How Bad Biology Is Killing the Economy," *RSA Journal*, December 20, 2009, http://www.emory.edu/LIVING_LINKS/empathy /Reviewfiles/RSAJournal.html.

12. Elizabeth Levy Paluck, Hana Shepherd, and Peter M. Aronow, "Changing Climates of Conflict: A Social Network Experiment in 56 Schools," *PNAS* 113, no. 3 (January 19, 2016): 566–571.

13. Kevin J. Jones, "A Grave Problem—NJ Ban on Religious Headstone Sales Could Violate Constitution," Catholic News Agency, March, 2015, https://www .catholicnewsagency.com/news/a-grave-problem-nj-ban-on-religious-headstone -sales-could-violate-constitution-58838.

14. Tanya D. Marsh, "A Grave Injustice to Religious and Economic Liberty in New Jersey," *Huffington Post*, August 28, 2016, https://www.huffpost.com/entry /grave-injustice_b_8057730.

15. Daniel Carpenter and David A. Moss, *Preventing Regulatory Capture: Special Interest Influence and How to Limit It* (New York: Cambridge University Press, 2014), p. 13.

16. Quoted by Robert S. Smith, "Compensating Wage Differentials and Public Policy: A Review," *Industrial and Labor Relations Review* 32 (1977): 339–352.

17. Richard A. Posner, *Economic Analysis of Law* (Boston: Little Brown, 1973).

18. Ronald Coase, "The Problem of Social Cost," *Journal of Law and Economics* 3 (1960): 1–44.

19. See, for example, Natasha Dow Schüll, *Addiction by Design: Machine Gambling in Las Vegas* (Princeton, NJ: Princeton University Press, 2013).

20. Jonah Berger, *Contagious: Why Things Catch On* (New York: Simon and Schuster, 2013).

Chapter 11

1. Arthur C. Pigou, *The Economics of Welfare* (London: Macmillan, 1920).

2. Curtis Carlson, Dallas Burtraw, Maureen L. Cropper, and Karen Palmer, "Sulfur Dioxide Control by Electric Utilities: What Are the Gains from Trade?" *Journal of Political Economy* 108, no. 6 (December 2000): 1292–1326; A. Denny Ellerman, Paul L. Joskow, Richard Schmalensee, Juan-Pablo Montero, and Elizabeth M. Bailey, *Markets for Clean Air: The U.S. Acid Rain Program* (Cambridge: Cambridge University Press, 2000); and Nathaniel O. Keohane, "What Did the Market Buy? Cost Savings under the U.S. Tradeable Permits Program for Sulfur Dioxide," Working Paper YCELP-01-11-2003, Yale Center for Environmental Law and Policy, October 15, 2003.

3. Gabriel Chan, Robert Stavins, Robert Stowe, and Richard Sweeney, "The SO_2 Allowance Trading System and the Clean Air Act Amendments of 1990: Reflections on Twenty Years of Policy Innovation," Harvard Environmental Economics Program, January 2012, https://dash.harvard.edu/bitstream/handle/1/8160721/RWP12-003-Stavins.pdf.

4. Henry Goldman, "New York City Council Approves Manhattan Traffic Fees," Bloomberg.com, April 1, 2008.

5. Holly Jean Buck, "The Need for Carbon Removal," *Jacobin*, July 24, 2018, https://www.jacobinmag.com/2018/07/carbon-removal-geoengineering-global-warming.

6. Brad Plumer, "New U.N. Climate Report Says Put a High Price on Carbon," *New York Times*, October 8, 2018.

7. University of Michigan Energy Survey, "Carbon Taxes and the Affordability of Gasoline," September 2017, https://www.umenergysurvey.com/assets/C-taxG-aff_12Sep2017.pdf.

8. Motoring FAQs: Environment, RAC Foundation, 2018, https://www.racfoundation.org/motoring-faqs/environment#a22.

9. Coral Davenport, "White House Pushes Financial Case for Carbon Rule," *New York Times*, July 29, 2014.

10. Megan Geuss, "Energy Jobs Reports Say Solar Dominates Coal, but Wind Is the Real Winner," Ars Technica, May 17, 2018, https://arstechnica.com/information-technology/2018/05/energy-jobs-reports-say-solar-dominates-coal-but-wind-is-the-real-winner/.

11. Maria Panezi, "When CO_2 Goes to Geneva: Taxing Carbon across Borders without Violating WTO Obligations," *CIGI Papers* 83 (November 2015), https://www.cigionline.org/sites/default/files/cigi_paper_no.83_web.pdf.

12. "World's Richest 10 Percent Produce Half of Carbon Emissions, While Poorest 3.5 Billion Account for Just a Tenth," Oxfam International, December 2, 2015, https://www.oxfam.org/en/pressroom/pressreleases/2015-12-02/worlds-richest-10-produce-half-carbon-emissions-while-poorest-35.

13. Justin Gillis, "Forget the Carbon Tax for Now," *New York Times*, December 27, 2018.

14. Hal Bernton, "Washington State Voters Reject Carbon-Fee Initiative," *Seattle Times*, November 6, 2018.

15. Reuters in Ottawa, "It's No Longer Free to Pollute: Canada Imposes Carbon Tax on Four Provinces," *Guardian*, April 1, 2019.

16. Brad Plumer and Nadja Popovich, "These Countries Have Prices on Carbon. Are They Working?" *New York Times*, April 2, 2019.

17. I was pleased to accept Mankiw's invitation to become an inaugural member of the Pigou Club. At this writing, a partial list of the club's diverse membership, living and deceased, includes Anne Applebaum, Kenneth Arrow, Katherine Baiker, Jack Black, Alan Blinder, Michael Bloomberg, Judith Chevalier, Noam Chomsky, John Cochrane, Tyler Cowen, Laura D'Andrea Tyson, Thomas Friedman, David Frum, Jason Furman, Bill Gates, Al Gore, Lindsey Graham, Alan Greenspan, Kevin Hassett, Katharine Hayhoe, Dale Jorgenson, Juliette Kayyem, Joe Klein, Morton Kondrake, Charles Krauthammer, Paul Krugman, Arthur Laffer, Anthony Lake, David Leonhardt, Steven Levitt, Ray Magliozzi, Megan McArdle, Daniel McFadden, Adele Morris, Alan Mullaly, Elon Musk, Ralph Nader, Gavin Newsome, William Nordhaus, Grover Norquist, Bill Nye, Leon Panetta, Richard Posner, Robert Reich, Kenneth Rogoff, Nouriel Roubini, Jeffrey Sachs, Bernie Sanders, Isabel Sawhill, Brian Schatz, George Schultz, Joseph Stiglitz, Andrew Sullivan, Laurence Summers, Richard Thaler, John Tierney, Hal Varian, Paul Volcker, Sheldon Whitehouse, and Neil Young.

18. Alan Hunt, *Governance of the Consuming Passions* (New York: St. Martin's Press, 1996), p. 19.

19. Ibid., p. 24.

20. Robert H. Frank, *Luxury Fever: Why Money Fails to Satisfy in an Age of Excess* (New York: The Free Press, 1999), pp. 199, 200.

21. James K. Glassman, "How to Sink an Industry and Not Soak the Rich," *Washington Post*, July 16, 1993.

22. Irving Fisher and Herbert Wescott Fisher, *Constructive Income Taxation: A Proposal for Reform* (New York: Harper & Brothers, 1942).

23. Laurence S. Seidman, "Overcoming the Fiscal Trilemma with Two Progressive Consumption Tax Supplements," Working Papers 14-04, University of Delaware, Department of Economics, 2014, https://ideas.repec.org/p/dlw/wpaper/14-04..html.

24. Amy Bell, "401(k) Plans and All Their Benefits," Investopedia, November 2, 2018, updated June 25, 2019, https://www.investopedia.com/articles/investing/102216/understanding-401ks-and-all-their-benefits.asp.

25. Richard H. Thaler and Cass R. Sunstein, *Nudge: Improving Decisions about Health, Wealth, and Happiness* (New Haven, CT: Yale University Press, 2008).

26. Brigitte C. Madrian and Dennis F. Shea, "The Power of Suggestion: Inertia in 401(k) Participation and Savings Behavior," *Quarterly Journal of Economics* 116, no. 4 (November 2001): 1149–1187.

27. Eric J. Johnson and Daniel Goldstein, "Do Defaults Save Lives?" *Science* 302 (2003): 1338–1339.

28. Alain Samson, "A Simple Change That Could Help Everyone Drink Less," *Psychology Today*, February 25, 2014.

29. Robert Cialdini, *Influence: Science and Practice*, 4th ed. (Needham Heights, MA: Allyn & Bacon, 2001).

30. N. J. Goldstein and Robert B. Cialdini, "Using Social Norms as a Lever of Social Influence," in *Science of Social Influence*, ed. Anthony R. Pratkanis (New York: Routledge, 2014).

31. Jane Black, "Small Changes Steer Kids toward Smarter Lunch Choices," *Washington Post*, June 9, 2010.

32. "Policy Makers around the World Are Embracing Behavioral Science," *Economist*, May 18, 2017, https://www.economist.com/international/2017/05 /18/policymakers-around-the-world-are-embracing-behavioural-science.

33. David Meyer, "Congestion Pricing Was Unpopular in Stockholm, Until People Saw It in Action," Streetblog NYC, November 28, 2017, https://nyc.streets blog.org/2017/11/28/congestion-pricing-was-unpopular-in-stockholm-until -people-saw-it-in-action/.

34. Ibid.

35. Ibid.

36. Jesse McKinley and Vivian Wang, "New York State Budget Deal Brings Congestion Pricing, Plastic Bag Ban, and Mansion Tax," *New York Times*, March 31, 2019.

37. Winnie Hu, "Congestion Pricing. N.Y. Embraced It. Will Other Clogged Cities Follow?" *New York Times*, April 1, 2019.

Chapter 12

1. Richard Wiseman, "Ten of the Greatest Optical Illusions," *Daily Mail*, September 25, 2010.

2. Richard H. Thaler, "Toward a Positive Theory of Consumer Choice," *Journal of Economic Behavior and Organization* 1, no. 1 (March 1980): 39–60.

3. See, for example, Elizabeth A. Phelps, "Emotion and Cognition: Insights from Studies of the Human Amygdala," *Annual Review of Psychology* 57 (January 10, 2006): 27–53.

4. Brad Plumer, "U.S. Carbon Emissions Surged in 2018 Even As Coal Plants Closed," *New York Times*, January 8, 2019.

Chapter 13

1. This characterization was described to me by psychotherapist Karen Gilovich, who has long treated victims of sexual abuse, and Heather Campbell, executive director of the Advocacy Center of Tompkins County, New York. It is also consistent with material in teaching programs for domestic violence counselors,

as described, for example, by Liana Epstein, *Domestic Violence Counseling Training Manual*, Cornerstone Foundation, 2003, https://www.scribd.com/document/273282828/Domestic-Violence-Training-Manual.

2. Alison Wood Brooks and Leslie K. John, "The Surprising Power of Questions," *Harvard Business Review*, May–June, 2018.

3. Ibid.

4. Alison Wood Brooks, Karen Huang, Michael Yeomans, Julia Minson, and Francesca Gino, "It Doesn't Hurt to Ask: Question-Asking Increases Liking," *Journal of Personality and Social Psychology* 113, no. 3 (September 2017): 430–452.

5. Ronald D. Vale, "The Value of Asking Questions," *Molecular Biology of the Cell* 24, no. 6 (March 15, 2013): 680–682.

6. Ginat Brill and Arnat Yarden, "Learning Biology through Research Papers: A Stimulus for Question-Asking by High-School Students," *Cell Biology Education* 2 (Winter 2003): 266–274.

7. W. Lee Hansen, Michael K. Salemi, and John J. Siegfried, "Use It or Lose It: Teaching Economic Literacy," *American Economic Review* 92, no. 2 (May 2002): 463–472.

8. Robert H. Frank, *The Economic Naturalist: In Search of Explanations for Everyday Enigmas* (New York: Basic Books, 2007).

9. Paul Sloane, "Ask Questions: The Single Most Important Habit for Innovative Thinkers," InnovativeManagement, https://innovationmanagement.se/imtool-articles/ask-questions-the-single-most-important-habit-for-innovative-thinkers/.

10. Christopher A. Bail, Lisa P. Argyle, Taylor W. Brown, John P. Bumpus, Haohan Chen, M. B. Fallin Hunzaker, Jaemin Lee, Marcus Mann, Friedolin Merhout, and Alexander Volfovsky, "Exposure to Opposing Views on Social Media Can Increase Political Polarization," *PNAS* 115, no. 37 (September 11, 2018): 9216–9221

11. David Broockman and Joshua Kalla, "Durably Reducing Transphobia: An Experiment on Door-to-Door Canvassing," *Science* 352, no. 6282 (April 8, 2016): 220–224.

12. Ibid., p. 221.

13. Ibid., p. 220.

14. Ibid., p. 223.

15. Brian Resnick, "These Scientists Can Prove It's Possible to Reduce Prejudice," Vox, April 8, 2016, https://www.vox.com/2016/4/7/11380974/reduce-prejudice-science-transgender.

16. Brian Resnick, "Most People Are Bad at Arguing. These 2 Techniques Will Make You Better," Vox, November 20, 2018, https://www.vox.com/2016/11/23/13708996/argue-better-science.

17. Kiran Bisra, Qing Liu, John C. Nesbit, Farimah Salimi, and Philip H. Winne, "Inducing Self-Explanation: A Meta-Analysis," *Educational Psychology Review* 30 (September 2018): 703–725.

18. Matthew Baldwin and Joris Lammers, "Past-Focused Environmental Com-

parisons Promote Pro-Environmental Outcomes for Conservatives," *PNAS* 113, no. 52 (December 27, 2016): 14953–14957.

19. Jonathan Haidt and Jesse Graham, "Mapping the Moral Domain," *Journal of Personality and Social Psychology* 101, no. 2 (2011): 366–385; Jonathan Haidt, *The Righteous Mind: Why Good People Are Divided by Politics and Religion* (New York: Pantheon Books, 2012).

20. Matthew Feinberg and Robb Willer, "From Gulf to Bridge: When Do Moral Arguments Facilitate Political Influence?" *Personality and Social Psychology Bulletin* 41, no. 12 (October 7, 2015): 1665–1681.

21. Vasanti S. Malik, Barry M. Popkin, George A. Bray, Jean-Pierre Després, and Frank B. Hu, "Sugar Sweetened Beverages, Obesity, Type 2 Diabetes and Cardiovascular Disease Risk," *Circulation* 121 (March 23, 2010): 1356–1364.

22. M. Arantxa Colchero, Juan Rivera-Dommarco, Barry M. Popkin, and Shu Wen Ng, "In Mexico, Evidence of Sustained Consumer Response Two Years after Implementing a Sugar-Sweetened Beverage Tax," *Health Affairs* 36, no. 3 (March 2017): 564–571.

23. Greg Lukianoff and Jonathan Haidt, *The Coddling of the American Mind: Good Intentions and Bad Ideas Are Setting Up a Generation for Failure* (New York: Penguin Press, 2018).

24. Robert H. Frank, *Success and Luck: Good Fortune and the Myth of Meritocracy* (Princeton, NJ: Princeton University Press, 2016).

25. Shanto Iyengar and Douglas S. Massey, "Scientific Communication in a Post-Truth Society" (November 26, 2018), *PNAS* 116, no. 16 (April 16, 2019): 7656–7661.

26. Bail et al., "Exposure to Opposing Views on Social Media Can Increase Political Polarization."

27. Broockman and Kalla, "Durably Reducing Transphobia."

28. Elizabeth Levy Paluck, Hana Shepherd, and Peter M. Aronow, "Changing Climates of Conflict: A Social Network Experiment in 56 Schools," *PNAS* 113, no. 3 (January 19, 2016): 566–571.

29. Juan David Robalino and Michael Macy, "Peer Effects on Adolescent Smoking: Are Popular Teens More Influential?" *PLOS ONE* 13, no. 7 (July 12, 2018), https://journals.plos.org/plosone/article/comments?id=10.1371/journal.pone.0189360.

30. Andrew Merle, "Why You Should Ask More Questions (and Actually Care about the Answers)," Medium, November 13, 2017, https://medium.com/@andrewmerle/why-you-should-ask-more-questions-and-actually-care-about-the-answers-6abddcd25a2d.

31. Robert H. Frank, *Passions within Reason: The Strategic Role of the Emotions* (New York: W. W. Norton, 1988).

32. Robert H. Frank, *Choosing the Right Pond: Human Behavior and the Quest for Status* (New York: Oxford University Press, 1985).

33. Dan Moulthrop, "The Art of Asking Questions," TedxSHSS, December 18, 2015, https://www.youtube.com/watch?v=hZSY0PssqH0.

34. Brooks and John, "The Surprising Power of Questions."

Epilogue

1. Wallace-Wells, *The Uninhabitable Earth*, pp. 226, 227.

2. Ibid., p. 219.

3. William Samuelson and Richard Zeckhauser, "Status-Quo Bias in Decision Making," *Journal of Risk and Uncertainty* 1 (1988): 7–59.

4. For a comprehensive survey of this literature, see chaps. 5 and 6 of my *Luxury Fever* (New York: The Free Press, 1999).

5. Wallace-Wells, *The Uninhabitable Earth*, p. 189.

6. Ibid., p. 225.

7. Katharine Wilkinson, "How Empowering Women and Girls Can Help Stop Global Warming," TEDWomen, 2018, https://www.ted.com/talks/katharine_wilkinson_how_empowering_women_and_girls_can_help_stop_global_warming?language=en.

INDEX

Note: Page numbers in italic type refer to figures.

A NOTE ON THE TYPE

This book has been composed in Adobe Text and Gotham.
Adobe Text, designed by Robert Slimbach for Adobe,
bridges the gap between fifteenth- and sixteenth-century
calligraphic and eighteenth-century Modern styles.
Gotham, inspired by New York street signs, was designed
by Tobias Frere-Jones for Hoefler & Co.